Ayurveda and Thai Yoga

Religious Therapeutics Theory and Practice

By

ANTHONY B. JAMES

Meta Journal Press

Ayurveda and Thai Yoga
Religious Therapeutics Theory and Practice

by Anthony B. James, DNM(P), ND(T), MD(AM), PhD, DPHC(h.c.), RAAC

Inquiries should be addressed to:

Meta Journal Press
Anthony B. James, DNM(C), ND, MD(AM), DOM(C), DPHC(h.c.), PhD, M.Sc., RAAC, SMOKH

5401 Saving Grace Ln. Brooksville, FL 34602
(706) 358- 8646
Email: NativeAIC@gmail.com

Websites:
www.ThaiYogaCenter.Com
www.SomaVeda.Org
www.ThaiMassage.Com
www.BeardedMedia.Com
www.ThailandStudyTours.Com
www.CafePress.com/thaimassage

ISBN 13:   978-1-886338-28-9 (Trade Paper)
ISBN 10:   1-886338-28-0 (Trade Paper)

Printed in the U.S.A
Cover Illustration by Anthony B. James
Original art and photography by Anthony B. James
Typography by Anthony B. James
Design art and original design by Anthony B. James
Editorial Assistance by Dr. Arianna B. Coe CATP, CTT, DSNM

This book is an entirely new edition based on previous work by the author under the title: "Lines, Wheels, Points and Remedies", Anthony B. James, Meta Journal Press, 1991, 2007, 2012.

THAILAND *is situated in the southeast part of Asia between 5 degrees north parallel, and 21 degrees north parallel, 97 degrees east latitude and 106 degrees longitude. It is bordered by the countries of Myanmar (Burma), Kampuchea (Cambodia), Laos and Malaysia. The terrain is quite diverse with sub-tropical lowlands bordered by the gulf of Siam in the south, the spacious great central plains of Menam Chao Phraya, and the craggy mountains of the Northern Highlands.*

Note how centrally located in South and S.E. Asia the country of Thailand is. Not far geographically from India, China and the Philippines by land, river or ocean.

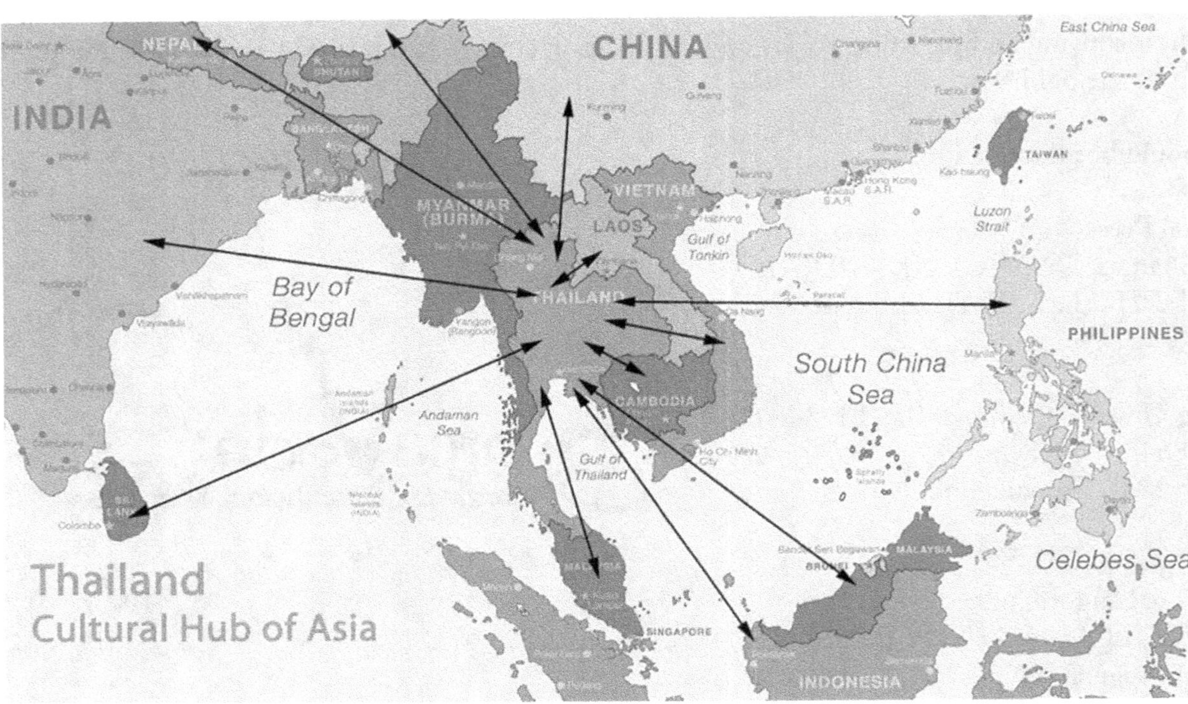

Authors Forward

The bulk of this book is based on the Thai Ayurveda, Indigenous Traditional Thai Medical theory and practices. This material is then compared and contrasted with the Indigenous traditional "Classical" Indian Ayurveda which is the principle origin of the Thai Medical practices. I have resourced heavily from understandings of Classical Ayurveda text such as Charaka Sushruta Samhita, Charaka Samhita, Mahabharata, Atharvaveda, Yoga- Upanishads, Pradapika, Patanjali and other similar works which would have been not only extant but historically foundational in the formulation of indigenous, traditional Thai culture from earliest times. The influence of the classical Indian Ayurveda concepts and traditions on "What is Traditional Thai Medicine" continues to the present day both in Thailand proper and the world today.

I also have made an effort to bring understanding and clarity from modern science, scientific and philosophical understandings which either support or clarify the traditional medicine perspective.

This book is an entirely new edition based on previous work by the author under the title: "Lines, Wheels, Points and Specific Remedies", Meta Journal Press, Chicago 1991". Additional material was obtained from a series of both video and audio lectures given at SomaVeda Integrated Traditional Therapies® Thai Yoga Practitioner trainings given over a five year period from 2002 to 2013. Transcripts of these original lectures
Page 4

were made and then the conversations and commentaries were integrated into the present edition. Chapter Two: "History of Ayurveda in Thailand" was extracted with references from my book " Ayurveda of Thailand, Indigenous Traditional Thai Medicine and Yoga Therapy" [66].

Other materials I have used are derived from original articles and posts which I have over the years published independently on several websites such as www.ThaiMassage.Com, www.Somaveda.Org and www. ThaiYogaCenter.Com. Unless otherwise noted all graphics, art, photographs and illustrations were created by myself for the purposes of
illustration and elaboration.

It is important as one of my former teachers explained to me to give credit where credit is due! To that I must once again say thank you to my many Thai Aachan and teachers who gave me open access to their insight and teachings, to their lineages of indigenous Traditional Thai Culture and medicine. We pay respect to all of our personal Grand Masters and teachers in the Thai Traditions we honor.

- PhraKru Uppakarn Phatanakit: Wat Po 1983- 1985
- Aachan Moh Boonsorn Kitnyom 1983 - 1994 (Wat Po Director/ Professor)
- Aachan Phaa Khruu Samaii Mesamarn: Buddhai Sawan Institute, Nogkam/ Ayudthaya 1980 to 1998
- Aachan Moh Velowong Sidtisopong : Wat Po 1983 to 1995
- Aachan Phaa Khruu Sintorn Chaichagun: Buntautuk Northern Provincial Hospital (Old Medicine School) 1989-2005
- Aachan Chongkol Settakorn: ITM Chiang Mai (1991-2010)
- Aahan Pichest Boonthumme Buntautuk Northern Provincial Hospital (Old Medicine School) 1988-1990
- Venerable Prakhru Pipitpattanapirat Wat Wat Pra Kaew Don Tao and Wat Suchadaran, Lamphang 1990-2010
- Aachan Phaa Khruu Anantasuk: Wiangklaikangwan Industrial College 2004- 2010
- Aachan Nanthipa Anantasuk: Wiangklaikangwan Industrial College: Anantasuk School of Thai Traditional Medicine Hua Hin/ Lak Sii 2004- 2010
- Mr. Surasak Srinoi (Wat Po Association for Traditional Thai Medicine, Anantasuk School for Traditional Thai Medicine and Wangklaikangwon Industrial Community & Educational College)
- Dr. Aram Amaradit, Member Parliament of Surin Province, Chairman of the Committee on Public Health, President: The Union of Thai Traditional Medicine Society (UTTS), Ministry of Public Health (2009)
- Aachan Moh Mama Lek Chaiya: Lek Chaiya Nerve Touch Massage, Chiang Mai (1990-2015)
- Aachan Moh Tawee: Wat Sawankhalok School for the Blind
- Aachan John: Wat Loi Khro, Chiang Mai: 1988-1994

I want express gratitude to several Ayurveda professors who I have been fortunate to train with in both India and the US and or who have otherwise have been inspirational to my work and research: Prof. Dr. K Muraleedharan Pillai (Vishnu Ayurveda College, Shoranur, Kerala), Dr. Suresh Kumar Agarwal (Institute of Health and Healing), Dr. C. P. Asghar (Greens Ayur Hospital, Azhiyur. Calicut, S.India), Dr Janardhana V Hebbar B.A.M.S., MD (Ayu), PGDPSM (Rajiv Gandhi University of Health Sciences, Mangalore), Dr. Shekhar Annambhotla R.M.A.S.(Association of Ayurvedic Professionals of North America AAPNA). Last and not the least grattitude and appreciation to my wife Dr. Julie James and Head Teacher at the NAIC/ SCNM: Thai Yoga Center Khruu Daniel Kram for their support and tireless efforts to bring the healing arts and sciences of SomaVeda Integrated Traditional Therapies® Thai Yoga to all of the students.

Table of Contents

Chapter 1: What is Thai Yoga?

The basis of SomaVeda Integrated Traditional Therapies® is Indigenous Traditional Thai Ayurveda & Thai Yoga Therapy. So, what is Thai Yoga?

Indigenous Traditional Thai Yoga and or "Traditional Thai Massage" (slang) represents the most authentic vision of Traditional Thai Ayurvedic Medicine (*Pâet pǎen boh-raan* แพทย์แผนโบราณ), Thai Culture and related healing arts. Our instructors are directly authorized teachers, representatives and traditional lineage holders in several different traditional Buddhist schools: Buddhai Sawan Institute: Ayudthaya and Nongkam (famous for martial and healing arts for 900 years!), Phra Wat Chetuphon (Buddhist Temple, Wat Po Traditional Thai Medical School...One of the oldest schools of traditional arts), Buntautuk Hill tribes Northern Provincial Hospital and Training Institute also known as "The Old Medicine Hospital of Shivago Komarpai"; ITM (International Thai Massage, Chiangmai), Mama Lek Chaiya (Lek Chaiya Jap- Sen Nuad/ Nerve Touch), The Foundation for the Blind (Wat Sawankhalok), Buddhist Temple Wat Wianglock.

In addition to the Traditional and colloquial Thai Medicine we include the standardized systems promoted by the Thai Ministry of Public Health referred to as TRADITIONAL THAI MEDICINE (TTM) (*Pâet pǎen tai* แพทย์แผนไทย) and taught in colleges all over Thailand. It is also based on ancient texts and has been modified as recently as the late 1990s. Although this system is primarily derived from recognized royal traditional medicine sources, the western medical influence is noticeable and growing. Both the Wangklaikangwon Industrial Community & Educational College program originally sponsored by HM. King Bhumibol, (Anantasuk Traditional Thai Medicine) and The UTTS or Union of Thai Traditional Medicine Society as well as several other significant lineages, teachers and Grand Masters are key in modern TTM practices and standards..

And most importantly, the Buddhist medicine associated and derived from the famous Saint Jivaka Komarabjacca (*Th. Shivago*).

In the states, Traditional Lineage and teaching is primarily passed on via the educational programs of the SomaVeda College of Natural Medicine (SCNM: Thai Yoga Center in Brooksville, Florida, USA). Additionally, we recognize any schools formally licensed as legal Thai Yoga and or Traditional Thai Massage schools by the Royal Thai Ministries of Health, Education, Thai Traditional Medicine and UTTS (Union of Thai Traditional Medicine Society) whether listed or not. The type of Thai traditional therapy that most people will be directly exposed to is *rǎksǎa thaang nûat* (healing treatment using the hands). This is what is more commonly known as the Nuat Thai or Nuad Boran styles of Thai Yoga therapy or the spiritual massage, healing work of Thailand.

Please note: for clarity although in common english we use the word "massage" we do not mean it in the same context as the typical western usage. In the west "Massage" means something like a "Rub Down" for money and is primarily referring to systems derived from Swedish Massage and Massage Therapy. "Thai Yoga and or Thai Massage" (*Th. Phaen Boran Rǎksǎa Thaang Nûat*) is completely unrelated! It is a healing art derivative of Theravada Buddhism, Buddhist medicine, Classical Indian and Tibetan Ayurveda and Yoga Vedanta.

It is not required that one become a practicing buddhist to practice this healing art. Although it would be more accurate to call this medicine either by its traditional name or "Ancient, Anachronistic or Old Thai Way of Healing with The Hands", the slang form of "Thai Massage" is in use, and as long as this is so there will be some understandable confusion.

Primary Outcomes Of The Practice

The primary outcomes associated with the practice of Thai Yoga Ayurveda and Religious Therapies are called "*ProMiiWihan Sii*" or Four Divine, Boundless or States of mind without limitation. They are Love, Compassion, Joy and Equanimity. As long as these four qualities are communicated, transmitted and exemplified during a session, we say it was good and successful. For this reason it is possible to have a Thai Yoga healing session with little or no actual touching. In addition to the Four Divine States of Mind we practice and perform Puja (*Th. Bucha*) ritual healing, a multi step protocol to first Acknowledge the sacred space shared by client and Yogi, to honor and acknowledge the Boddhisatvas and progenitors of our way and teaching, to generate the Boddichitta or perfected mental processes of enlightened beings through Mantra (recitation of OmNamoShivago, the Metta Sutra or similar), invoking and inviting of the essences and energies of love and healing to move within the body of ourselves and our client, listening, and sacred attunements. This prayerful and thoughtful meditation and attuning of various energies and petitioning of sacred and symbolic metaphor of deity and ancient guides and role models provides the basis for all further communication and expression of the ideals.

Secondary Outcomes Of The Practice

On the surface, Thai Yoga may share characteristics similar to many forms of western massage such as the secondary outcomes (considered less important in the Thai perspective), such as stress and pain relief, and increased range of motion (with Thai therapy this list goes on).

Thai Yoga Therapy may additionally use many similar looking techniques such as effleurage (stroking and kneading the muscles), manipulation (manipulating or moving/ aligning osseous or skeletal parts) and pressure point or acupressure style technique (applying deep, consistent pressure to specific nerves, tendons, ligaments, trigger points, acupoints or Lom). However, all of the applications of therapeutic intent are performed in order to balance the functions of the Four Body Elements called *thâat tháng sìi* in Thai (ThAkaat/ Lom, Fai, Naam , Din).

Thai Yoga therapy incorporates elements of classical Ayurvedic assessments of Prakruti, Vikruti, Dosha Imbalance with spiritual, energetic and Prana assessment. The Hands on healing or Chirothesia therapies include counseling, mindfulness, gentle rocking, Asana positional release, deep stretching, focused breathing or PranaYama, Chakra balancing, Prana Nadi or Sen line balancing and rhythmic compression to create a singular healing experience.

However, as we said previously any and all applications of physical pressure are intended to convey the primary intentions of ProMiiWihan Sii to balance and harmonize the *thâat tháng sìi* or four elements, Tridosha or Three Winds, Humors and or energetically based body types. Much like a hug can convey care and consideration and love with physical pressure, the only difference here is with the level of sophistication in exchanging this love with pressure. Borrowing from India's Ayurvedic tradition, some practitioners employ Pali-Sanskrit terms for the bodily elements:

Ether Element:	(*Th. Akat/Lom*) (*Sans. Akashadhatu*)
Air Element:	(*Th. Lom/ Prana*) (*Sans. Vayudhatu*)
Fire Element:	(*Th. Fai*) (*Sans. Tejasdhatu*)
Water Element:	(*Th. Naam*) (*Sans. Apodhatu/ Apasdhatu*)
Earth Element:	(*Th. Din*) (*Sans. Prthvidhatu*)

(More details on the elements in Chapter 6)

Let me say this with emphasis, Thai Traditional Ayurveda and Yoga Therapy (Traditional Thai Massage) is not LIKE Yoga, IT IS YOGA. It is Yoga Therapy. From the Ayudthaya period until early this century, the Thai government's Department of Health included an official massage division (*Th. phanâek mãw nûat*). Under the influence of international medicine and modern hospital development responsibility for the national propagation/maintenance of Thai Ayurveda was eventually transferred to Phra Wat Chetaphon (Wat Pho) in Bangkok, where it remains today. Traditional Yoga therapy has persisted most in the provinces, however it has recently enjoyed a resurgence of popularity throughout the country. The Wat Po system is divided into two completely separate and distinctive categories: A) the tourist massage pavilion and Tourist massage school, (*Th. Rongrian Sala Thaang Nuat*) and B) the School for traditional Medicine for training and certification of *Maw Nuad* (Ayurveda and Traditional Massage Doctors). There are huge differences in the term and quality of training.

For example a tourist may receive an introductory massage certificate in as little as 10 days, whereas the full program for Maw Nuad is 12 to 14 semesters or four full years. In the states we have many different levels of recognitions for Certified

Thai Yoga /Massage Practitioners. The SomaVeda® Thai Yoga based Doctorate of Sacred Natural Medicine (DSNM) program is a four year program which qualifies graduates to sit for the Traditional Naturopathic National Boards (ANMA). A traditional western Naturopath (Nature Cure Physician) is considered by many to be the top of the holistic pyramid. We now have an established program to educate Doctors of Indigenous Traditional Sacred Medicine in the traditional healing methods of Thai Ayurveda and Yoga.

Indigenous Traditional Thai Yoga and or Thai Massage is not the same as "Massage, Massage Therapy", and or "bodywork" as commonly defined in so called "Massage Laws". The term "Thai Massage" is western slang, mostly promoted by tourists in Thailand. Although the use of the term is now common, it still is misunderstood and misused by the un and/or misinformed. It is easy to be confused as both use the word "Massage" but legally there are distinctions and differences in definitions. In law, specific words may have different meaning than those same words used in ordinary "Non-legal" or in lay speech/ speak. For example: "Massage and Massage Therapy" definitions are based on the general practice of what is termed "Swedish massage".

So called "Swedish Massage" is new (less than 100 years), Western (Europe and America) and defined legally as "the application of a system of structured touch, pressure, movement and holding to the soft tissues of the human body with the purpose of positively affecting the health and well being of the client. The practice includes the external application of water, heat, cold, lubricants, salt scrubs and other topical preparations and devices that mimic or enhance the actions of the hands." Thai Yoga Therapy sounds a bit similar at first glance, however, what is not mentioned in the preceding definition is that Thai Yoga and or Traditional Thai Massage is a system of movement education (Yoga). It is based entirely on principles of energy balancing (Ayurveda, Sen, Tridosha, Lom, Chakra etc.) and the actual touching, contact or soft tissue manipulation is incidental to, and not the central aim of the practice.

As described above: The primary outcomes associated with the practice are called "*ProMiiWihan Sii*" or Four Divine, Boundless or States of Mind Without Limitation. They are Love, Compassion, Joy and Equanimity. As long as these four qualities are transmitted and exemplified during a session it was successful. That's why it is possible to have a Thai Ayurveda and or Yoga Therapy session with little or no touching, however, touching is good! Thai Yoga may incorporate elements of mindfulness, gentle rocking, deep stretching and rhythmic compression and focus to create a singular healing experience.

This work brings fundamental elements and energy into harmony and creates wholeness of mind, body and spirit. SomaVeda® Thai Yoga/ Thai Traditional Massage is a religious therapeutic. It is a somatic technique and profession, a modality with standards originally established in the ancient indigenous Ayurvedic practices of the Hindu physicians of Taxila and Nalanda and then the Buddhist medical centers and temples of asia and southeast asia thousands of years in the past. It has an established code of ethics derived from the Buddha Dharma and other similar sources. There is an established educational criteria for training and professional practice for services which are unrelated to "Massage" or "Massage therapy". There are actually quite a few different "schools" of Traditional Thai Yoga. They range from the big university supported programs of Bangkok, to the "Family" style oral and traditional lineages of the Northern Hill Tribes people such as of the Karen, Lisu, Lahu and Akha people. Their influence is a growing factor in the modern expression of Thai Ayurveda especially in the North.

In the north of Thailand, as it is closer to mainland China, you see more Chinese and Laotian influenced therapeutic techniques. For example a well known Teacher and practitioner in Chiang Mai, Mama Lek Chaiya and her family, teach what is called nerve-touch massage (*Th. nûat jàp sên*), a Chinese-style massage technique that works with the body's nerve meridians much like acupuncture. Some of the plucking techniques are reminiscent of Tuina and can be quite unpleasant. However, the ultimate aim of balancing the chi takes precedence over comfort. Within the traditional Thai medical context, a massage therapist (*Th. mãw nûat*, literally, 'massage doctor') usually applies Thai massage together with pharmacological (herbal) and/or psycho-spiritual treatments as prescribed for a specific problem or specific imbalance of the Dosha or winds and humors of the body, mind, spirit. It is becoming quite popular for many Thais to also use traditional massage as a tool for relaxation and disease prevention, rather than for a specific medical problem. However, once you leave the big city and move into the country you see more reliance on the application as energy based medicine.

The most famous traditional school in the north is The Buntautuk Northern Hill Tribes Medical Hospital or "The Old Medicine Hospital" as it is more likely called. Under the auspices of Grand Master Aachan Sintorn Chaichagun

(Transitioned November 2005) it has become a national and international phenomenon. Teaching various levels of programs to Thai and falang (foreigner) alike, Aachan Sintorn was also famous for his daily recitation of the Pali mantra "Om Namo Shivago", a prayer and invocation for blessing. Every day, twice a day he would lead the entire community in this rhythmic and beautiful traditional mantra for healing. In the north they say you don't know Thai Ayurveda/ Thai Yoga until you know this mantra! Today the Wat Po Association of Traditional Doctors and member schools and Aachans or Master Instructors are bringing this work into the modern world. Famous schools and their head Masters such as Anantasuk Rongrian (school of traditional medicine) under Aachan Nantipa Anantasuk work with the King's Rajaprajanugroh projects to document completely the traditional medicine and preserve its rich heritage.

Notes on Ayurveda

Thai Ayurveda is not exactly the same as classical Indian Ayurveda. For reasons that I discussed earlier which mostly have to do with the geography of Thailand being in the center of Southeast Asia.

Ayurveda of Thailand is heavily influenced by the original Mon-Khymer culture, classical Indian and Myanmar (Burmese) culture, Chinese, Laotian, Cambodian and Vietnamese culture, as well as heavily influenced in the south by Javanese, Malaysian-Indonesian culture, all coming together in Thailand.

Several of the countries that are heavily influential like Tibet, Bhutan, Nepal, and Burma are Buddhist countries. To the south toward the Indian side, we have Sri Lanka which is probably the oldest Buddhist country still practicing a real fundamentalist sort of Buddhism.

There actually are three different kinds of Ayurveda in India. There is the Hindu Ayurveda, Buddhist Ayurveda and the Muslim Ayurveda. These are the major populations of the continent of India, South and South East Asia. Without comparing and contrasting the colloquial cultural influence on their practices, you can't have a clear overall picture. It's not thorough to rely on only a few western resources. It's easy to cherry pick from a few sources or the popular Yoga schools' explanations and variations of what is Ayurveda. Schools, systems and or organizations like the Ashtanga School, Iyengar school, Sachidananda school, Friend school, Yin Yoga school, Yoga Journal Magazine and Yoga Alliance each represent what they think or believe the sum of Ayurveda and Yoga practice to be. Every one of them puts their spin on whatever is their particular exposure to it. In a way, they're all good and useful and from another point of view, they're all not so useful since none of them are representative of classical Indian Ayurveda and Yoga.

Ayurveda today in India is quite different than you might imagine. For example: to be licensed as an Ayurvedic doctor anywhere in India today, you have to be an expert in western, Hahnemann-Austrian derived Classical Homoeopathy.

Homoeopathy came into India during the late Raj period and was the one western medical practice or system of medical thought that the Indian Ayurvedic doctors accepted immediately with no conflict.

Homeopathy uses all natural remedies. They are vibration/ energy based, easily available or manufactured and there're no side effects. So the community of India and classical Indian schools of Ayurveda and traditional Indian Naturopathic medicine adopted Homoeopathy. Now it is a requirement that you have the equivalent of a diploma or diplomat in Homoeopathy to be able to take either the national boards or any of the State boards of Ayurveda in India. If you want to practice Ayurveda in the largest state in India, Bengal State, you have to pass a Homeopathic board. If you want to practice Ayurveda in Kerala and South India which is maybe the second largest state of India, same requirement.

What is Ayurveda? More specifically the Ayurveda of Thailand? Thais have a long history of simulation and adoption. There is such a thing as traditional Thai culture, but the Thais have been very quick and adept, especially over the last 20 years. There are places all over Thailand that are unrecognizable compared to how they were 20 years ago based on the development and based on the dress. When I first went to Thailand most people wore Sarees and Sarongs. Now you have to go way out in the country before you see Thai people wearing Sarees and Sarongs in normal daily life. Everyone except western business people dressed traditionally 20 odd years ago, now everybody wears jeans, slacks, T-shirts and button up shirts and various other western attire.

Ayurveda is part of traditional Thai culture, but Thai culture is Buddhist, and so the flavor of the adoption, the interpretation of terms, is sometimes a little different. Those of you who have had other Ayurveda or other Yoga training might notice when we get to the Eight Limbs discussion that there are some little differences. Ayurveda of Thailand has been practiced that way for millennia. Even today's Indian Ayurveda may be different from what you anticipate. As with a western concept like Homeopathy for example, that has become part of classical Ayurveda for the last 50 years. If you go to these countries to practice you will see things that you won't expect if all you've done is read Deepak Chopra's, Dr. Vasant Ladd's, or Mark Halpern's books. If you go there you will be shocked at the variety of innovation using modern western concepts like biologic testing for example in the hospitals. Blood tests, urine tests, using microscopes and dark field microscopy is quite common now. There is much that is similar though, and so we still look at India's classical Ayurveda for deeper insight.

Chapter 2: History of Ayurveda in Thailand

Origins of Indigenous Traditional Thai Medicine and Massage

Indigenous, Traditional Thai Massage (Indigenous Thai Yoga Therapy), also called *"Ryksaa Thang Nuad Phaen Boran Thai"* or the "ancient Chirothesia (Yoga Therapy) or hands-on healing" of Thailand, is born of a long tradition. This unique system of indigenous, traditional, natural medicine and Yoga therapy finds its ancient roots first in the traditions of classical Ayurveda as far back as the 5th century BCE. Subsequently the Vedic health and medical practices that eventually became common practice in SE Asia, Burma (Myanmar) and Thailand were heavily influenced by succeeding generations of Buddhist influence, philosophy and practice. Some form of this traditional medicine has been taught and practiced in various locations for about 2500 years.

When Theravada Buddhism arrives in the region (400-600 C.E.) it is firmly established as a colloquial and unique variation still founded primarily on its Vedic roots but progressively influenced by the diversity which is found in early Thailand beginning in the Sukhothai period, followed by the Ayutthaya and Bangkok eras. Beginning in the Ayutthaya period (1351) we see influences from the Burmese, Japanese, Chinese, Malay, Philippines and Portuguese [3] consistent with the immigration and trade of the kingdom during that time. This is also when we note the first documented arrival of western doctors. Traditional Burmese medicine especially came to the forefront before and after the sacking of Ayutthaya between 1765 and 1767 [4].

The classics of Indian literature and Ayurveda were known and being distributed and or used by the Royal Court in Ayutthaya such as the haraka Samhita, Ramayana, Rig Veda, Athara Veda, Pradapika and Sushruta Samhita. Additionally, the Thai Royal court from earliest days was likely

knowledgeable, by way of local culture and the literature of the Vedas and the Puranas, of the Hindu deities and in particular the deity and iconic symbols associated with Dhanvantari (*Tha. Pra Narai, Narayana, Jagannath*). It is interesting to note that one of the oldest bronze statues in Thailand, now located in the National Museum in Sukhothai is that of Vishnu. Dhanvantari is an avatar of Vishnu in Hinduism. He is the physician to the Gods and generally the deity/spiritual icon of Ayurveda.

Vishnu or Pra Narayana statue in Huytungtao, Chiangmai Thailand

During the periods of war with neighboring Burma, many tens of thousands of Thai people were taken as prisoner and held for over 40 years establishing their freedom and returning to their homes, including the famous Thai Prince, later King Naresuan [5] [6]. When they returned they brought with them knowledge and practices obtained during their captivity including medicine, martial arts, music, food and more. These were incorporated into the dominant Thai culture over time and remain influential today by way of the many generations of Burmese people who immigrated and now live in Thailand.

OM NAMO SHIVAGO

Historically, the initial credit for the origination of what became Indigenous Traditional Thai Medicine and Massage is given to one individual, a famous Indian doctor called Jivaka Komalaboat [12] (Shivago) other spellings include Jivaka Kumar Bhaccha and Jivaka Amravana. Jivaka, of Indian origin, is alleged to have been born in what is today the city of Rajgir, the ancient capital of the Magadha Kingdom (Later Majapahit/ Bihar). There are several different accountings of his birth, life, education and teachings.

Jivaka statue from authors collection

I found several references that were more detailed and or which offered historically verifiable references to the life of Jivaka. One specific account cross referenced several other however, without specific references it is hard to verify all details. I am including it here under fair use to present the details for further research and or verification: According to one author (Salina- Nalanda University) "According to the Anguttara commentary he was the son of Salavati, a courtesan of Rajagaha with Abhayarajakumara (Son of Raja Bimbisara) but some accounts maintain Jivaka was Ambapali's son with Raja Bimbisara. As per the Vinaya sources the child was placed in a basket right after birth and thrown on a dust-heap, from where he was rescued by Abhayarajakumara. When questioned by Abhaya, people said "he was alive" (*Sans. jivati*), and therefore the child was called Jivaka; because he was brought up by the prince, he was called Komarabhacca (child of a Prince). It has been suggested, however, that Komarabhacca meant master of the Kaumarabhrtya science (the treatment of infants); VT.ii.174; in Dvy. (506-18) [12] he is called Kumarabhuta because of his medical profession."

When he grew up, he learns of his antecedents, and went to Takkasila without Abhaya's knowledge and studied medicine for seven years. When he returned to Rajgir, Abhaya established him in his own residence. There he cured Bimbisara of a troublesome fistula and received as reward all the ornaments worn by Bimbisara's five hundred wives.

The 12th century Chinese commentator of the Susruta Samhita, DalhaSa, says that Jivaka's compendium was regarded as one of the authoritative texts. Another text that quotes Jivaka's formulas is the "*Navan taka*" (meaning 'butter'), a part of the Bower MSS discovered in 1880 from Kuchar in Chinese Turkistan. Based on earlier standard sources, this medical compilation of the 4th century AD, attributes two formulas dealing with children's disease to Jivaka, saying 'Iti hovaca Jivakah, i.e. thus it spoke Jivaka. One formula is: i.e., Bhargi, long pepper, Paha, Payasya, together with honey, may be used as linctuses against emeses due to deranged phlegm." A "Linctus" is a form of cough medicine [13].

In researching Jivaka, Rajgir and the ancient Nalanda University, there are references to Jivaka and also separately in connection with the Buddha from the Chinese authors Xuanzang (Hiuen Tsang) and Yijing, especially those of Xuanzang (Sixth Century between 630 and 643 CE). In one of his accounts he writes "North-east from Srigupta's Fire-pit, and in a bend of mountain wall, was a tope (stupa) at the spot where Jivaka, the great physician, had built a hall for the Buddha. Remains of the walls and of the plants and trees within them still existed. Tathagata often stayed here. Beside the tope the ruins of Jivaka's private residence still survives."

Referred to in some ancient references as the Thrice Crowned King of Medicine, he was a classically trained Ayurvedic physician probably in the tradition of Atreya (Atreya Punarvasu/ Takkasila). Jivaka was known to be influenced by Buddhism and was possibly the personal physician to Raja Bimbisara, the Magadha king of that period and to the Buddha and local monks' community on appointment of the king.[12]

It is possible today to travel to see Jivaka's home and the ancient Nalanda University in Rajgir still today.

His name is mentioned in the traditional Pali canon or writings of Theravada (Hinayana) Buddhism (Zysk, Kenneth, G. 1982). Pali is the anachronistic/ancient Sanskrit language still in use today by Theravada Buddhist monks. "Studies in Traditional Indian Medicine in the Pali Canon: Jivaka and Ayurveda", (Kenneth G. Zysk, Journal of the International Association of Buddhist Studies 5, pp. 309–13) [15]. There are numerous additional references to him, his life and healing practices in the Pali Canon. In fact, there is some support for the idea that the "Giving of Robes" (Vin.i.268-81; AA.i.216) [16] where he made a gift to the Buddha of "a celestial shawl he received from a king named Chanda Pradyotha prompted the Buddha to give a famous sermon leading to the practice still followed today.

Another example found in the Pali Canon has Jivaka directly treating the Buddha for specific ailments using Ayurveda. "Once when the Buddha was ill, Jivaka found it necessary to administer a purge, and he had fat rubbed into the Buddha's body and gave him a handful of lotuses to smell. Jivaka was away when the purgative acted, and suddenly remembered that he had omitted to ask the Buddha to bathe in warm water to complete the cure. The Buddha read his thoughts and bathed as required. (Vin.i.279f; DhA. ii.164f)" [17]

The above is an example of the therapeutic adjuncts we use in ITTM today: Chirothesia, Anointing, Oliation, Herbology, Aromatherapy, Pancha Karma, Marma Chikitsa etc.

During his time in association with the Buddha he became a Buddhist monk (Sot panna) and continued to practice
medicine and develop the strategies that would be the foundation for medical and healing practice in Buddhist temples until the present day.

Jivaka was eventually declared by the Buddha chief among his lay followers loved by the people (*Pali. aggam puggalappasannanam*) (A.i.26)[18]. He is included in a list of good men who have been assured of the
realization of deathlessness (A.iii.451; DhA.i.244, 247; J.i.116f) [19].

He seemed to follow, teach and or exemplify the doctor's moral obligations (Doctors Code of Conduct) as found in the Pali scripture, the Vejjavatapada. Attributed to actual practices and teaching directly from the Buddha. In the seven articles, excerpts from four passages in the Pali canon, the Buddha lays down the attitudes and skills which would make "one who would wait on the sick qualified to nurse the sick." (Anguttara Nikaya III, p.144) [20]. The Vejjavatapada likely predates the Greek Hippocratic Oath. It does not just exhort doctors to practice ethically, it clearly specifies a true holistic practice of medicine addressing the spirit, mind and body in an integrated fashion.

The Vejjavatapada

The Lord said: "Health is the greatest gain." He also said: "He who would minister to me should minister to the sick."

I too think that health is the greatest gain and I would minister to the Buddha. Therefore:

(A) I will use my skill to restore the health of all beings with sympathy, compassion and heedfulness.
(B) I will be able to prepare medicines well.
(C) I know what medicine is suitable and what is not. I will not give the unsuitable, only the suitable.
(D) I minister to the sick with a mind of love, not out of desire for gain.
(E) I remain unmoved when I have to deal with stool, urine, vomit or spittle.
(F) From time to time I will be able to instruct, inspire, enthuse, and cheer the sick with the Teaching.
(G) Even if I cannot heal a patient with the proper diet, proper medicine and proper nursing I will still minister to him, out of compassion.

Translated from Pali into English by Bhante Shravasti Dhammika

The Brahmajala Sutra says: "If a disciple of the Buddha sees anyone who is sick, he should provide for that person's needs as if he were making an offering to the Buddha." [12] Brahma Net Sutra, STCUSC, New York, 1998, VI,9[21]'

Jivaka is revered to this day. Many modern practitioners and schools begin every healing session with recitation of a Pali Mantra called OM NAMO SHIVAGO. Royal practitioners generally do this quietly while in the North of Thailand the Mantra may be recited out loud, sometimes with the receiver participating as well.

The Wai Khruu or paying of respect to Jivaka (Shivago) is still done partly in remembrance of his contribution to the present day art. It is impossible to say to what extent other styles of medicine and massage have contributed to Indigenous, Traditional, Thai Medicine (TTM/ ITTM) development.

Development of Indigenous Ayurveda in Thailand

The current capital of Thailand, Bangkok, was established in 1782 with the coronation of Chakri King Rama I in 1782. According to Thai historians the first meaningful building to be erected in the new capital was the rebuilding of the new Wat Pho (1789-1801). The original in the former capital (Ayutthaya) having been burned by invading Burmese armies.

Primarily ITTM has been passed from one generation to the next in the form of an oral tradition, whereby one would serve an apprenticeship under a teacher, often for several years before practicing as a practitioner. In general, the teachings were preserved and cherished by the monks and nuns of the Buddhist Temples. In addition to the oral tradition there have been several treatises, hand written papers, Codices and or books written mostly for or by the Royal Court and not easily obtained by the general public. The most accessible documents detailing the practices of the Royal Court Traditional Medicine, were the stone carvings, built into the walls and pavilions of Wat Po in Bangkok. More on these later.

Important to note also is that there have always been, from earliest days to the present, two different corollary systems of practice, two types of traditional curing methodologies in the way healing and traditional medicine was practiced in Thailand. The urban or variant descendant practice from the Royal schools of traditional medicine, and the country/ rural or common practices found in the villages, jungle and countryside. The urban represents efforts at standardization and training, the rural or country incorporates the more indigenous ideas and practices restricted by tribe or geographic location. Most researchers agree that there has always been and still is cross sharing of ideas, influences and practices of both systems.

Similar variations of this indigenous traditional medicine are practiced in Sri Lanka, Burma, Laos, Cambodia and, of course, Thailand. There is also a dramatic similarity to Traditional Tibetan Medicine, Amma/Tui Na of China, the Anma/Shiatsu of Japan, and Filipino Hilot.

History is unclear as to when specific developments were incorporated into the traditional medicine catalog of practices. Additionally there is a lack of documentation of the family, tribal and village specific practices passed on through oral tradition and not documented in the "official" or sanctioned records and historical texts. There were significant differences, both historically and in contemporary, between "Official" Traditional Medicine practices and the "Rural" traditional medicine practices found in remote villages and tribal communities.

We don't see the first official documentation until King Rama commissions the medical tablets (epigraphies) made and enshrined at the new Wat Pho in the 1830's. According to the custodians of Wat Pho, after the capital (Ayutthaya) was destroyed in 1767 by Burmese invaders, rescued fragments of the original documents were used by King Rama to make the new ones.

These tablets are a text of the theory behind ITTM and show the Sen, lines of energy, running throughout the body. The stone charts stone depict sixty figures, thirty of the front and thirty of the back with channels and points clearly displayed. Many channels directly correspond to Chinese meridians and special or Extraordinary vessels, others correspond to the concepts of Prana Nadis from classic Indian Ayurvedic medical science. The charts detail many major and minor Marma/Chakras or centers of energy. In Traditional Thai Medicine these centralized point locations of energy/wind/breath/air are called "Lom" or Wind Gates.

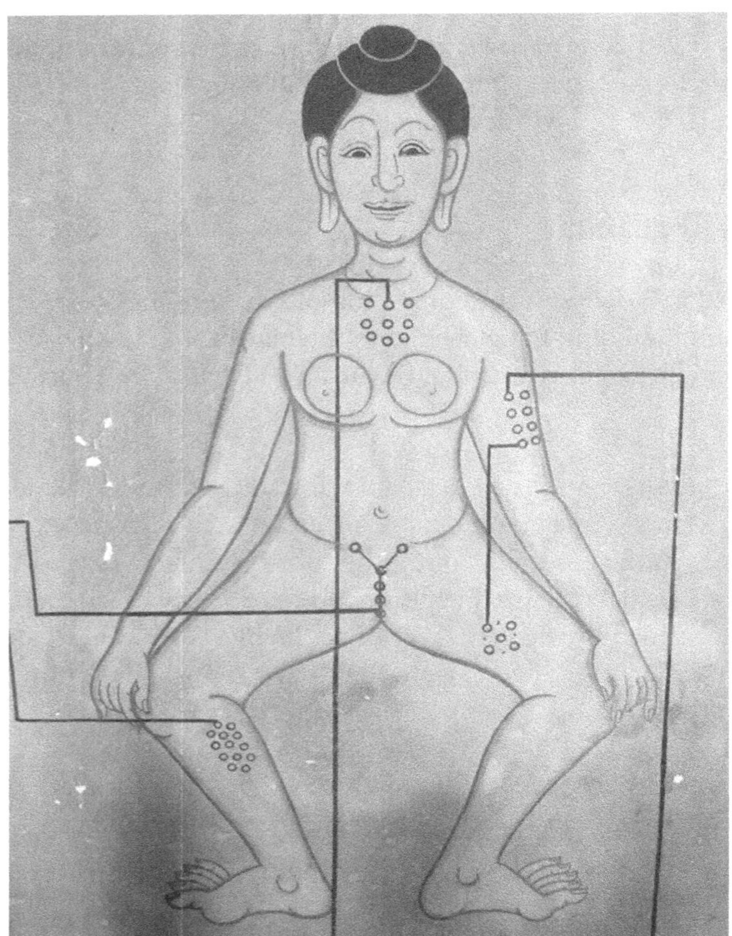

"Chart depicting female balancing points: Wat Po Massage Pavilion"

The depiction of the knowledge of traditional medicine at Wat Po (Bangkok) and also at Wat Raja Orasaram Ratchaworawiharn (Thonburi) were considered incomplete. This was perhaps intentional as the "Secrets" of healing practiced by the Royal Court Doctors (Maw Nuad) at that time were closely guarded. The Royal practice of medicine was more likely passed on from one generation to the next within the family... father to son or nephew in formal apprenticeship.

ITTM detail: Engraved stone plaque:
Wat Raja Orasaram Ratchaworawiharn

In addition to the famous "Epigraphies of King Rama" (Carved stone medical texts) located at Wat Po and Wat Raja-Orasarem (King Rama III: in the Thai/ Chinese style called "The Royal Favorable Art" style), there are also gunite statues of Thai Reishi Yogis practicing the various Asana or traditional Yoga postures - The Thai variation of Hatha Yoga or self treatment. In the past there were more than 100 of these figures scattered about the courtyards of Wat Po. Over the years many were damaged or deteriorated due to weathering and have been retired for preservation. The Yoga of the Thai Reishi is referred to as Reusi Dottan.

In Thailand's past, people came to the temples for just about everything from medical help to education. Anyone could come to the temple for food, shelter, medical or spiritual healing. ITTM (Traditional Thai Medicine/Traditional Thai Massage) contributed to the emotional, physical and spiritual well being of the ancient Thais, and continues to do so today.

Thai culture as a whole is a blending of many cultures from east to west (India to China and from Tibet to Indonesia) and ITTM reflects this. Today, there are two primary schools of indigenous traditional Thai medicine and indigenous traditional Thai massage (Thai Yoga), and several minor. As well there are many private teachers and monks or nuns passing on multi-generational teachings in the oral tradition. Many have grown up in families that have practiced for several generations and are quite knowledgeable.

It is relatively recent in Thailand's history (1990's), that the Royal Thai Government under various ministries has made dedicated efforts to catalog the various traditional schools and teachers from the entire country. Initially the emphasis was on the "official" or Bangkok styles and schools but over the years wider research has included many more variations. There is now standardized practice and curriculum for the traditional practices under the Union of Thai Traditional Medicine Society (UTTS) which has been recognized by the United Nations formally as the Indigenous Traditional Medicine of Thailand (1978: WHO UN DESA, recognition Indigenous and Traditional Medicine).

There are well known traditional schools such as the Traditional College of Medicine, Wat Pho, Bangkok; Wat Raja-Orasanem, Thonburi; Anantasuk School of Thai Traditional Medicine: Wiangklaikangwan Industrial College: Hua Hin and Lak Sii (Aachan, Phaa Khruu Anantasuk); Ayurved Vidyalai: Bangkok and the Foundation of Shivago Komarpaj, Buntautuk Old Medical Hospital in Chiang Mai (Founded by Aachan Sintorn Chaichagun in 1973). There are also satellite or derivative medical schools in the Wat Po tradition in various areas of the country outside of Bangkok located in Lamphun and Chiang Mai.

Indigenous, Traditional Thai Medicine and Massage is also taught in other local temples, temple auxiliaries and by various competent individuals from Chiang Mai to Sri Lanka. I refer to the Wat Sawankhalok Medicine School for the Blind (Aachan Tawee), The School of Traditional Medicine at Wat Suandok in Chiang Mai, and Wat Amperwa, as well as in traditional sword fighting schools such as the Buddhai Swan Institute formerly located in Nongkham now in Ayutthaya. The practices of ITTM are found in the Muay Boran and Muay Thai Boxing Traditions. Lastly, you see the practices and Ayurvedic influences in the Reusi Dottan or "Reishi/Yogi" still practiced and currently experiencing a renewed interest.

PLEASE NOTE: Today the official designation of the Indigenous, Traditional Thai Medicine abbreviation in common use is TTM. Because we wish to emphasize the indigenous and traditional origins of both what is formally recognized and the oral traditional practices passed on in common use by family, tribal and temple institutions, we will use ITTM.

Much progress has been made towards formal recognition of ITTM in Thailand. It is now officially recognized with parity of its primary competitors: the institutional and or corporate based western Allopathic medicine and that of Traditional Chinese Medicine. The Thai government defines the highest standard on ITTM practitioners i.e. Traditional Doctors (Moh Boran and or Moh Phaen Boran) as those "practicing the healing arts by means of knowledge gained from traditional text or study which is not based on science." [22][23][24][26][27].

This is not to say that the essentially traditional practices are unscientific! Many aspects and uses of ITTM for the reduction of suffering and the curing of disease have been clinically verified in published scientific articles and clinical trials. Today's path for formal recognition in Traditional Thai Medicine (TTM) [24} of the traditional doctor follows a rigorous and defined course of study and National examinations followed by licensing.[27] Training duration, depending on area of specialization can be anywhere from two to four or more years. This is due to the long catalog of traditional areas of specialization from the Hands-on/Chirothesia to practices of Midwifery, Bone Setting, Herbal Medicine and more. The historical records appear to concur that from the earliest time the practice of medicine and traditional healing was a sacred act, performed by individuals obligated under oath to perform healing as a spiritual practice and sacred duty.

Origins of the Thai people

There is some controversy and differing opinions as to the historical origins of the Thai people who came to found the country of Thailand. Formerly the country was called Siam, a designation which likely originated with the Portuguese, who were among the first westerners to visit the region.

Some historians estimate that the origin of the Thai people is in the north of what we today call Siberia. In a latter period, these people immigrated in a southerly direction and eventually settled in China in an area from the Huang Ho River downward. About 2,500 years before the Buddhist Era (about 4,500 years ago) displaced Chinese people crossed the Thien Cham Mountain and began to infiltrate the basin of the Huang Ho River. They met the "Ai Lao" or "Thai" people there. The Chinese called these people "Tai" meaning powerful and prosperous. The Thai themselves have always preferred to refer to themselves as "Meung Thai."

Recently, this migratory theory has been challenged by the discovery of prehistoric artifacts in the village of Ban Chiang in the Nong Han District of Udon Thani province in the Northeast [28]. There is evidence of bronze metallurgy going back 3,500 years, as well as other indications of a far more sophisticated culture than any previously suspected by archaeologists. Based on these discoveries a new origin theory has been proposed: the Thais may have originated here in Thailand and later scattered to various parts of Asia, including China.

A significant to note about the history of Thailand is that the Thais were not the first inhabitants of Thailand. Although over time the Thais became dominant through military conquest, the majority of their subjects were not Thai. They were the remnants of the Mon/Khmer dynasties that ruled from India to Vietnam. The Mon/Khmer cultures had originally been part of a great Hindu empire that stretched from Tibet to the Philippines by way of South and Southeast Asia. Historically this Hindu empire dating back to the lifetime of the Buddha (500 BCE) was known as the Majapahit (Maharlika) empire (Virgil Apostal: Way of the Ancient Healers). Thai rulers in their expansion and southward migration gradually adopted many of the ways and cultures of the people they came to rule.

According to researchers (Braun and Schumacher: Traditional Herbal Medicine in Northern Thailand: White Lotus 1994) [2] "The Thai Court followed a pattern of adopting (and adapting) the indianized culture of the people they conquered. During the Ayutthaya period Indian influence thus became firmly established in many domains: the concept of divine kingship replaced the original Thai version of feudalism; Indian Law - The Code of Manu - became the model for Thai law; The astrologers surrounding the king were Hindus; the alphabet was modeled after the Indian (and Khmer alphabets); Indian literary genres and metrics were introduced and of course Buddhism became the national religion.

Please note: The Thai did not entirely abandon their original Chinese influenced heritage, according to Braun and Schumacher and other sources (Andaya, Reid, Wyatt, Wood). The Thai Kings up to this last century,

looked to the emperors of China for official recognition. They maintained relationships formally through tributes made to the Chinese court and through trade. Large numbers of Chinese have always been part of the great migrations into Thailand bringing with them their cultural identities. We can see the Chinese influence in Wat Raja-Orasarem (Korat) and in Wat Po (Ayudthaya/ Bangkok) temple design. Wat Raja-Orasarem is literally a Chinese style temple built according to Feng Shui principles with eight sides, large circular doors, Chinese style mosaic decorations throughout and a grand multi-tiered pagoda right in the middle. Wat Po has adjacent to the Reclining Buddha statue an actual Taoist shrine and large guardian statues in the Chinese style posted at all entrances and exits.

The Thais apparently split up into two main groups as they traveled along the southern part of China. One group eventually settled in the area of what is now Northern Thailand establishing the Lanna kingdom.

The second group settled further south and after being conquered by the Khmer (Angkor: Kampuchea) founded the kingdom of Sukhothai.

The Thai united and set up a large territory which they called "Narn Chao." They controlled this area from approximately 648/B.E. 1192 to 1253/B.E. 1797, for a total of about 600 years. The Chinese continued to press the Thai people until finally a famous Chinese emperor, Ng Quan Lee Cho or Kublai Khan, lead a large army against the Narn Chao and conquered the territory. Most of the Thai's fled further South, although there are still ethnic Thai people in the area of Yunnan China today.

The remaining Thai people settled in the area in which they now predominate and set up independent kingdoms (Ngoenyang, Sukhothai, Chiang Mai, Lanna) much like those of India of the same period. These kingdoms were assimilated into the kingdom of Ayudhya around 1369/B.E. 1913.

Krungthep Dvaravati Sri Ayutthaya (also spelled Ayudhya, Ayudthaya or Ayuthia) was capital of Thailand for 417 years under 33 kings of the Ayudhya Dynasty. At its peak, this capital was larger and cleaner than contemporary European capitals. Ayudhya was founded on an island bordered by the Lopburi River on the North, the Pasak River on the East, and the Chao Phyra River to the West and South.

In the 11th century A.D., before the Thai settled, there existed a small outpost settlement formed and named Ayudhya by the Khmer who dominated this region of the Menam Chao Phraya. Ayudhya was of some importance because it formed a boundary with the U-Thong (a vassal State under the Sukhothai - the first integrated Thai kingdom called the "Cradle of Thai Civilization"). The first King of Ayudhya was Somdej Phra Ramathibodi. The kingdom was ruled in succession by 33 kings for 417 years, from A.D. 1350 to A.D. 1767.

When the original buildings of the new capital were completed in A.D. 1353, King Ramathibodi built the temple Wat Buddhai Swan on the site of his first residence at Wienglak. It is this wat or temple which became the home and training ground for the Kabri-Kabrong Fighting Arts. These Arts were practiced by the monks as a form of meditation and physical exercise, and the monks themselves were responsible for training the royal family and the military. Essentially, this tradition still continues.

Similarly, Wat Chetuphon (Wat Po- later rebuilt in Bangkok) was also established as a teaching center for traditional healing and medicinal arts. In addition to the Chinese influence which the Thais brought with them and the integration of the Indian culture via the Mon/Khmer cultures they conquered, there was significant and continuous migration, trade and exchange directly between all of the neighboring states and cultures such as India, Burma, Malaysia, Indonesia, Cambodia, Laos and as far away as Persia and Japan.

It is said there was one king of the Ayutthaya period whose entire
personal retinue of bodyguards were Japanese Samurai! [7] This is part of the Buddhai Sawan history of the development of the Thai Martial Art Kabri-Kabrong which includes the use and techniques appropriate for the Katana and the Thai equivalent the Maha Deo or Great Sword.

*Wat Buddhaisawan, Ayudthaya: Khymer style Prang
in center of temple courtyard.*

Phaa Khruu Samaii Mesamarn once gave a lecture on the Japanese influence in Thai Sword fighting and in Thai healing arts saying the Budo arts and Japanese (Chinese) Amma was influential beginning during the Ayutthaya kingdom period. Some of the Samurai allegedly returned to Japan where we suspect they shared Thai teachings of medicine and martial arts as well.

Two possible examples of this:
1) The "Extraordinary meridians" of Shiatsu Anma (Massanauga/ Ohashi Schools), which are virtually identical to the depictions and stated functions of Thai Sen Lines. I corroborated this in discussions with Dr. Do An Kaneko, PhD researcher, University of Tokyo in 1989 and 1991.

2) Historical accounts of Japanese merchants and Samurai in Ayudthaya from the Twelfth century through the fall of the old capital[8] [9] [10] [11]. ("Thai-Japanese Relations in Historical Prospective" (1988), edited by Chavit Khamchoo and E. Bruce Reynolds; and "From Japan to Arabia: Ayudhya's Maritime Relations with Asia" (1999), edited by Kennon Breazeale.) From Japan, besides historical material, come numerous tales narrating the adventures of Yamada Nagamasa (ca. 1585-1630), the most prominent Japanese figure in the history of Ayudhya" [7].

Yamada, a Samurai was first famous as a warrior and later in life as a merchant. There was a vibrant Japanese enclave in Ayudthaya for hundreds of years. There were also many accounts of commerce and communications, trade and exchange between the Thai Kings and Japanese Shoguns." It is estimated that the Japanese district, in its heyday in 1620, counted 1,000 to 1,500 inhabitants[29], making Ayudhya's Nihonmachi the second largest in population of the Japanese enclaves in southeast Asia.

Phaa Khruu Samaii Mesamarn performing Buddhai Sawan Khruu Blessing ceremony dating to Ayudthaya period. 1983

To the present day you will see ancient and famous Japanese weapons: Katana, Daisho, Yori etc. in the Royal Museum Weapons Armory in Bangkok. Thai Kings in Royal Regalia wear and/or hold a Japanese sword decorated in the ornate Thai style.

Burma (Myanmar) was certainly one of the primary sources of cultural influence with a periodically contentious and warlike relationship. The period of settlement in the old Capital of Ayudhya is significant in that it was marked with numerous altercations and battles with the neighboring country of Burma. The Burmese captured the Capital of Siam (as it was called in 1568/B.E. 2112) and took most of the population as prisoners back to Burma (Myanmar). During this period, Siam was a vassal State of the Burmese.

Around 1582/B.E. 2126, the Thais, led by the self-declared Thai King Naresuan, revolted against the Burmese. King Naresuan was famous for being a great boxer or fighter and founder of Buddhai Sawan. King Naresuan and the Burmese Crown Prince met in single combat mounted on elephants they dueled fiercely and King Naresuan defeated the Prince and the Burmese army was routed. (A monument to both King Naresuan and the Kabri- Kabrong fighting arts is located in Phitsanolaok not far from the night market.) In 1781/B.E. 2325, King Phra Buddha Yodfa Chulaloke ascended the throne as the first King of the Chakri Dynasty.

Thailand continued as an independent State from this time to the present day where it is currently under the patronage of H.M. King Maha Vajiralongkorn tenth King of the Chakri Dynasty. The capital of Thailand presently is Krungthep or Bangkok, where the King resides in the Grand Palace next to Wat Phra Kaeo, the Temple of the Emerald Buddha, and Wat Pho, the Temple of the Reclining Buddha.

Epigraphies depicting Sen Lines: Wat Po, Massage Pavilion, Bangkok

Khmer/Mon/Sumatra/Majapahit Cultural Influence

The influence of the Indianized Khmer/Mon culture in all aspects of traditional life in much of the central and western regions of Thailand should not be underestimated. Most aspects of life reflected this influence including the colloquial traditional medicine practices of the era. For a little over 300 years Mon/Khmer and Sumatran cultures were the dominant cultures of the region. Khmer culture was a Vedic culture, revering the Hindu art, culture, and text of classical India including the practice of traditional or classical Ayurveda.

According to the World Health Organization (WHO) Legal Status of Traditional Medicine and Complementary/ Alternative Medicine: The use of traditional medicine is documented in the stone inscription of the King Chaivoraman (around 1182-1186) who ruled the Khmer Kingdom (Thai/Cambodia) which is in the northeastern part of Thailand. Traditional medicine was used in 102 hospitals which, at that time, was called *Arogaya sala'.*[25] [31] "

Khymer/ Mon style architecture detail: Srisatchanali/ Sukhotai

Khymer/ Mon style deorative detail: Sukhotai

It can be inferred that Khmer doctors practiced Ayurveda and Vedic medical astrology (Jyotish). Remnants of this practice may be seen today in the Anantasuk TTM practice of medical astrology (Anantasuk Korosot) as taught at the Wiangklaikangwan Industrial College TTM curriculum in Hua Hin.

From the 9th to the 11th century, the central and western area of Thailand was occupied by the Mon civilization called Dvaravati. The Mon share the same lineage as the Khmer and settle in southern Burma later. The influence of Dvaravati includes Nakhon Pathom, Khu Bua, Phong Tuk, and Lawo (Lopburi). Dvaravati was Indianized culture, Theravada Buddhism remained the major religion in this area.

After 1157 CE [25](Chockevivat, Chuthaputti, Chamchoy), Mon heavily influenced central Thailand. Khmer cultural influence was brought in the form of language, art and religion. The "Sanskrit" language entered in Mon-Thai vocabulary during the Khmer or Lopburi Period. The influence of this period has affected many provinces in the north-east such as Kanchanaburi and Lopburi.

The Architecture in "Angkor" was also constructed according to the Khmer style. The Khmer built stone temples in the northeast, some of which have been restored to their former glory, those at Phimai and Phanom Rung and further cultures are stone sculptures and stone Buddha images. "Politically, however, the Khmer cultural dominance did not control the whole area but exercised power and cultural influence through vassals and governors." [32] Sumatra/Sumatran culture, a Buddhist culture until the 1300's when it became officially Muslim, controlled or ruled southern Thailand and especially peninsular and coastal Thailand. Originally called the Melayu Kingdom (Malayu, Dharmasraya Kingdom or Jambi), it was absorbed by the Kingdom of Srivijaya. Sumatra was a vassal state in the Majapahit Empire which stretched from Sumatra to New Guinea.

The Indianized Sumatran/Majapahit culture and trade were factors in early Thai history from the Ayutthaya and Bangkok periods first because these were the culture and belief systems of the indigenous people who lived there before being assimilated into the Thai Kingdom and secondly due to trade and exchange. The common traditional medicine of the Majapahit was Ayurveda and their famous martial arts were based on Kalaripayattu. Thai Kings, traders and military would have encountered all of them. The vast Majapahit Empire controlled the seas and trade routes of the Asian, SE Asian, Malaysian, and Indonesian archipelago all the way to the Philippines. Keep in mind trade is a two way system and ancient trade always included medicine and medicine practices.

The history and research I have given here is far from complete! My intention is to give a background and context for the birth and development of the Royal Thai Traditional Medicine and Healing system (Indigenous, Traditional Thai Medicine: Indigenous, Traditional Thai Massage: ITTM) which we simply call the Southern or Royal style.

- *Aachan Moh Boonsorn Kitnyom (Wat Po Director/ Professor) , Wat Po School of Traditional Massage: 1983*

Chapter 3: SomaVeda® Noble Eightfold Path

1. **YAMAS:** Good Way of Life (Internal: Not expressing negativity. Think good thoughts. Generate BoddhiChitta.)

2. **NIYAMA:** Good Way of Life (External: Bring love into the world. Practice external consideration: Use of prayers, chants (Mantra), study and charity, do good things. (Practical Generosity)

3. **ASANA:** Practical Exercise (For yourself and others), SomaVeda®, Martial Arts, Hatha Yoga, Invest in personal development for yourself and others. Develop yourself and others. Keep yourself as healthy as possible.

4. **PRANAYAMA:** Breath Science (Facilitation of 5 Pranas), Bandhas (Locks and Windgates), Mudras and Mantra (Focus and direct energy). Cultivate awareness of breath and Intention. Breathe on purpose!

5. **WAI KHRUU:** PUJA (*Th. Bucha*): Paying Respect to the Teachers (Pratyahara). Give credit where credit is due. Make acknowledgement a way of life.

6. **SAMATHA:** (*Sans. Shamatha, Dharana*) (Calm Abiding Meditation). Don't Panic! Wait and things will change.

7. **VIPASSANA:** (*Sans. Dhyana*) (Insight Meditation). Three kinds of meditations: Walking, Sitting, and sharing Thai Yoga. Find your real abiding mind in thought, action and deed.

8. **PROMIIWIHAN SII:** (*Sanskrit: apramāna, Pāli: appamaññā*) Four Divine States of Mind (Love, Compassion, Joy and Equanimity) (*Sans. Samadhi*)

Make the four divine states of mind your basic motivation... Work toward love, stay with it, come from that place. When we talk about SomaVeda® and SomaVeda® Thai yoga, we are also talking about it as a code of ethical conduct. It's not just a system or methodology of healing. It is the art of being. We say that there are basically 8 things that you want to incorporate in your life in some way, shape or form in order to have a noble or ethical way of life as a healer.

Noble Eightfold Path: #1: Yamas

Yamas are good way of life internally, your internal way of life vs. your external. We have two parts here: thinking good thoughts and generating Boddhichitta, and not expressing negativity. The concept of Yamas is to question: how do I intentionally craft a thought life that will generate a good way of life in the external? The way to do this internally is to think good thoughts. In order to think a good thought and not express a negative one, you have to know the difference between them. You have to have an idea of what is a good thought.

In the back of the SomaVeda® Fundamentals of Thai Yoga and Thai Massage: Level 1 workbook, there is a copy of the Metta-Sutra. It has this concept of wishing well to all living beings. May all beings be free and happy. May they be free of suffering whether they are high, middle, or low, etc. the traditional, classical idea is that thinking those kinds of thoughts generates Boddhichitta. It is the perfect thinking. Boddhichitta means 'the mind of the Buddha'. Boddhi means 'perfect intellect' or perfect understanding. It means to generate the mindful character of an individual who perfectly understands the value of being intentional about thinking. Yamas is very important.

Yamas are the activities and pursuits that you do to craft a healthy way of thinking. That could be reading health books or literature that inspires you and causes you to have thoughtful, considerate and truthful kinds of thinking. There is this idea of discretion and discernment as far as what you are exposed to. It could be watching movies and videos that have themes that are truthful and lead to higher thoughts like love, compassion and joy…correct thinking about the way of the world and so on.

Not expressing negativity is very important. We know, for example, that the cause of all illness and negative emotions are disturbances in the body's energetic field. We also know that negativity and its expression, saying it and acting it out cause disruptions in the body's energy field. These disruptions then cause more negative emotions. These negative emotions support negative thinking. These disruptions and negative emotions, cause postural and physical distortions which push us toward a negative expression of who we are in life, which is less than what we could be or what we are designed to be; less than our capacity for being. These kinds of ideas, this disruption and distortion and acting out, these negative emotional states of fear and phobia do not support the work of the human, biologic, transformational machine. Anything that doesn't support the work of the human organism we want to stop and change.

The word Yamas translates literally as a "binding" or a "restraint". In other words, when I'm practicing Yamas I am binding myself to a principle, a way of being. It infers consciousness and that you have the capacity and will to do. That's asking a lot. Maybe you don't have will. Maybe you don't have discipline, or consciousness or the ability to make a conscious decision that you will be different at this time, and ten minutes from now that will still be true. These are ideals however and we want to work toward them.

Doing these eight things on a daily basis will keep you healthy while you're practicing. If you do these a little bit everyday you will be mentally, emotionally and physically healthy, which is your platform to bring healing to others.

Constituents of Yamas: There are five traditional attributes of Yamas: Ahimsa, Satya, Astya, Brahmacharya, Aparigrata.

Ahimsa: Ahimsa is the practice of nonviolence. We get the definitive statement of what nonviolence is from the Metta Sutra. And the last line of the Metta Sutra is "may I no longer participate in the origination cycle for the creation of suffering for myself and for others". That is the core concept of Ahimsa. Sometimes it's stated as "do no harm". But how do you do no harm? That's why I like the Metta Sutra's statement better than simply saying Ahimsa means do no harm or nonviolence. (Appendix #14, page ????)[65][66]

There's a Karmic element in all violence, so the statement "may I no longer participate in the origination cycle for the creation of suffering for myself and for others" is more fundamental than just "do no harm" and just "be nonviolent", it's proactive. For example, for me the answer to the question "how do I no longer participate in the origination and creation cycle of suffering for myself and for others?" is that I do healing work. It creates positive, beneficial karma. It is not creating harm but it's doing more than that, it's actually creating karma which is the opposite from the karma that creates violence. So doing healing work, crafting love, compassion, joy and equanimity in practical ways is in fact a way of creating meta or beneficial karma. By definition those things are not participating in the origination cycle of suffering. The only way to be nonviolent is to not start down that pathway in any respect.

We all have karma. We come with baggage: no one's clear, no one's hands are clean, no one's not bloodied. In some religions like for example, the Christian religion, they say "we are born into a body of sin." I don't disagree with that, it meets the criteria of independent origination of karma which is manifested through life. When you read a little bit further into these ideas you find that it's not enough for you to be a good person. It's insufficient to slow down the inclination to express harmful karma. We have to make a conscious effort. We have to create positive karma on purpose.

Just being a good person is not enough, you have to be a good person on purpose. There's nothing wrong with being a good person by nature. But the ancient teachings say if you want weight on the good side of the scale you have to put it there on purpose. That's where we get into value of declarations, affirmations and agreements. It's the value of the cultivation of discipline and the way of right action, way of right livelihood and the like. It's where intention comes in as a counterpoint to creating suffering; all the unconscious ways that we create suffering is where the counterbalance lies.

 So every action, word or thought or as the Tibetans say every "thought, action and deed" creates karma. We bring attention to our thoughts, action and deeds. We see if by force of will, determination and commitment, that instead of expressing harmful things, we can express something else and generate beneficial karma.

      Satya: Satya means truthfulness. The root word of Satya is "Sat". Sat means truth. Satya Creation Principles [page ????] or "Samkhya Creation Principles" in Thai, both mean truth. This is about developing honesty. Avoiding deceiving others and one's self, to cultivate truthfulness. Work on avoiding lies and exaggerations, things that you know are not true. Another concept of Satya, is disclosure. In our culture we have this idea (perhaps in other cultures too) that not telling a lie is the same as telling the truth. According to this principle of Satya they're not the same. Satya principle stresses absolutely that disclosure is required. It's actually better to have the disclosure and then take your lumps than it is to be closeted and withhold the truth thinking that it is the same as not telling a lie. Being truthful is different than not lying because you're not telling the truth. If we lie to our self we will absolutely lie to everyone else. We will also lie about everything else.

      Astya: Astya is non-stealing. In Fourth Way teachings, we call the inclination or tendency to steal "tramp feature". That's a good name for it. When you steal something from somebody else, you're being a tramp. Tramp feature covers all kinds of little things. Tramp feature is pretending someone else's idea is yours. Tramp feature is theft by attrition, example: I borrowed something from my friend and I never gave it back and so at some point I just actively believe it's mine. However, if they didn't give it to me, no matter how long I've had it, it's not mine.

That process is called theft by attrition. "oh, I didn't really steal the car. It was unlocked, running and the keys were in it. That's not stealing, right? They obviously wanted someone to take it away." It is stealing. It's theft by attrition; you came to possess it without the expressed intention of the owner (however that comes about). In practical terms we say things like copyright, trademark etc. In spiritual terms we have the same thing. There is an implication to give credit where credit is due. It behooves us to credit the source because that's one way to avoid tramp feature.

Tramp feature could also be the way that we rationalize the defective part of our expressional life. In other words, if I'm not being the whole good person that it is my intention to be, I'm being some other way. The process of how I rationalize that as opposed to just owning it and disclosing it is tramp feature. Every time I do the opposite of hide something I don't like about myself, when I disclose it I am practicing Astya. It starts inside the head. It doesn't mean that you always have to disclose everything to everybody else around you; you do not. But honesty, integrity, honor and generosity begin in your head. You have to practice allowing yourself to speak the truth about yourself in your head first. Eventually you'll notice that sometimes something true escapes your mouth. When people give you a true and authentic reflection of yourself and you go into denial, judgement and defensiveness that is not the practice of Astya. An example being: trying to prove that obviously they don't see what they see. "Are you going to believe your lying eyes or what I tell you?"

It is a high standard but these are qualities to work toward everyday: a little bit of disclosure, a little bit of t ruthfulness, a little bit of owning something that ordinarily I'd like to hide, justify or explain away. It also has to do with holding agreements and then making note when we don't. We make agreements with ourselves in our head all the time and don't keep them. We make agreements with each other all the time and don't keep them. If this lack of integrity and consistency is ever pointed out, we identify, justify and try to explain it away. Saying things like "maybe I meant something else and what I agreed to was conditional." We try to wiggle out of it.

Astya is the practice of not wiggling out of it even inside your own head. When that voice which we call our conscience (the still small voice of the emotional realization of the truth about us) speaks to us, practice taking whatever part of us is trying to get away, and don't let it. This principle of Astya is a foundational principle. If you practice this cultivation of truthfulness, avoidance of identification, defensiveness, justification, practicing disclosure, practicing keeping agreements and so on and so forth. These disciplines create a foundation for being that's relatively solid and clear. From this point of view you're more stable in respect to the events that happen to you.

One of the issues that took me a while to sort out because I was identifying and justifying it, was acceptance of undeserved praise. In other words, when you get kudos but inside you know you don't really deserve them. It doesn't mean not to be gracious because a lot of times people will praise you or give you gratitude and so on as very genuine expression. But if you're getting praise or gratitude for something that you didn't actually do you should be clear about that at least within your own head. It doesn't necessarily mean that you'll be self-deprecating telling everybody that you don't deserve what they're giving you as that also comes across as disingenuous or insincere. Mostly I'm talking about inside of your head.

      Brahmacharya: Brahmacharya is control of appetites. Now, that's an interesting one to me because we're nothing but appetites, every part of us. I think that's part of what the many I's are. Each of the different I's that are psychological aggregates within us are personality aggregates. Many of them express appetite and craving. This has to do with food, sex, personal space, anything that you think you need. Hoarding is on one end of the spectrum and control of appetite is at the other. In Zen philosophy, like Zen meditation and so on, there is the idea of reducing to the most essential. Zen stresses the elegance of singularity, the elegance of simplicity. Why? Because that is a treatment for out of control appetites.

      Aparigrata: Aparigrata has to with non-grasping and to avoid the accumulation of unnecessary possessions. It's purpose is to become free; not from possessions themselves, but from the attachment to them so one is unaffected by their loss or gain. It's about being able to let go. For example, many monks take vows of chastity and charity. The vow of charity is about non-attachment to possessions and things. In the Thai way this is essentially what one does when one becomes a monk: you're literally stripped naked, your head and body is shaven. And then from that point forward the only thing you own is what someone else gives you and that's a loan, you don't really own it.

The monks don't buy their robes, the public donates the robes as a gift and the monks get what they're given. When those wear out they hope that somebody notices and gives them a new robe or they wait for the Buddhist Lent in July when it is traditional to give new robes to the Monks.

This is a practice of Aparigraha and the concept of non-grasping and non-possessiveness. It is elief from the attachment to things. A concrete practice to cultivate this is to practice generosity. Cultivate a practice of spontaneous acts of human kindness and generosity. At the end of your day ask yourself, "have I given more than I have received?" There is a universal law of reciprocity. If you want more but without the attachment that goes with craving and grasping, then give away. Be generous. When we're generous we do get something, it's not always what we think it will be, but it's always good. Active generosity is a practice of Yamas.

Noble Eightfold Path: #2: Niyama

Niyama is a good way of life externally. Bring love into the world. Practice external consideration. It also includes use of chants, mantras, study and charity. Do good things or practical generosity. The concept of Niyama is that now I'm taking what I've been working on as far as internal qualities and I am generating a practical expression of that. The fact that I'm a good person and that I think happy thoughts in and of itself is not enough. There has to be a tangible expression of your thought life in order to fundamentally change your being. It's an algorithm. That's something we get from the ancients. They said that if all you do is think and there's no practical expression of your thought life, then you are unsubstantial or ungrounded. You are air-headed and not practical, dysfunctional. You may have lofty thoughts with grandiose healthy themes. You may be a very loving person but with no expression of that, something's out of balance. The work in your life and the progress on yourself will be limited. You not only have to have the practical development of internal states of being which are good, but you then have to also cultivate what's called work, the art of expression of your being.

Niyama has several kinds of specific attributes: (*Sans. Saucha, Santosha, Tapasya, Swasthya and Isfarpranidhana*).

Niyama is the practical expression of love; the idea of bringing love into the world in concrete terms. Practicing external considerations, use of prayer and chants and mantras, study, charity and doing good things and again, practicing generosity. So this idea of expressing and practicing generosity is both a Yama and a Niyama. Practicing external considerations: "excuse me, pardon me, no, please, you go first", those are little considerations. A good place to practice external consideration is when driving on the highway. If someone looks like they want to cut in front of me I let them. Let people in line. Some consider it a crime if someone breaks in line waiting for tickets at the theater or at a ball game -- people have literally lost their lives due to this. If external consideration is practiced instead of violence then there is no trauma to be passed on to the surviving generations.

Here's a dramatic example of what can happen when we are Not practicing Niyamas. A road rage incident which happened in Chicago where a family of nine, a preacher and his wife and seven children, died in a fiery car crash because an individual thought their minivan had cut them off changing lanes on the expressway. The angry driver forced them to crash their van. The van burst into flames and the entire family perished. Imagine how pitiful and sad it was, the person who did this survived. They tried to explain, "well, I got mad because they changed lanes too abruptly". Notice the justification. That person was in a state of non-generosity, not practicing Niyama long before the incident.

The grasping, the competitiveness, the violence is automatic, literally happening faster than thought because that is the habit. The habitual response is the first blush of a response that you have before consideration. That first response is actually the one that defines your level of practice of previous discipline in history. If you've been practicing your first response would not be to do a bad thing, an inconsiderate action. Your inclinations act as a Niyama thermometer. If you're first response is to do harm, then you haven't been practicing. Even if you catch it and nobody notices.

Saucha: The first Niyama is Saucha or purity: Think cleanliness of the body and purity of the mind, as the body and mind are interdependent. Purification of the body is a way of controlling the mind. External cleanliness i.e. hygiene on a daily basis, daily bathing, clean clothes, living in a clean house on a subtle level is purity of action or selflessness. It's interesting that simply bathing regularly is an example of selflessness. It's an external consideration in consideration of yourself, your environment, others and future burdens. Think about disease processes, for example. How many disease processes and disease conditions have their fundamental origin in poor hygiene? There are too many to count. This extends to accumulation of waste products and toxicity, and so many other things.

We could talk about hygiene as it relates to bacterial and or parasitic infections caused by not washing your hands. For example: why colds and flu are communicated through populations? People don't wash their hands regularly. The cruise ship example of the Hanta/ enterovirus that causes the explosive diarrhea. It's transmitted throughout the cruise ship by one person who has the infection and does not wash their hands. Everywhere they go on the cruise ship and on everything that they touch they deposit the virus. The next person comes and touches that: door knob, handle, railing, chair arm and picks up the virus. Consider that the average person touches their face several hundred times a day. You touch a surface, now it's on your hand. It's guaranteed at some point in the day you're going to touch your face. The mechanism is failed hygiene. All it takes to interrupt that cycle is, one, keep the outside surfaces clean (housekeeping) and two, practice good personal hygiene.

Health and wellness require good hygiene. How does this relate to practice of spiritual philosophy and discipline? There is a correlation between hygiene and meditation and the ancients knew this. This is why the ancient spiritual communities were the first places where people practiced indoor plumbing. It wasn't in households of people where these concepts were refined and developed it was in the spiritual temples, the sacred areas, in the sacred places because that's where the concept "cleanliness is next to Godliness" comes from. There is a correlation between good personal hygiene and the health that this engenders. Hygiene directly affects your ability to contemplate, your ability to meditate, your ability to have a clean and clear mind without confusion and distraction, your ability to think of other things than how good or bad you feel.

The ancients knew this. They tried to pass this information on to us. The systems I have studied share many things in common, one thing they all share in common is this concept of hygiene as being part of the disease process. There is a story in the Atara Veda of how a group of the Reishi Ayurveda doctors got together to discuss what they perceived as epidemics on the horizon. They got together to discuss this new thing called a "village" and how if people starting moving into villages there were going to be whole new pathways of disease. The one thing you can't do with a village is keep it clean. Villages are dirtier than homesteads mostly because everyone assumes that someone else going to clean it up. At least when you're on your own you're not under that illusion. But when you live in the city everyone assumes someone else is going to clean it up. If everyone assumes that, then that looks like the city. It's not very clean. That's a hygiene issue. It's also a health issue; hygiene and health are the same concept but different.

Santosha: The second Niyama is Santosha or contentment. It's more than a passive state of mind, it's a virtue to be actively cultivated in order to free the mind from the effects of pleasure and pain. It's about recognizing happiness in the now, not when this and that occurs or that it only occurs when pleasant situations are experienced. This idea that you can cultivate a state of mind, a way of being in yourself that is buffered from what happens to you. Elizabeth looks at me one way, I'm really happy; an hour later she looks at me another way and I'm not happy anymore. I want to think is it possible for me to cultivate a state of mind where I am well and happy regardless of what Elizabeth's face is doing at any particular time. The ancient Reishi have indicated that, yes, it is possible but it will take some work.

Tapas: The third Niyamas is Tapas or austerity. Usually in yoga communities they talk a lot about Tapas. And in my community, we talk a lot about tapas and where can we get some! Not to be confused with the famous Spanish delicacy, this Tapas is about austerity. It means literally to burn, to burn it up. In yogic terms Tapas burn off all desires by means of discipline, purification and penance. Austerity is perfected when it seeks control over the body and senses without attachment to the austerities themselves.

The way we interpret that is to actually practice the discipline that you say you believe or that you follow. That requires effort and discipline. Sometimes that looks like you're doing things that you don't want to do at the moment. You're doing things because you have a higher commitment. The difference between the comfort of you doing what you want to do and the discomfort of working through an issue because you committed to it creates friction. This friction is the fire, the burn off, the Tapas.

If I'm always on cruise mode and I go with the flow I have no austerity, no friction, no effort. Author Jim Hightower says, "Even a dead fish can swim downstream." It takes effort and energy to swim upstream. Even a dead fish can go with the flow. We want to live, to have a full and rewarding life. We want to not always go with the flow. Sometimes our discipline and our commitments don't go with the flow. In fact, sometimes it looks like we're standing still in the current and sometimes it looks like we're going upstream.

There is a difference between going with the flow and the struggle to have integrity, to be yourself and to do the work that you need to do to become the possible person that you could be. That difference is what creates friction. That friction is the fire that forms the (your) self. So, if you really are comfortable with your daily meditation then chances are that your meditation is no longer beneficial for you. The moment it becomes entirely comfortable like an old comfortable pair of shoes, you know, just before they wear out when they're just right. That's when you need to be looking for new shoes because you know what? They are going to die unless you're in the frame of mind that duct tape is a form of shoe repair.

Swasthya: The third Niyama is Swasthya (study); self enquiry, reflecting deeply on the question of who am I. Study by one's self or to study with the necessity to review and evaluate your progress. At least once a day everyone should ask themselves "Who Am I?" It's an existential exercise by definition. Why am I here? Who am I? Every day you want to confirm that you're who and where you're supposed to be. Every day you want to go through some process of validation and confirmation that your life has meaning. Overtime instead of just looking at your life like an unknown blur, eventually you can get to a place where you look at your life and it actually makes sense.

If you recognize these trajectories and inclinations, wheels within wheels, then overtime you may start to understand what is true to your nature and what is tangential. What are the kinds of things that will take you way a from your good life? You learn to recognize them earlier and earlier so that you have less tangential evolution and can remain in some semblance of integrity according to your true nature.

Isvara Pranidhana: The fourth Niyama is Isvara Pranidhana or the art of surrender. Isvara Pranidhana is recognition that the limited ego based self is an illusion. Channeling of energy towards realization of truth. One who sees the self in all being and has surrendered the ego, for being the doer is a true practitioner. Now, many times in our school we come to this conversation from the idea of many "I's". The concept that there is no singular "I" when referring to the self. Unless you've really been working on yourself in a very specific way for an extended period of time, when you say the word "I" at this particular minute and you say the word "I" an hour from now, it's two different people (personality constructs) talking. The little things are where you see this dramatically. Someone says, "it's really good for the kitchen to be clean," everybody nods their heads and says, "yeah, clean kitchen. Yeah, that's a good thing." And so we really want people to step up and volunteer to be part of the project of keeping it clean. "I'll do it!" You say. Then in some future time, seven minutes later, there's the dirty kitchen and all the "I's" have something else to do that's more important.

And the "I" that wanted to do it is not in the room, he left immediately as soon as he said, "okay. I'm on it,". Intuitively you know this.

You're not going to say no, you are not going to say "I'm not going to do it now", because you hear the echo of that first "I" still ringing from the rafters from seven minutes ago. You said you would do it happily because it's a "joy of life". What actually happens is, you make yourself do it, but you do it with the resistant grumbling "I". It still gets done. Technically you met your agreement. However you didn't say when you volunteered "I'll do it badly. I'll do I grumbly." You didn't volunteer and say "I'll do it resentfully with constant under the breath criticism." The "I" that cleaned the kitchen wasn't the "I" that agreed to do it. It's a completely different personality (personality construct). In those little behaviors you can see the many "I's" because they are different personalities. Those different personality constructs are the "EGO".

So, what is the self? There is no self. What we say is you've got to find one to have one. You want to have a self? Great. Ambitious. Find one "I" that hangs around more than the others and that's a good starting place. If every minute you're somebody else, then there is no self that you're working on. Many of the exercises we do about holding attention and crafting the ability to hold a long thought are about that. Whatever has that capacity within you to be unified or singular in focus is more authentic and more true than all the other parts. When I say things like "I have the attention span of a gnat" that is not the "I" you want to be in charge of your soul development. I want another "I" to be in charge or a group of work "I's".

We work with aggregates of ego constructs that have similar goals and similar resonance. I find those parts and feed them. Then between them they can sustain a long thought. To craft a soul requires effort sustained over a period of time. I said "to craft a soul", but that's not really accurate as you already have a soul or Atman that is infinite and which has existence outside of the limitations of time and space. What I'm trying to do is get in touch with it in real time. I've been led by my ancient forefathers to believe that it's possible. However, just because some ancient person became transfigured doesn't mean that you're going to, or that I'm going to. Just because Jesus walked on the water, doesn't mean that I'm going to. It means that I might; it doesn't mean I will. To even come close to a metaphor of what that represents is going to take a bit of effort and a lot of help.

I surrender my ideas about the ego and the attachment to them. The first exercise that I recommend is to consider that the ego is not real. In fact, think that if a personality is a reflection of the ego, then the personality is not real. Then think if virtually everything about us is defined by our personality then virtually everything about us is not real. But something might be! The trick is, over time, we want to sort out how we can be not so distracted by the not real that we might actually be able to see past it or through it to see the real.

Another reference from the Bible, Saul of Tarsus, after his epiphany seeing the spirit of Christ in his first letter to the Corinthians explains "When I was a child, I spoke and thought and reasoned as a child. But when I grew up, I put away childish things. Now we see things imperfectly, like puzzling reflections in a mirror, but then we will see everything with perfect clarity". (1 Corinthians 13:11, Holy Bible, New Living Translation copyright 1996, 2004, 2007 by Tyndale House Foundation.) Previous to this epiphany of transformation he could see and he thought he saw the world as it really was. But in comparison to the sight of an enlightened person (a person of knowledge of the truth), the previous state of being was as if he was looking through a very dark glass. When we talk about the ego we see ourselves as we are defined by the ego. Since the ego defines what we see, then we are not seeing our true self, we're seeing a shadow of our true self. That's what this teaching is about.

Noble Eightfold Path: #3: Asana

Asana is the concept of practical exercise both for yourself and for others. SomaVeda® is a practice as are martial arts and Hatha yoga. The concept is to invest in personal development for yourself and for others. When

I say exercise, I mean literally to exercise. We have different centers inside of us: emotional, intellectual, moving and instinctive centers. Each of these centers requires different kinds of input, stimulation, food and effort to balance them. To balance the moving center, you have to have exercise. Move on purpose. We practice martial arts, Hatha Yoga, dance. We do Nuad, intentional movement on the mat with another person.

One of the benefits of practicing SomaVeda® is that it's as good for the therapist as the client. One of the reasons is that it has an element of intentional movement, which balances your moving center. It also brings a balancing and compensatory influence to the moving center of the person that you are working on. The ideas of flow, Vinyasa, sequential coordinated release in line with the breath and maybe with affirmation and visualization is balancing to the moving center. That's one of the classifications of benefit that we get. I receive it for myself and I also engender it for my client. I need more, so I also practice Hatha Yoga, Reishi Yoga, Chi Gung, and martial arts. I won't say here that there's any preference. Virtually anything can work. If you don't have access to martial arts, for example, find a place to dance, or a Hatha Yoga studio.

Intentional movement is necessary for balance and health. Anyone who doesn't have that, to the degree that they are lacking it, is going to be unhealthy. That is one of the big issues with a sedentary lifestyle and as people get older with atrophy. There is no excuse. As long as you are in the shell, it's required for you to move.

All of these steps together are what we call an algorithm or formula for enlightenment. Devotees of Paramhansa Yogananda say 'self realization' not enlightenment. That may be enough. Fourth Way people might say we are working towards a fully self-consciously elevated person or being. Develop your self and others, keep yourself as healthy as possible. Asana is sometimes referred to as the "Third Limb of Yoga", the word is generally translated as a posture or seat with the main purpose of preparing the body for sitting for many hours in meditation and shifting and awakening the kundalini energy.

In traditional medicine development, it was very logical to develop a systematic practice of religious therapies of medicine. Imagine that you lived 2500 years ago and there was a discipline being taught, an art being practiced that could in a single lifetime lead to elevation, enlightenment or at least inner peace. This teaching is in just one spot in the world. There is a teacher with a group of people who follow the teachings and you have to travel there to learn it. You decide to learn this discipline. It attracts you enough that you're going to leave your family, friends, town, farm, job and activities to go to where this teaching is, so off you go.

Now imagine this process from the perspective of the place where the teachings happen, the centre. People start to come who want to learn. They arrive from everywhere, all ages, all shapes and sizes and all physical conditions.

One of the conditions for this practice however, is that you have to be able to sit in one spot long enough to craft a long thought. There are many preparatory exercises and there are many supportive disciplines both Yogic disciplines of physical exercise maybe martial arts and others but you are all part of this meditation practice.

The new people show up and by and large the vast number of people who want access to this teaching, are not healthy; not healthy in mind, body, emotions, or in spirit. They show up with whatever they brought with them, whatever baggage or parasites. Now imagine your first lesson. For example, in traditional Vipassana training in Thailand the first Vipassana training is a 28 day silent retreat with 18 hours of sitting a day. Even today in really traditional Bhavanna schools in Thailand the dropout rate with new students there for their first training of the Vipassana meditation is around 90% or higher.

       A) Unable to Sit: People can't sit for 12 or 14 or 18 hours a day if they're not perfectly healthy. What if you had a bad back, a bad knee, a bad ankle, a shoulder problem, migraine headaches, parasites, problems with your guts and with your bowel, arthritis, what if you have diabetes? All these things have a direct concrete impact on your ability to sit. And a direct and concrete impact on your ability to do the exercises.

        B) Unable to Walk: What if the exercise in the Vipassana is walking? What if you can't walk or even stand? What if you got there in a wheelchair or in a cart or on the back of some friend and once you get there they tell you the only way to do this meditation is to walk? What if on the way to the meditation you were attacked by bandits and are wounded? You survived and you managed to get to the class, but you are wounded and have an infection.

Picture all the issues represented if an average group of people decided to go and do one thing in whatever condition that they happen to be, and that discipline that was there was very strict. Luckily part of their tradition was the practical expression of generosity and compassion, so when people showed up and they didn't have the capacity to participate, someone was prepared to help them.

They would have had to organize a filtering system called a system of medicine. This system was to take in the public, assess them, give them the therapy that they needed, give them the remedial exercises that they needed in order to get them in shape, mind body and spirit to start day one in meditation to have even a little chance of being successful.

This is why over time there was always a medical/ hospital function that was within and adjacent to the Temple/ Self work function. This was observed by the Buddha himself at a very early time in the development of his system. He addressed it directly and placed for example the Ayurvedic Doctor Jivaka (Shivago) in charge of organizing this medical function for the early Buddhist community.

Some of the monks instead of tending to their self-interest all day and every day, and by self–interest I mean "I'm not here to take care you I'm here to become enlightened". The Monks looked at these new people, these prospective adherents and they said "actually my ultimate enlightenment is contingent on yours". There was also this theory or philosophy concept "that no one gets out until everyone gets out". No one's free until everyone's free. The ones who got that the quickest would be the first to volunteer to help.

If I absolutely understand that my personal evolution as a conscious being is completely dependent on the slowest person's progress, then I roll up my sleeves and get real helpful. "Come on, you can do it, let's clean that up, let's practice Yoga. We need to get you on a diet, do a detox, balance that energy. We need to fix that broken leg." And so it was inevitable that medical/ religious therapeutics function became a big part of the Asana practice.

The Asana is the physical practice, the external physical practice same as with martial arts. That's why martial arts was always part of these healing disciplines Kalari Payat in India, Kabri Kabrong in Thailand, Tai Chi, Tsing-I, Ba Gua, Chi Gung and Taoist Gung Fu in China, Kali, Silat and Armas in the Filipino Hilot, the martial arts traditions practiced by the Aztecs, the Incas and Mayans, and they would've been quite sophisticated because all spiritual communities in the past had an external defensive mechanism or they wouldn't have survived.

If you don't have an internal practice of hygiene and an external practice of hygiene you will not survive. You will become toxic, infested with parasites and you will waste away. You have to have medicine and therapy if you are going to survive. Spiritual disciplines have the same needs as our physical body.

This is why we get into the idea of Asana: develop yourself and others but develop yourself for others. Keep coming back to this idea that the reason I do any yoga at all is really not just for me. The reason I do yoga at all is to stay healthy, strong, able and agile so that I can be of service to others. That's my primary motivation now, however, when I was in my 20s and 30s my yoga practice was really for me, it was performance
Page 36

oriented. I wanted to look good and be good in front of others so that's why practiced and I was highly motivated. I practiced very, very hard but over time I realized that practice for self-aggrandizement, self-elevation, self-importance was actually all practice for self. What I wanted to do was cultivate a practice that was not for the self but was for others. I wanted to cultivate a diminishment of the self, i.e. the Ego. Asana are really about keeping yourself as healthy as possible because your health is an absolute limitation on your creativity, capacity and motivation to help other people.

Noble Eightfold Path: #4: PranaYama

Breath science is the facilitation of the five Pranas. Pranayama, traditionally called the "4th limb of Yoga", is practiced in many forms and is generally defined as breath control. There are different things we can do to bring emphasis and explore the different kinds of Prana. Learning how to breathe may be one of the most important things a person can do. As a practitioner coaching your client how to breathe (that they should have an intentional element in their breath life) is a miraculous intervention. When you are working with people, you can show them first hand and directly the value of the participatory experience in breathing. That is for you also. Bandhas, locks and wind gates, Mudras and Mantras, focusing and directing energy. Mantras are the manipulation of energy with your mouth making sounds – it is Prana and sound. A mudra is Prana and movement. Mudras are motion and breath, mantras are sound and breath. These both focus and direct energy.

Cultivate awareness of breath and intention. In other words, breathe on purpose. One thing I like to say is, "when in doubt, breathe it out." If you don't know anything else to do at any given moment in time, you know there is one thing you can and must always do, that is breathe. Breathe with intention. If you can't do anything else in a situation in life where there is literally no other choice before you – physically, emotionally, intellectually or otherwise, take a breath. Since breath is the basis for life, we are brought into life with breath, it never goes away. From first to last, the breath is what defines our incarnation in the world of organic life. Our story of life is a story of breath.

When I start to consider this, I realize that Pranayama is worth more investigation. Pranayama might be a key to many things. In fact, Pranayama might even be the key to every darn thing. When you bring breath focus into any possible activity, it changes.

Pick something that you normally do without an intentional breath focus. It can be anything, reading a newspaper, listening to a song, even making dinner. Do that activity from beginning to end with a focus on your breath. See how that goes. It will show you something. That's why in everything we do and in every position, with every touch, it is meant to be an extension of the breath. If everything you do on the mat is not an extension of the breath, you are not doing SomaVeda®. You are doing something LIKE SomaVeda® Thai Yoga. In SomaVeda®, all of the pressure is meant to be an extension of the breath. That's the first extension of consciousness in the organic world. Physical pressure in the world of me communicating my intention and attention is through the tool of the breath. That's the tool we've been given.

The word Pranayama is made up of two roots, Prana plus Ayamma. Prana means vital energy or life force, this life force exists within all things. Pranayama is more than just breathing exercises providing oxygen to the body for increasing energy. It works on a deeper level. Ayamma is extension or expansion. Pranayama has its mysterious power to soothe and revitalize an entire body, a flagging spirit or an unruly mind, the mind is calmed, rejuvenated and uplifted. The focused breath also leads us internally to a deep level of meditation.

One of the teachings that I emphasize in SomaVeda® is the idea that Prana is vital life force and what I'm trying to do with my clients is to support the increase of their vital life force, that everything I do is an extension of the vital life force, the breath. Every conscious application of pressure, I visualize as an extension of my breath. I don't push or pull people. I don't paw, prod, squeeze, poke, jab, scrape, twist, fold, spindle or mutilate. I extend my Prana, my breath. I'm constantly working to reaffirm that visualization.

It automatically keeps me breathing so I never run out of gas. When you stop breathing you run out of energy. When I breathe, I also find that my clients breathe. And so this breath focus and occasional breath coaching, when we specifically give instructions like, "Breathe here now. Be here now with your breath." is Pranayama. Pranayama is not just a Lion's breath or "Udjaya" breathing or "Mulabhanda" with Udjaya Breathing.

Having a breath focus as you extend a Rolling Thumb is Pranayama as much as Udjaya breathing is Pranayama. I'm creating a circuit of the traveling breath throughout my body, all the chakras, the macrocosmic orbit, transferring into my hands through the microcosmic orbit driven by Anahata Chakra or the Heart Chakra's expression of the pranic energy to the body of my client. I am visualizing the circulation of Prana within the body of my client. It is creating a circuit between the sky, the earth, my heart, my body, their body, their heart, their heaven, their earth and back again. That is a big circuit. That's what I'm doing when I am doing Nuad as Pranayama. The essential concept of Pranayama is to breathe on purpose. However, the visualization of the breath as pure vital energy which is conscious and consciously circulated makes it unique.

Noble Eightfold Path: #5: Wai Khruu or Puja (*Th. Bucha*)

To Wai Khruu is to pay respect to the teachers. In Sanskrit it's called "Pratyahara". Give credit where credit is due. Make acknowledgment a way of life. Classically in Wai Khruu we are paying respect to three teachers. The first teacher is "whatever is your conscious conception of ultimate origin or God". In other words, all good things come from God. Wai means we put our hands together and bow our head and perform Namaska Mudra (Sans. Namaste Mudra). Wai first to Great Spirit, to God to the ultimate original source of consciousness. Whatever that is for you.

The second teacher is the physical embodiment or representation or earthly manifestation of that ultimate original source, a person. The first teacher is big, cosmic even, the second teacher is flesh and blood. We have big and small examples of second teacher. Big examples are like Jesus, or Quan Yin (Th. Guan-een) Bodhisattva. Big teachers are like Saints or sages who have a life just as troublesome as yours and yet overcome it to be an embodiment of holy or sacred ideas. The small second teachers are your direct physical teachers who teach you anything that could be true, that's the nature of the whole circuit. Truth comes from the origin of all things. Truth exists whether worlds exist or not. Worlds exist as a result of truth manifesting. We might qualify this truth as a truth of love, a truth of light.

There are many truths, but the idea is that all that there is, is actually a manifestation of truth and these ancient sages, second teachers, are an embodiment of truth in human form. When I Wai the second time, I Wai to my literal teacher such as to Phaa Khruu Samaii, but in the very same moment, in the form of a hologram, I see a reflection of his teacher and his teacher's teacher as far back as back goes coming all the way back to me. That also relates to family for example, when I do the second Wai and Wai Khruu I pay respect to my grandmother who taught me many important truths.

If there's any truth within you, you learned it from a person and you owe them an acknowledgment. When I Wai Khruu, I say all the teachers in my life which have given me that which I believe to be true, which has enabled my life to have truth in it as an operative principle, I pay respect to you. We want to pay respect to each other. It is very important to acknowledge the spiritual beings you find yourself with in life. It's very important that we don't get caught up in the minutiae and forget why we're here. Wai Khruu is not something we do once in awhile. Wai Khruu is a continuous state of being. Give credit where credit is due. Pay respect to everybody. Give respect to the girl at the checkout counter. Pay respect to the mailman. Pay respect to the service processor who brings you the wonderful notice that someone is going to sue you today. Don't be rude to them. Pay them respect because all lessons originally come from spirit, no matter what it looks like.

When you study books that are related to our discipline like the Tibetan "Bardo Thodol" commonly known as the "Tibetan Book of the Dead", you learn that some of the most powerful teachers look like they will eat you alive. They are there on purpose. They are there to help you make your progress. We have to reframe how we see the people around us. We have to constantly work at it because it's very difficult to stay in this place constantly through the day.

There are always challenges for what I call discursive thinking, which is thinking that leads me to have other thoughts than this. The discipline is to come back to it at the first moment when you are back in your right mind. Pick it right back up and get back on that horse. Wai Khruu is something that is important everyday, cultivate this into your life. Make acknowledgement a way of life. Affirmation can be imagination. Acknowledgement is really to see, to notice what's in front of you and clearly think the thought. We can affirm things that we never see. You cannot acknowledge things that you cannot see.

The third teacher in the Wai Khruu is the Innate or inner teacher, that which we call the conscience. We define conscience as an "emotional realization of truth" and so the voice of conscience is that voice that sometimes speaks inside of your head, as if from a gallery observing you from the sidelines, but which always speaks the truth. That voice is the inner teacher, the third teacher.

In Wai Khruu we pay respect to those three teachers because we want to keep connected to them. We want to be in the way of them. In every generation as we are that teacher for the next generation. We honour and perpetuate that tradition.

Group Wai Khruu ceremony at Buddhai Sawan Nongkam, Thailand 1983

Noble Eightfold Path: #6: Samatha (*Tibet. Shamatha*)

Samatha is called Calm Abiding Meditation. I think of the phrase "Don't panic, things will change"".

Why do we meditate? What is the purpose of meditation? The purpose of sitting in meditation is so that you can actually observe what's happening inside and outside. We get so caught up in what's going on in and around us that we don't see it all. We only see little bits of it. Just like your eyes are attracted to motion automatically. If something is moving in front of you, your eye is drawn to it. You have no control over that. Life is in motion, so automatically our attention is drawn to what's happening to us in our life. It's automatic, it's mechanical. It's part of the machine.

But we have other capacities. We have the capacity to separate, to create a meta-state. Meta doesn't just mean love but also above. It also means extra to, or aside from. We can create a meta-state that we can objectively see what's happening inside and see what's happening outside. This is "don't panic." When something happens you don't panic. What you do is to observe. Observation is better than panic. Panic is entirely reactive and reactive is entirely mechanical. It's a 50-50 chance that your reactive expression, whatever that is, will be inappropriate.

It is just as likely to be inappropriate as appropriate. If you add a third step, a third force the idea of a calm place where you can observe what's going on inside and outside, you are more likely to do something that's cogent with what's actually happening. You will be more likely to make a better choice. Most of the wrong choices that people make in life are because they make those choices too quickly, with too little information, and without taking a minute to really look inside, really look outside for what is actually happening.

 Calm Abiding meditation is object focused or no object focused. It is passive and introspective. Object focused, calm abiding meditation or Shamatha is when you have some thought or image, a picture, a person, an icon, a passage or place… singular within your in your head. You try to hold that thought, try to sustain it. For example sitting and looking at a candle flame or "Tratak" meditation is Samatha meditation. Because the object is the flame, calmly abiding on the flame. It's passively introspective. There is nothing to do except to sit and look. Maybe someone will throw in a real twist and you have to breathe a certain way when you're looking at the candle.

Maybe you have to sit in Seiza or in warrior or in Lotus posture or there might be some other constricting criteria, but the basic outline of the meditation is the same. You sit and you look at an object and that object is the flame.

The reason why we look at the flame is because the flame is motion. Motion automatically attracts the consciousness. The eye is drawn to it. The reason we meditate on the candle is that it is easier to meditate on the candle than to meditate on a lawn chair. But honestly, if you could meditate on a lawn chair you could get the same insight. There's nothing special about the candle. You could meditate on a Yantra or a Mandala. You could write any word on a blackboard and you could calmly abide and meditate on that word. You would get the same result as meditating on the Yantra. The Yantra is better than just writing a word on the board, because the geometries draw your attention to a point.

Meditating on an odd object, a word written on a board, the tripod that the camera is sitting on, lawn furniture, an item of clothing, or a natural thing is all the same. That's what we mean by "object focused meditation". It's all good. You don't have to meditate the same way as anyone else. You do need to spend a few minutes of the day in contemplative attention of some thing. It can be short, just for a minute or two or three.

The idea though, is that the time spent is intentional. You will intend to consider this object for an expressed period of time without distraction or consideration of anything else. Then you do it. You will get the benefit of creating attention and cultivation of the ability to be present when something happens. You don't necessarily instantly and automatically have to lose your mind. It's not required that every time something happens to you that you jump with a startle reflex, jump over the stove, make a loud exclamation, run around in circles for a few minutes, "which way did they go! Which way did they go! Which way did they go!" before you finally settle down and think "what just happened?". You go straight to "what just happened?" first without all the mania, but it takes practice and discipline.

Samatha is the same as Dharana. It means calm, abiding meditation. When I go into Savasana or corpse pose and do my extension and go into my breathing and calmly abide, I am doing Samatha meditation and using the asana to facilitate it. I could do this in many other Asanas. You can do everything you do in Savasana while sitting. It's more difficult which is why we don't do it in other postures, it may even be painful. Pain comes into
Page 40

bear when you do long, sitting meditations. If you have ever done a whole day of Vipassana or Samatha meditation your body notices after about 4 hours. You get a wake up call after about 8 hours; you are wondering why you are there. After about 12 hours, you might be absolutely miserable. At 18 hours, you either have breakthrough or you just feel lucky to be alive. If you do that every day for 30 days, eventually it might get better, but sometimes it doesn't.

Sometimes, it takes years to be able to sit comfortably just for one day. It varies from person to person. It is the number one reason why millions of people don't do long seated meditations, because it is so painful. If it weren't, more people would do it. The beauty is, we have another tool, Savasana. Everybody can do Savasana. Everybody can learn meditation. I know in a lot of yoga schools, it's not even cool to say meditation anymore because they are going more for the exercise thing. They still have people in Savasana. When I was growing up, Savasana was the meditation at the end of our practice, it wasn't naptime. It was 'now that we've opened the channels and balanced the chakras and we have handled the body issues and shut down all the miscellaneous conversations of all the organs and the imbalanced areas, moving the Prana through the restricted places, we can be still, meditate and have a more enlightened and free reign inside of ourselves, without all the body distractions.' That's what I was taught. Now for many people it is a nap break after a hard practice. You can tell that just by listening to all the snoring during Savasana. In my meditation training, if you went to sleep in any posture, my teachers would come over and kick you or slap you or hit you with a wooden stick. This was old school. If you went to sleep somebody would whack you, sharply. Sharp enough that the guy who is almost asleep on the other side of the room jumps. The people who are not asleep but are meditating don't jump, only the ones who are almost or who are asleep jump.

Samatha is calm, abiding meditation. Don't panic. It's from the Hitchhiker's Guide to the Galaxy. The first rule is to not panic. Remember with Pranayama, if there's nothing else to do, take a breath. That's the metaphor for the towel in the hitchhikers guide. If you don't have anything else in the whole universe, make sure you have your towel. What is that towel? The towel is "Don't panic". Why? Wait and things will change.

What if they never change? Well then, you'll die, that's change. If you hang out long enough, one way or the other, things will change. There is no reason to be hopeless even if you are in a hopeless situation unto your death. People who understand this have different ideas about death and dying than people who don't. If death cannot cause you stress or separate you from yourself, what can?

Noble Eightfold Path: #7: Vipassana

In Sanskrit language sometimes called "Dhyana". Insight meditation is active where Samata/ Shamatha is passive.

Samatha: Passive introspective. Vipassana: active extroverted or extra-spective. We practice three kinds of meditation: walking, sitting and sharing Nuad Thai. Find your real abiding mind in thought action and deed. Vipassana is the idea of maintaining a state of mind while doing something. Traditionally the basic Vipassana medicine is taking a short walk, turning around taking another short walk and turning around again, so you're facing the original starting spot. Vipassana could also be a 10 mile hike on the Appalachian Trail. It could be a canoe trip or walking in your living room, or walking on the mountain. You can do Vipassana sitting. That's an interesting thing. How do you do an active extroverted meditation while sitting? For example, instead of having a singular object as the focus of your meditation, perhaps you have a long mantra. Perhaps you see a sequence or series of images. Some monks visualize a series of Buddhas… they might have the hundred Buddhas to meditate on as a formal meditation.

Christian monks in many disciplines, have Saints. They will often do a meditation where they visualize every saint, now the next saint, now the next saint, and so on because all the saints on some level are supposed to be a mirror of God. They are all a little different and yet all the same and so although I'm meditating on many, I'm really meditating on one. However, I'm doing it actively.

In Thai one of the highest levels of Vipassana meditation is when you do the meditation on or with another person. Generally speaking walking meditation is always done in groups, people standing side by side. Rows could be 10 or 20 across, could be 10 deep or 100 deep. The elder monks in the front, novices and initiates in the back.

The elder monks lead the exercise "taking a walk". The new people follow closely. There is always someone within an arm's length so if you're not paying attention you'll step on the person in front of you, or back up into the person behind you or tip over into the person next to you on the right or bump into the person on your left. When you are doing the meditation, everyone has to stay relatively in the same space the whole time. That alone takes a lot of attention. In fact, it's quite normal for the newbies in the back to fall down. We are going to take eight steps… eight simple steps forward. We are going to turn around and walk back eight steps. Then turn around and stop. In those 16 steps and 2 turns somebody falls down, and somebody bangs into somebody else. So in the front of the group Vipassana parade, though cohesive and calm like water flowing, in the back little ripples, like a tail that's got a little wiggle on the end of it.

The difference from front to back is level of attention. In front, the practice discipline is grounded in stability and motion. It doesn't matter if they are standing still. It doesn't matter if they're walking, it's the same. In the back people take three steps, if they have to stop they fall over, if they have to stop and turn they fall over. The theory is that this state of being is what we actually do in life. We have a little flash of consciousness and then we throw ourselves forward into space hoping to land in a good place.

When we land we have another little spark of consciousness and we again throw ourselves into space hoping to land in a good place. There's a gap, a moment where we are not completely present. We don't see the gaps. We have the illusion of continuous consciousness, continuous attention. It's an illusion as we have a little bit of attention "we're here", "we're not here". "We're here", "we're not here". But this changing state happens so fast that we think we are here all the time.

The closest illustration I can give to something similar that you might be able to relate to, is a movie, a motion picture. I use the word motion picture more than movie because it is the motion of individual pictures that gives the illusion of a movie. You have a photograph, and then another photograph, and then another photograph, etc. until you have many hundreds or thousands of them. If you show the photos in sequence fast enough you lose the ability to discern the single image and your brain thinks that it's one continuous image, although it never is.

We watch a movie and we think we are seeing something seamless and with continuity. It almost looks like real life. We think it's actually happening in front of us as it appears. It is not, it is "one image, stop, space", "one image, stop, space". A conventional movie shows somewhere between 24 frames per second (FPS) at the lowest and 60 FPS to give you the appearance of continuous motion. If it's slower than 24 FPS you see a flickering image. That is, you can actually see the gaps between each frame (photo). If it's going too slow you know the movie's playing but you can't tell what your looking at, but soon as you get to 24 FPS you have a sense of continuity, of continuous motion. By the time you hit 30 FPS, just six frames faster per second, (the standard speed of the standard movie 30 FPS which is 60 gaps per second) there's actually more space between what you see i.e. gaps, where there's nothing, than there is the content of what you see. That is enough to give us the illusion of continuity because we no longer see the gaps.

The purpose of Vipassana is to show the gaps. In this metaphor it's not a movie, it's my consciousness "I'm here, I'm not here", "I'm here, I'm not here". I think I'm always here but the practice of Vipassana, the practice of Nuad on the body actually slows the mental frames down, slows the film down until we start to see the gaps and eventually come to the conclusion that you're mostly gaps. What you think of when you think of continuous motion is similar to the SomaVeda® Thai Yoga practice exercise of doing Flow.

You think you're moving and you're not. You think you can just say "I'm going to move from here to there without stopping" and that you can do it. Everyone learns relatively quickly the this is an impossible task! Learning to Flow is an impossible request. It's so hard that there has to be a point in your practice where you think it's unduly ridiculous to even expect that you could do it. No one can do Flow, initially. First have to find the gaps, you have to see them. You put something in the gap that wasn't there before. That something is consciousness. As you fill in the holes with consciousness reality can be more easily seen. That's the theory. Vipassana: which I mentioned originated with the Thai monks. We actually know approximately the place where this meditation form was developed, who the monks were, who first codified it. We know approximately where it was first widely taught, and practiced in Thailand. A place called Sukhothai. If you ever get a chance to go visit Sukhothai it is one of the most amazing places on the planet. If you want to talk about planetary vortices, points and places that are significant, Sukhothai is one of those places.

Sukhothai is very interesting, it's been extensively researched by anthropologists with many excavations over a period of about 50 years. There are many hundreds of ruins of old temple around the Sukhothai area, aside from the primary area which is which is called the Grand Palace. If you excavate down 10 ft. there are remnants of older temples, dig down another 10 ft. you find remnants of another set of structures and temples, in fact you can dig down 30 ft. and still find that their temples were built on top of temples which were built on top of temples over a period of thousands of years with, many years between them.

There was a period of time where for over a thousand years there was some kind of monastic and spiritual life being practiced. Then there was a period of 500-1000 years where no one was there, then followed by another group who happened build the next set of temples right smack on top of the other ones. Then a great period of time passes and another culture came along and decided to build their sacred site right in the same place on top of all the others. Like a parfait of sacred sites built on top of sacred sites, built on top of sacred sites.

We have concrete archaeological evidence supporting this history. The oldest known intact kilns on the planet are in Sukhothai, Thailand. It is believed that the Chinese brought the technology of making porcelain and terracotta from the Thais. Celadon is the glazed terracotta and the porcelain originally from Sukhothai. There's a museum that's been excavated a little over thirty feet straight down and there are Kilns that were built on top of each other over a period of ten thousand years. Kilns of virtually the same identical style and if you built a traditional kiln in that style today, it would essentially look exactly like the kilns that were built there, centuries and centuries and centuries ago. There're millions of pieces of pottery that have been collected from there.

Sukhothai was one of the first cities that we know of that had indoor running water and indoor plumbing, indoor bathrooms and flushing toilets. Sukhothai had a fine understanding of the value of hygiene and health in the 11th century a time period where the European cultures were still walking in their poo. Europeans at that time would either deficate outside the house or just dump it out the window when they were done. This is literally a thousand years before the Europeans discovered that you shouldn't live in your excrement.

The role of health and spiritual life and development originated in the oldest Khymer- Mon Vedic cultures and their Ancient Reishi Vidya and Yogis.

When we talk about meditation in general we say there are 3 kinds of meditation:

        Standing: Walking (Vipassana)

        Seated: Sitting- stationary (Vipassana, Samatha)

        Sharing Nuad- Chirothesia: (Laying on Hands as a dynamic and shared experience)

Traditionally speaking the actual practice of doing sessions on people is a form of meditation. There are meditative benefits that you get from doing flowing or other sessions on people, they do not get from any other kind of meditation. Sitting meditation is calm, it's object focused it is introspective and it is passive.

Vipassana: Vipassana is active, it's dynamic. It's extroverted and it's almost always done with other people. You walk with them so that you have to be mindful of who's in front of you, who's behind you, who's to either side of you, who's moving too fast and who's moving too slow. You have to observe the cadence of the mantra, the cadence of the meditation. You're beating and banging around other people while you are trying to meditate, to find the space, the tempo that's just right. That's one level of insight meditation and it's considered a fairly advanced form of meditation.

When you start talking about mediation on the body of another person it's a whole other level. Not only are you dealing more personally with the person and their resistance and their openness, their mobility or lack of motion and so on, but you also have to deal with yours. You've got to deal with your restrictions of motion, you have to deal with the pain in your body.

You've have to work not only with their issues but you have to work with your issues, at the same time. It is a fine and very sophisticated idea of meditation this idea of laying hands on another person and taking them through a sequence of Yoga Vinyasa flow as a form of meditation, dancing meditation. It's not linear, it's not just walking. You use every part of your body and you move in every direction. You go up and down and out and back, you bring in and push up, you project and call forth. You use of all your faculties of mind, body and spirit. It is an advanced form of meditation. It is in the Vipassana tradition way of thinking. The idea that by emphasizing the between space, the meditative space, between one technique and another, you are looking at the in-between space for your answers.

My first Vipassana teacher was a Thai monk, his name was Phaa Khruu Aachan Chaa. He used this little description which you have perhaps heard as it is common. It's been shared by many people. Vietnamese Buddhist teacher ,Thich Nhat Hanh who I mentioned previously, also studied with Aachan Chaa in the Bhavanna Vipassana tradition.

The venerable Aachan Chaa said that the way the mind works is like you're standing outside and looking at the sky. You see stuff in the sky called "weather" or "clouds", or "storms" or what have you. Some days you go outside and look up and all you see is clouds, you can't see anything else but clouds. And if you just look for a moment you might not realize that the clouds are moving.

The clouds are in motion and if I look at the sky right this minute. And I look again at the sky 10 minutes from now, even though it might look the same, it's not the same. Why? The clouds are in motion. The clouds I see now are not the same clouds that were there a few minutes ago. On some days you look up and see clouds, and between the clouds, you see something else. You see what Aachan Chaa called the "clear blue sky" behind the clouds. He said, that is actually the sky. The stuff between the clouds.

The stuff that the clouds are in is the sky. The clouds are not the sky, the clouds are something temporary. The clouds are transitory moving across the landscape of the sky. And so it is in our head. Ideas, thoughts and feelings are clouds. They're impermanent, temporary. They're transitional and associative, subject to change at any time. It is their nature to move, to change always and at all times. That never is not the case. But that is

Page 44

not your mind. Your mind is the clear blue sky, the template, or the tableau, the between space. Whatever is between the thought A and thought B. Picture A and picture C. Emotion A and emotion B. Whatever is not those things, that's what your mind is. The function of Vipassana is to give you a way to practice looking at the between places while not being overly considerate of that which is obscuring your vision of it.

From our point of view, the sky above the clouds is eternal and never changes. Yes we have the moon, planets and the sun, but for the purposes of the metaphor, the life of the planets and the life of the stars is pretty much immortal, compared to our consideration of them. The same thing is inside of our head. We actually have something inside of us that is more like that sky than it is like the clouds.

We want to find ways to be able to see that and then to move into it. If we can find ways to move into that space, then we're actually beginning to be more considerate of a consciousness which is not temporary, not transitory, which is not in motion, and not subject to any random influence, which is in fact completely outside of the normal limitation of time and space.

Vipassana is a practical exercise to find your real abiding mind in thought action and deed.

People spend a lot of time doing Samatha meditation on things that are very negative and harmful for them. In other words, they think about images and words that disturb them. They spend a lot of time, effort, and energy on it, that is object-focused meditation. Our recommendation is that the object of meditation is positive. Vipassana is a dynamic form. Working on another person in a thoughtful, deliberate, and conscious way while following the breath is Vipassana. What's the benefit of Vipassana? The benefit of Samatha is calmness and serenity, which are the antithesis of the stress of life. The result of Vipassana is insight. Who couldn't benefit from a little bit of insight? It's not random insight. It's insight into the reality of life, of you, and of nature. What's between this and that that you are so occupied with?

Find your real abiding mind in thought, action and deed. In other words, this means irrespective of events and circumstances. There's a way to be you and to know yourself in every possible situation of life and that's what Vipassana is for. Vipassana is a way I can learn to meditate and do my meditation no matter what is going on around me. I can meditate next to my car, which just broke down on the road. I can meditate in a war zone. I can meditate in a hospital room. I can meditate when I'm in pain. I can meditate in any circumstance. By practicing Vipassana, we learn how to consciously take control of our inner states irrespective of external environments.

Noble Eightfold Path: #8: Promiiwihan Sii: *(Pali.Brahmavihāra)*

The Brahmavihāras (sublime attitudes, lit. "abodes of brahma") are a series of four Buddhist virtues and the meditation practices made to cultivate them. They are also known as the four immeasurables (*Sanskrit: apramāna, Pāli: appamaññā*).[64][65]

Promiiwihan Sii is a Thai term. It means the Four Divine States of Mind. Other ways to say the four divine states of mind are: the four boundless, the four unlimited, the four infinite states of mind or even the godlike states of mind, exemplary of conscious beings manifest. They are Love, Compassion, Joy and Equanimity. The Thais say that if you do not have all four of these things, you are sick and in need of therapy. If all four divine states are not apparent in your life, there's something that is imbalanced within you.

     LOVE: (*Pali. Mettā pāramī*): loving-kindness) Love is the first one, love is understood as the clear mind of God. It is the infinite source of consciousness and it is substantial, love is not something that is without substance. Love is a formative energy in the universe, it is in fact the source of direction for the creation of suns, the creation of solar systems, the creation of all of the primary elements, the fundamental elements of the universe on the atomic periodic scale, and it's the source of light. In fact light is a manifestation of love and many sacred scriptures say that, light is the first manifestation of love. What is the dark matter of the universe? The original plasma energy, binding, the engaging force that generates all life and light in the universe is objective love. Love is what literally makes the world go round. Life itself is a manifestation of this concept of love. However, love in a philosophical context is not good enough.

To have a balanced life, there must be appreciation of love, knowledge of love, an experience of love and a practical expression of love. If I have love but no way to express it and no experience of love with the world and other people, I am unbalanced. I could be a person who is nothing but love and I could also be completely imbalanced. This is a hard concept to consider. There are many loving people who have a miserable existence, who languish for lack of the expression of love in their lives. They languish for the lack of reciprocity. They're loving and genuine in their love but because they haven't conquered the hurdle of practical expression, their love is unrequited, unsatisfied, and unreal. In order to be more balanced, we have to have the practical expression of love. (Appendix #10, p.46)[65][66]

COMPASSION: (*Sans., Pali. Karunā*) Compassion is defined as the practical expression of loving-kindness. Compassion only comes into being when you do something. To be compassionate is not a way of thinking, though we might use the term that way. To be compassionate does not mean to think loving thoughts, to be compassionate is to do loving acts.

That means that the thoughtful person who understands this and does not have a way to act out of love and manifest their love in practical terms in their life, house, relationships and community are incomplete in their health. They might have an emotional, mental or physical imbalance. Unrequited and unexpressed love is a seed of much mental illness. By definition, in Thai, it is a symptom. If I look at someone and don't see the evidence of their expression of love, that explains why they are imbalanced.

Doing healing work is a compassionate activity. We define Nuad Thai as the practical expression of loving kindness. That means that we grab someone and we love him or her in real terms. I show you that I have love in my life by making concrete efforts to reduce your suffering. The most convincing argument that you love someone is that you take practical steps to reduce their suffering.

If I love you but can't or won't help you or only practice 'tough love', it's different. It has to be practically expressed. Love without practical expression is just an idea. Love practically manifested into something tangible, something that can be weighed and measured, is an act of compassion, the manifestation of compassion. When compassion manifests, there is a side effect, the fuel gauge of compassion. If the compassionate act is an unqualified, unconditional, expression of boundless, unlimited loving kindness, there will always be evidence. That evidence is Joy.

JOY: (*Sans., Pali. Muditā* मुदिता) Joy is the evidence or proof that love is actually being practically manifested. Joy is actually very important in life. This Joy is the pleasure that comes from delighting in other people's well-being. It is the litmus test of true compassion. For example, a wealthy person can give money to charity to get a tax break, but they will not experience the side effect of joy because that expression of philanthropy was completely conditional, judgmental and attached to outcomes and results which have nothing to do with love. Therefore they don't get the joy and maybe nobody else does either. There's no guarantee that just because you practice philanthropy and make a gift of money that you will get any benefit from it, especially if it is not an act of compassion or love. In ancient literature, they mention this as the reason rich people seldom get to spiritual enlightenment.

Page 46

We find that many charities are corrupt, when people do give millions or billions of dollars to charity, the money is mostly used for other things. If the giving is not compassionate, if it was for tax breaks, shelters, to set up bureaucracies, infrastructure, grafted… everything but to help the people. If the gift was so they would look like compassionate people. That is not an expression of loving-kindness. It can be very confusing for some people why all this good work is being done but there are no examples of good occurrences happening as a result. It makes sense when you understand the principle.

Joy is a side effect of compassion. If there is no joy, there is something lacking in the practical expression of loving-kindness. This is known in all classic situations of traditional medicine, whatever culture, Vedic culture, Thai culture, Chinese, Native American. There is a point where to gain certain attributes or qualities of life, requires that you be of service to someone else. If there's no service aspect in your life, concrete, define-able service, practical expression of compassion, then you will not have these good side effects. You can't get them any other way. You can't wish them into existence, they require action. What Dr. Amrit Goswami calls. "Do, Be, Do". They require you to do something. There's another side effect that only comes about when there's joy, it's called equanimity.

EQUANIMITY: (*Pali: upekkhā* उपेक्खा; *Sans. upeksā* उपेक्षा*)* Equanimity is a fancy word, it means equal disposition, or balanced mind. Classically speaking, an imbalanced mind, is any mind that doesn't have joy, compassion and love in it. It's not about your intellect, or how smart you are. If you have no love, compassion, or joy, you are mentally unbalanced, you are sick. That's how we define mental illness. The ancient Yoga Reishi said, you have to do all these steps. The result of you doing these steps is that you will have periods of clarity. You will have periods where your mind works in the way it's should, clear thinking, making sense and functioning. However, as westerners we try to put understanding ahead of everything else.

We put understanding, and intellectual competency above everything else. We make everything that we might do, contingent upon our understanding. According to the ancient Yoga Reishi we have it backwards. Understanding is something that only a balanced mind can do. In order to have a balanced mind there must be other qualities in that space which create the basis of the mental activity. We must support working in harmony with nature so we can know the true nature of the universe. And so, Promiiwihan Sii gives us this, in traditional yogic terms these states together are also called the state of Samadhi.

When you take the triad of love, compassion and joy, three different kinds of influences, all deriving from love (love is just another word for Prana), you get equanimity, a balanced mind. By definition, you cannot have a balanced mind and be a healthy minded person if you do not have love, compassion and joy as a practical process evidenced in your life. A life without joy, a practical expression of loving-kindness, and you are not balanced. A life without love is imbalanced. The strategies in our system were specifically designed to correct imbalances in these four areas.

Ayurveda is specifically designed to correct imbalances in these four areas. When we talk about our system of healing, or any system of healing, we might talk about primary outcomes. If I expose you to this medicine, what will be the primary outcome? If I give you medicine that might reduce a cancer but you will certainly lose all your hair, that's an outcome.

When we talk about our system of healing, or any system of healing, we often talk about primary outcomes. What I'm looking for in primary outcomes is not an increase in circulation, or range of motion. That's why I say over and over that range of motion is not important. The stimulation, the energy, attention, consciousness, breath and pressure are more important than pressure. Range of motion is an expression of pressure. Taking someone into a stretch is pressure equilibrium. It's not necessarily about consciousness or intention or affirmation or acknowledgement or breath. Pressure is the least important on the list.

The idea is that our therapeutic outcomes, that which we are trying to create with the client are fundamentally spiritual. Anytime I am on the mat or in my therapeutic mind, my intended outcomes are the same: that I am expressing unconditional love with active and practical compassionate acts, to balance the energy to reduce suffering and generate a sense of wellbeing and wellness in the client. It is practical, not airy-fairy. It's tangible, it's not a concept, the love is practical. I can prove the love by helping, comforting you and reducing your suffering. I can share that experience with you. As a result, we will have a more joyful life experience. All of us will then think well. We will become more ourselves and see our lives with more clarity and truth. With more truth we develop more balanced minds.

Student: What about something you are not excited about doing like volunteering for something? Your idea and you thought, was 'I should do this because I should help these people'. You drag yourself there. But once you're there and you do it, you feel glad that you did it and feel joy after that. What if your attitude was about 'should'.

Dr J: In nothing I've said here have I mentioned that you should want to do this. The knowledgeable and wise person will do this whether they want to or not. My internal progress is dependent on my acting on these principles and making these concepts in my life a reality. The very moment I explore love, express it practically, experience joy and create the possibility for balanced thinking my life changes. It might originally look like voluntary suffering. Voluntary suffering is when I put myself in a situation on purpose to cultivate one of these four divine qualities. That's a whole other conversation. Voluntary suffering is necessary. That is your coin of the realm. That is the only dollar you can spend in the coin machine of 4 divine qualities.

We have the vending machine of 4 divine states. The love soda, the compassion soda, the joy soda, and the equanimity soda in the machine. You can kick and knock the machine all you want but if you don't put in the coins of voluntary suffering in, then nothing will come out. That's different from unconscious, uncontrolled victim suffering. When suffering is put upon you, you don't necessarily get those benefits. You have to volunteer to accept the suffering. You have to make the extra effort to get the benefits. That's how these algorithms work.

The traditional Yoga Reishi would often have very strange, medical diagnosis. For example, you might come to them with this or that problem, and they would talk you and look at you. Maybe have you stick your tongue out. Maybe ask to hear some story about your issues or about your life.

Then they would then give the diagnosis: deficiency of love. We need to fix that. We need to manifest love in your life in such a way that you can identify it. The technique to do that, is that to begin to express yourself, and have an element of compassionate expression in your life. In other words, being good to yourself and being good to those around you in practical ways. Being helpful, being empathetic, being sympathetic and then finding ways to manifest that in something that actually materially changes your life. And then as you do that, love becomes not a concept, but something real. Then as that manifests you start to have these little glimpses, these little windows, little moments of experience where you are happy, where you are satisfied in your skin, where you are satisfied in your life, where you have a sense of joy in who you are and that your life has meaning and purpose and that the life of those around you has meaning and purpose. The Thai have this saying "If we're not having fun, why are we doing it?".

This is something you should always ask yourself, ultimately, if you're not having fun, why are you doing this and if you're not having fun, then the therapy is you've got to find a way to practically express your love and then the fun part, the joyful part is the side effect of that expression. If you have a deficiency of joy, that's another assessment, another diagnosis of disease.

Chapter 4: Lineage and Modalities of Expression

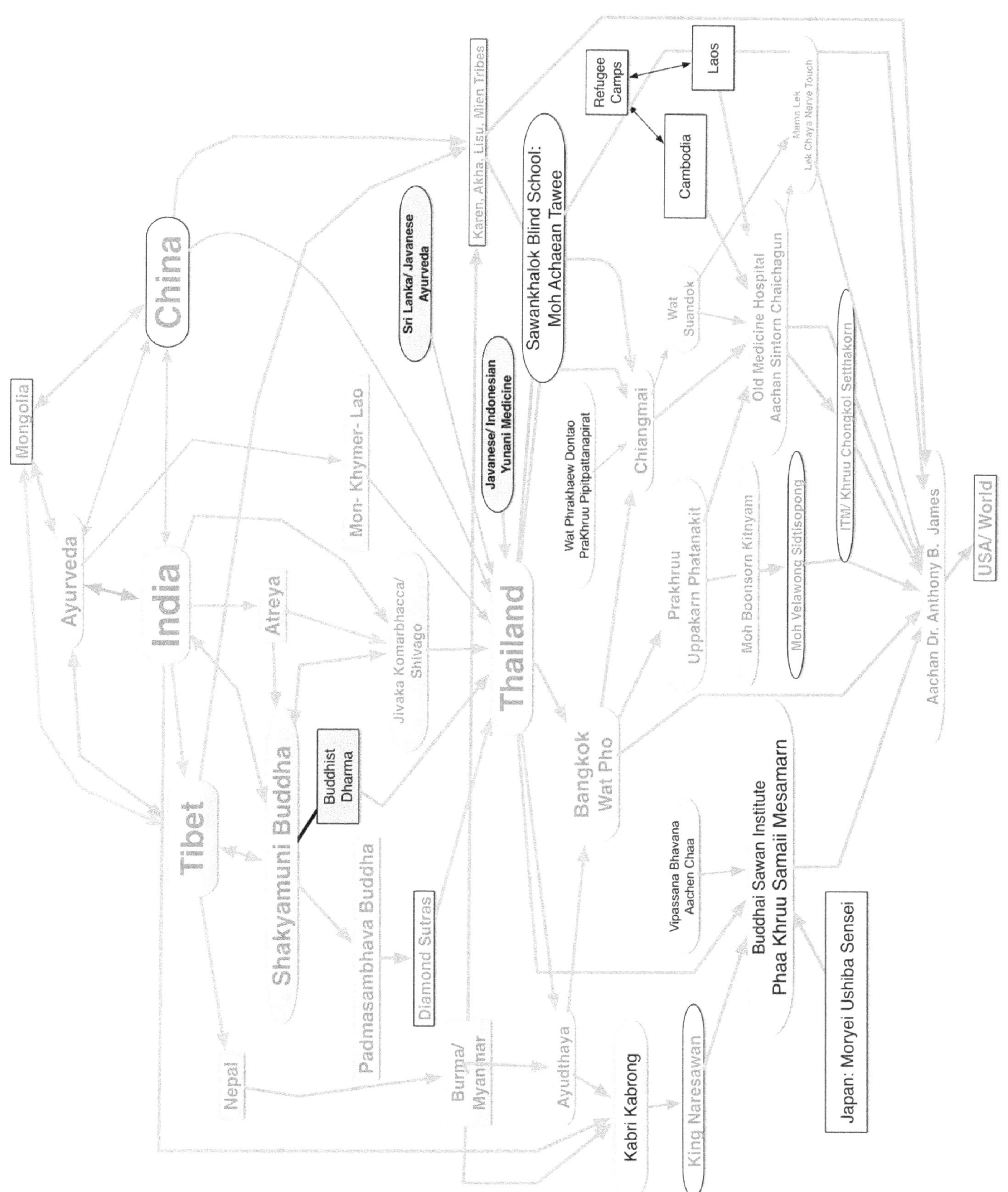

Therapeutic Modalities in SomaVeda Integrated Traditional Therapies®

The basic theory of SomaVeda®, Integrated Traditional Therapies is found in the following traditions and modalities:

A) Tibetan, Mongolian & Ayurvedic Medicine, Theory of Chakras and Chakra Body types and their correspondences. Panchakarma and Oil Massage. Twenty Three Assessments.

B) Theory of Thai Sip Sen or Prana Nadis. Locations, Indications

C) Theory of Flow (Filipino Kali, Jorge Lastra method/ Buddhai Sawan method)

D) Theory of PUJA (*Th. Bucha*), Prayer, Wai Khruu, Acknowledge Space, Lineage, Clean House, Petition, Listening, Bodhichitta

E) Theory of Promiiwiihan Sii, The Four Divine States of Mind (Love, Compassion, Joy & Equanimity)

F) Theory of Specific Remedies for Specific Problems (Traditional Formulas)

G)   Theory of The Laying on of Hands for Physical, Psychical, and Spiritual Healing

H)   Traditional Chinese Medicine Theory (TCM)
  1) Theory of Meridians and AcuPoints
  2) Yin/ Yang Theory
  3) Five Element Theory
  4) Modalities: Acupuncture, Moxibustion, Cupping, Tuina, Amma,
  5) Tai Chi, Chi Gung & Kung Fu
  6) Location and use of 20 primary points.

I) Western Therapeutic Hands-on
  1) Easlen Style Massage
  2) Manual Lymph Drainage
  3) Cranial Sacral Therapy
  4) Neuro-Muscular Therapy
  5) European Style Oil Massage
  6) Table and Portable Massage Chair
  7) Adjunct Modalities: Magnetic Therapeutics, Electro Acupuncture, Galvanic Iontophoresis, High Frequency, Photo-Bio-Modulation, Far infrared, Hot and Cold Contrast therapy, Sound therapy, Oxygen therapy, Colloidal Silver...

J) Thai Traditional Medicine: (*Th. Phaen Boran Ráksãa Thaang Nûat Thai*)
1) Laying On Hands, Spiritual Massage (*Th. Nuad, Jap Sen*)
2) Bone Setting (Th. Dat Kraduk) Healing of bone related injuries, reducing dislocations, setting broken bones etc.)
3) Yoga (All eight fundamental disciplines including Hatha & Tantric practices)
4) Prayers (Pali Chanting of traditional Mantra i.e.. OM NAMO etc.)
5) Acupuncture and Bloodletting (TCM conventionally taught and practiced in Thailand)
6) Moxibustion and Medicinal Incense (Use of heat and herbs)
7) Herbal Pharmacology and Medicines (Use of Medicinal Plants)
8) Herbal and Oil Massage (Panchakarma)
9) Therapeutic Herbal Steam Bath and Medicinal Baths
10) Pra Kob Sa Moon Prai: Steamed Herbal Compress or Herbal Poultice Treatment
11) Hot and Cold therapies (Massage treatment in water for hot syndrome)
12) Dietary Therapies/ Nutritional Counseling
13) Purging Therapies, i.e. Enemas, Purgatives and Emetics: detox strategies to help clean the gall bladder, liver and blood
14) Emergency Techniques for Trauma, Unconsciousness, Coma, etc.
15) Application of Buddhists Rituals in Mental Health: Meditation (*Pali. Jittanami*) (Samatha, Vipassana, Wai Khruu, Nuat Phaen Boran Thai)
16) Midwifery (Many practices prenatal and postpartum): nutrition, self-exercise coaching, counselling, structural correction, Sadung to evacuate the placenta
17) Chiwitanamai, Balancing Life Practices. (Bringing the elements into harmony through proper conduct and appropriate action.)
18) Death Practices (Chanting Abhidharma, Bardol Thodol-Book Of The Dead/ Clear Light Reading): functional death practices so the community continues to function after the loss of loved ones.
19) Krabi-Krabong (Traditional Thai Martial Arts, exemplified by the Buddhai Sawan Sword Fighting Institute of Ayudthaya/ Nongkam Thailand)

k) Native American Spiritual and Healing Ways: NAIC (Native American Indigenous Church)
1) Ceremony
   a) Tobacco Blessing
   b) Pipe
   c) Sweat Lodge
   d) Vision Quest
   e) Sun Dance
   f) Hunka or Making of Relatives
   g) Singing and Drumming
   h) Sacraments and Ceremony, (Ritual Healing techniques for balancing the soul and spirit such as those found in the Native American Indigenous Church, Mother Earth Spirituality, Crow, Lakota, Dakota, Bear Medicine Tribe (Sun Bear), Cherokee, Huichol, Tarahumara and other traditions of indigenous medicine from around the world. That is earth based medicine.)

Our Thai Lineage Masters

We pay respect to all of our personal Grand Masters and teachers in the Thai Traditions we honor:

- PhraKru Uppakarn Phatanakit: Wat Po 1983- 1985
- Aachan Moh Boonsorn Kitnyom 1983 - 1994 (Wat Po Director/ Professor)
- Aachan Phaa Khruu Samaii Mesamarn: Buddhai Sawan Institute, Nogkam/ Ayudthaya 1980 to 1998
- Aachan Moh Velowong Sidtisopong : Wat Po 1983 to 1995
- Aachan, Phaa Khruu Sintorn Chaichagun: Buntautuk Northern Provincial Hospital (Old Medicine School) 1989-2005
- Aachan Chongkol Settakorn: ITM Chiang Mai (1991-2010)
- Aahan Pichest Boonthumme Buntautuk Northern Provincial Hospital (Old Medicine School) 1988-1990
- Venerable Prakhru PipitpattanapiratWat Pra Kaew Don Tao and Wat Suchadaran, Lamphang 1990- 2010
- Aachan Phaa Khruu Anantasuk: Wiangklaikangwan Industrial College 2004- 2010
- Aachan Nanthipa Anantasuk: Wiangklaikangwan Industrial College: Anantasuk School of Thai Traditional Medicine Hua Hin/ Lak Sii 2004- 2010
- Mr. Surasak Srinoi (Wat Po Association for Traditional Thai Medicine, Anantasuk School for Traditional Thai Medicine and Wangklaikangwon Industrial Community & Educational College)
- Dr. Aram Amaradit, Member Parliament of Surin Province, Chairman of the Committee on Public Health, President: The Union of Thai Traditional Medicine Society, Ministry of Public Health (2009)
- Aachan Moh Mama Lek Chaiya: Lek Chaiya Nerve Touch Massage, Chiang Mai (1990-2015)
- Aachan Tawee: Wat Sawankhalok School for the Blind
- Aachan John: Wat Loi Khro, Chiang Mai: 1988-1994

- *Venerable Prakhru Pipitpattanapirat*
- *Wat Pra Kaew Don Tao and Wat Suchadaran*

Modern Adaptation and Integration Supported By Deep Roots

SomaVeda Integrated Traditional Therapies® is called such because it is a comprehensive religious therapeutic system of healing based on Indigenous and traditional Native and natural medicine philosophy and practices. SomaVeda® therapeutic practices are not limited to nor restricted by the practices of one indigenous source or tradition. We believe that all indigenous, traditional and Native systems have value. We also believe that we have the right as indigenous practitioners to access and make use of any and or all that we may be able to productively incorporate. Native people travel and have exposure to other native cultures wherever they may be found in the world.

Please consider that as a result of the diaspora and genocide which many native people and cultures have endured that many authentic and traditional medicine traditions were lost. Some tribal and aboriginal peoples lost their entire practical medicine traditions due to past medicine persons who were targeted specifically because they represented the core belief systems of the conquered peoples. This happened everywhere native people were conquered, colonized and disenfranchised.

Consider the banning of Ayurveda and Yoga practices by the British during the Raj period of colonial occupation in India. How much was lost over the more than 50 years of occupation? Consider the diaspora of the Native American tribes. How many original medicine traditions and the families responsible for their transmission were lost over the hundreds of years of subjugation and disenfranchisement, not to mention the various periods of wholesale slaughter?

Today, we are reclaiming and restoring the world heritage of Indigenous and traditional medicine. Native people and their supporters worldwide are sharing the body of their collective knowledge. SomaVeda Integrated Traditional Therapies® is entirely based on this movement.

Items A through K on the previous list represent our growing list of traditionally based effective therapeutic practices or "medicines".

The list is a survey. A caveat here on page [PageS 50- 51] (The basic theory of SomaVeda® Traditional Thai Yoga) is that this listing is not finished or complete. Here is presented an overview of some of the principal influences that are expressed in this SomaVeda® Ayurveda and Thai Yoga Therapy course. However, this list of inclusions is not comprehensive and continues to grow and evolve as new and complementary practices and concepts are either clarified and or added.

We have traditional answers to the traditional questions. We have as an example the 100 traditional treatments for the 100 traditional diseases. However, the challenge that we have, right now, right here, is that we deal with imbalances that indigenous cultures and their medicine systems never dealt with. We are dealing with illnesses and modern conditions that never existed in the history of the world.

For example: Diseases which relate to toxicity, poisoning and exposure to hard radiation and radioactive isotopes. So, pre-nuclear age and advent of the nuclear bomb, roughly beginning in the nineteen, late thirties and nineteen forties, this radiation did not exist in the world.

There is no Traditional Chinese Medicine, Herb or Acupuncture cure for radiation poisoning. There is no classic Indian, Thai or Tibetan Ayurveda treatment or cure for radiation poisoning. There is no traditional, Native American solution or cure for radiation poisoning. There's no such thing because there was no such thing. It's not listed as one of the hundred traditional remedies for the hundred traditional illnesses. Up until relatively recently, no longer than 200 years, the day to day diseases and concerns of the mass of humanity were quite well known and were quite well established. The treatments were pretty much straight forward.

You could go to a school and you could learn the top one hundred things that if you work on ten thousand clients the chances that they're going to have one of those hundred things is likely 99%.

As a practitioner you would know those traditional remedies for those top 100 things. Part of what it meant to become a doctor was to memorize, not just the herbs and the points and the positions, the mantras (sacred medicine prayers), but was actually that you memorized the algorithms for the 100 treatments any particular school represented. The set of those basic treatments and the conditions and way they were done would be the school style.

We live in an interesting time in that we deal with illnesses that never existed before. We are the first generation to have xeno-estrogen outgassing plastics. Xeno-estrogen by products of plastics and plasticizers never existed before. We're the first generation to have to deal with antibiotic resistant staph bacteria
(MRSA: Methicillin- Resistant Staph Bacteria).

We're the first culture to deal with air pollution from automobiles, coal fired power plants, CFC's from aerosols etc. Air pollution such as we commonly deal with didn't exist before our time. Lets add to this list of toxins, environmental and otherwise, that are new to us ELF/ EHF pollution, X-ray exposure from both medical origin and airport security. We have a whole list of things for which there is no traditional remedy, so when you study a system exclusively, like Ayurveda or Chinese medicine or Traditional Native American or other indigenous medicine, you will not find solutions for those things.

All those solutions are being developed right now. They're being developed and perfected. I believe, that's why we are here. It is our job. I believe it with all my heart. We're not accidentally incorporated into the most toxic period of the history of the planet and of the history of humanity. With an inclination to be able to learn and master healing and then to be able to creatively craft new solutions for issues that never existed before. It's no accident however it comes to be.

Chapter Five: Traditional and Modern Branches and Divisions

Eight Classical Branches Within Traditional Thai Yoga Medicine

1. **Surgery & Healing of Bone Injuries** (*Th. Kayaphabambat/ Sans. Salya*: Including "Bone Setting")
Surgery and the healing of bone injuries: That includes bone setting, in other words, all the adjusting, reducing of dislocations, healing of fractures and bone injuries. We don't teach that in SomaVeda® as we don't teach surgery and bone setting, although that is part of the training in Thailand.

2. **Treatment of Disorders of the Head and Neck** (*Th. Nuad / Sans. salakya*)
Manipulative Technology or Massage: primarily focusing on the spine and core, hips and   pelvis of the body. Manipulative technologies or pressure with the whole body on the whole body, primarily focusing on the spine, core, hips and pelvis. That's under the category of Nuad or salakia. Salia is surgery. Salakia is manual pressure or manipulation applied to the body. Much of what we call Thai Traditional Massage/ Thai Yoga Therapy is Nuad and or Salakya in practice. (Ryksaa Thang Nuad Phaen Boran Thai)

3. **General Medicine or Therapy of the Organism** (*San. kayacikitsa*) Peripheral Point Stimulation: Marma, Chakra, Lom, Bindu. Therapy is based on peripheral point stimulation based on Ti (marma), Lom (Secondary Chakra), Sen Line (Thai Prana Nadi/ Meridian, energy line) and Chakra. At each stage of the way it's quite typical to find practitioners that would specialize more on one of these areas than another. Anything that is so ancient, you are bound to see schools and individuals who will pick something out of the vast 10,000 things to specialize on. Much of what we call Thai Traditional Massage/ Thai Yoga Therapy is Kayacikitsa in practice.

4. **Psychiatry or Mental Diseases Caused by Demons** (*San. bhuta- vidya*: Karma related or origin) Application of Therapeutic Rituals or illness that is karma related or has karma as its origin. There are applications such as rituals and meditation that are specifically for this. Becoming a monk is one of the treatment protocols to handle mental illness. In my opinion, demons are the energetic embodiment of negative emotions. When negative emotions become fixated and are cultivated over long enough period of time, they can literally take on a life of their own, almost like another voice or being inside you. The Thai have always acknowledged that process and have always offered treatment protocols. Some of those protocols are ceremonial medicine, you could even say 'magic' ceremony to do an 'exorcism'. It's also an algorithm or formulaic way to approach the innate and to speak to the inner person in such a way as to dispel the energy that the negative emotional state is supporting. There may be many ways to do this. I will teach you a couple ways myself. My teacher also practiced these ritual ways.

5. **Midwifery, & Pediatrics** (San. kaumara-bhutya) Childhood Diseases Caused by Demons: A demon can be any sum of any energetic imbalance. It can be an aggregate of negative emotions. We have many demons. In the past, there was quite extensive charting of the locations of both the positive and negative spirits of each body part. There would be characters and Kanji (Hanzi) to identify both the demon and the benevolent spirit, or Kwan of any point or region of the body. It was a warfare type of situation between the positive and negative aspects of energy, the demon versus the angelic, the positive versus the negative and then in more modern times, instead of demons they started talking about qualities of fullness or emptiness or yin and yang and so on. In the olden days, yin and yang were treated more literal as far as being an intelligence that's at work in part of the body or overall disability pattern of a person.

6. Uses of Medicinal Plants and Substances (*Th. Nuad Prakhop Samun Prai*)
a) Toxicology- Medical Drugs for Poisons   (San. agada)
b) Rejuvenation, Elixirs   (San. rasayana)
c) Virilification: (San. vajikarana)
Virility, fecundity, Shakti, Sexual Prana and or Chi, Bone Marrow Chi, (Long life and bright mind), infertility issues.

#6, a, b & c may all be classified under a group heading of "Primary use in such applications as decoctions, steam baths, herbal compress massage, and in formulations of various pills."

Uses of medicinal plants or substances: (*Th. Nuad Prakhop Samun Praii*). Then we have several categories of using medicinal plants:

A) Toxicology: (Agada: Treatment for poisons-aghadam) which is Detoxification and treatment using medical drugs (Thai Ayurveda pharmacology) for poisons in traditional medicine even though in the USA none of them would qualify because they are not chemical synthetics and instead are made from whole plant and mineral substances) – the use of the word drug needs to be specified—it is not considered FDA approved pharmacopeia.

Thai Ayurveda Agada addresses the idea that all chronic illnesses have as part of their pattern of support either a severe deficiency or a severe excess of something that is vital. In Ayurveda we tend to focus on the excess. The primary culprit is too much of something. In TCM, they tend to focus on the deficiency and say that most illnesses and chronic conditions relate to being deficient in key nutrients and constituents either elementally, mentally or emotionally. They have lots of strategies for building up deficiency.

In Ayurveda we have strategies in reducing excess. That's where I really think Chinese medicine and Ayurveda are beautiful partners. In Thai, you see ideas and strategies that relate to both. This emphasis shows the blending of Thai and Chinese culture. Also, literal antidotes for poisons. In the past, in the Buddhist countries, it was considered very bad karma to spill someone's blood. So if you were going to kill someone and didn't want to have too much bad karma, then you would poison them. It was common practice for the maw nuad and the traditional doctors to have clientele concerned with poisoning. The Buddhist countries weren't famous for bloody bloodshed because that was really a last resort and generally reserved for open war with other countries. Because of that, they developed a medicinal focus on treating poison and snake bites, scorpions, centipedes, etc.

B) Rejuvination/ Elixirs: (*Sans. Rasayana*) Another part of Thai herbology is rejuvenations and elixirs or raciana. In modern terms, we would say this is the making of supplements. A Redbull energy drink is an elixir. It is a concoction meant to give you energy and sharpen your focus. We have many of these, there's the complex technology of mixing coffee drinks at Starbucks. Coffee is an herb and there are the many ways that you mix that herb, the different roasts, strengths, cream no cream, matcha tea, honey vs. raw sugar all the ways put together are variations of elixirs to give you a boost. This is the modern spin on rejuvenations and elixirs. All energy drinks are elixirs. All supplemental drinks and concoctions of any kind to give you some kind of energy, boost, vitality or whatever is an adaptation of this Vedic concept.

C) Virilification: (*Sans. Vajikarana, Vrishya chikitsa*), which is neither male nor female. It is also Vajikarana: the idea of virility, fecundity, Shakti, sexual prana or chi, bone marrow chi, long life and bright mind with infertility issues.

According to Vidya P.K. Dalal "Vajikarana or Vrishya chikitsa is a one of eight major specialty of the Ashtanga Ayurveda. This subject is concerned with aphrodisiacs, virility and improving health of progeny. As per Charaka Samhita, by proper use of these formulations, one becomes endowed with good physique, potency, strength,
Page 56

and complexion and sexually exhilarated and sexually potent." (https://www.ncbi.nlm.nih.gov/pmc/articles/PMC3705695/)

For mental, emotional attraction and so on was very important. It has always been so. I don't fault people for inventing Viagra. I fault them for giving people a drug that helps you have an erection but also gives you a risk of heart attack, stroke and permanent nerve damage among other things. People have always looked for the herbal equivalent of Viagra, as long as there have been people. Some say it began in the old days when there were harems with many partners. Certainly, considering the majority of a traditional family's labor force was other family members then the best long term plan for survival was to be more fertile and produce as many children as possible. That is an idea that anthropologists have suggested -as far as where this idea originates. No matter how far back we go in human civilization in the oldest records of any kind that relate to humans there is always a note on how to maintain an erection or how to be more successful as a female and have more babies. That's the way it was and it's also part of Thai medicine.

Virility is male. Fecundity is female. It refers to females being able to implant eggs and then create babies. Additionally, fecundity has to do the the ability to produce new ideas. For males it has to do with the production of sperm and the instrumentation of ejaculation. Both are vital to life. Shakti is the sexual energy or sexual life force or prana. In the Taoist way, we say bone marrow chi or life force itself is defined as sexual energy. When we are not making babies, it has other jobs. The shakti's job, when we are not having orgasms, is to stimulate the organs to stimulate the immune system and mind and strengthen the eyes, tone the skin, and balance the ph level or acid mantle.

Shakti is still prana. Shakti is more specifically relating to the kundalini Shakti or the sexual prana or the prana of regeneration. We experience that everyday when we have regenerative sleep and go into deep delta sleep. We create for a few minutes every day a moment when our bodies regenerate tissue from scratch, taking stem cells and telling them to become kidney or liver etc. That intelligence and directedness only takes place when you are in delta, a deep coma like sleep, not generally achievable through meditation. That is kundalini Shakti because it can make life in the body. Another old theory about yoga therapy was that it was about managing this energy and stimulating this energy when and where it's deficient and exploring how it manifests in every part of a person's life. That's the origin of yoga Tantra. Tantra and Tantra ideas and beliefs have always been part of the Thai way of looking at life.

7. **Natural Therapy:** (*Sans. Kayanamai, Jittanamai, Chiwitanamai*), (Hatha Yoga/ Martial Arts, Meditation, Proper Life Conduct: Longevity Science)

Hatha yoga (*Th. Reusi Dotton*), martial arts (*Th. Kabri-Kabrong, Muay Boran, Fan Dap* etc.), meditation (Vipassana, Shamatha), proper life conduct and longevity science (Noble Path) have always been considered branches of Thai Traditional Medicine – Martial arts, meditation, ethical instruction in how to live are practical expressions of the practice of longevity science in real life.

The ancient Thai healers and medicine practitioners were most likely Buddhist monks and other spiritual people. In one of the traditions all illnesses were divided up into two primary categories. All disease and malaise was either originating from Past Life Unresolved Karmic issues or Present life Karma. In many cases both past life and present life issues were indicated, although perhaps in different percentages and causing different symptomologies. The therapist, healer, doctor was supposed to determine the cause of origin and devise an effective treatment strategy based on the assessment. Tools of assessment could include Traditional Thai Korosot Astrology (see the book: Korosot Astrology by this author), palm and face reading, casting Joss sticks in the temple, and utilizing special persons deemed expert in medical intuition. Once a past life issue was determined then various means of relief were to be employed.

These almost always involved some spiritual ritual and evocation of various spirits who needed to be appeased, expelled or called home "Mat Kwan". Blessed water could be applied to affected parts or the whole body. Animal spirits and or totems could be invoked as aids such as calling for the Tiger. Sacred, magic candles could be prepared for calling, blessing or removing harmful Karma as necessary. Blessed objects could be tied to specific body parts including string, amulets and talismans. Sacred calligraphy, kongi and magic characters, geometries and sacred mantra could or would be tattooed over parts or in some cases the whole body. Many of these old Thai spiritual based therapies and rituals are still commonly practiced today. Look at the neck of the Thai scientist and most likely there will be an amulet there. Almost all Thai men have sacred tattoos, many as a mark of their time as monks in earlier days

8. **Sacred Medicine Tatoo:** (*Th. Sak Yan*) The Art and Science of the Sacred Tattoo
 Sak means tattoo in Thai, and yan is the Thai pronunciation for the Sanskrit word Yantra, a type of sacred and magical diagram used in Dharmic religions. Sak Yan Tattooing could be placed in any of these categories because characters, mantras and symbols can be used for healing in drawings, tattoos, on fabric and worn on the body. There are Thai Medical traditions which recommend to tattoo points for chronic disarray or issues with the Kwan or spirit of the marma or afflicted region of the body. There are charts that show all the Konji (*Th. Khom*) and balancing characters you would tattoo on a point you were having an issue with if for example the demon of that point was disturbed or it was too full or empty. Tattooing also relates to psychiatry in that classically the monks always were tattooed and used them for protection from virtually anything you can imagine. None of this was required for this medicine. Thai medical practitioners have never been classically required to learn or practice tattooing or get tattoos, it's just part of the culture.

Sak Yan Types and designs
There are many traditional types and designs of yantra tattoos, but some of the most well-known and popular include:
- Ong Phra (Thai: องค์พระ; translation: Buddha's body) - one of the most commonly used elements in Yantra tattooing, but can also be a more complex standalone design. Meant to provide insight, guidance, illumination, etc.
- Ha-thaeo (Thai: ห้าแถว; translation: five rows) - Typically tattooed on the back left shoulder. Each of the five lines relates to a different blessing for success and good luck.
- Kao-yot (Thai: เก้ายอด; translation: nine spires) - typically tattooed on the center top of the back in various sizes and levels of complexity. Simple version pictured at the top of this article.
- Si-yot (Thai: สี่ยอด; translation: four spires) - to influence the feelings or actions of others and protect the bearer.
- Paet-thit (Thai: แปดทิศ; translation: eight points) - represents protection in the eight directions of the universe. Round shape; typically tattooed on the center of the back. Pictured in gallery below.
- Sip-thit (Thai: สิบทิศ; translation: ten points) - a version of paet-thit, but protects in ten directions instead of eight.
- Maha-niyom (Thai: มหานิยม; translation: great preference) - to grant the bearer favor in the eyes of others. Round shape; typically placed on the back right shoulder.[12]
- Yot Mongkut (Thai: ยอดมงกุฎ; translation: spired crown) - for good fortune and protection in battle. Round shape; typically tattooed on the top of the head.
- Panchamukhi (Thai: ปัญจมุขี; translation: five Deva faces) - intended to ward off illness and danger.
- Suea (Thai: เสือ; translation: tiger) - typically depicts twin tigers. Represents power and authority. [62]

These are the schools or components of thought and practice of the Indigenous Traditional Thai Ayurveda which are concurrent with classical Indian and Tibetan Ayurveda.

Modern Branches of the Traditional Thai Ayurvedic Medicine

According to the Department for the Development of Thai Traditional and Alternative Medicine (DTAM) these seven traditional divisions are now divided into four distinctive areas.

Traditional Thai medicine (used as umbrella term for all medicine of Thailand) consists of five primary branches: Internal medicine - Primarily the use of herbs and diet to promote health. (*Pâet-sàat* แพทยศาสตร์) Pâet = medicine, doctor, drugs Sàat = knowledge, study, science & medical practice involving the diagnosis and treatment of diseases or symptoms. This branch includes the methods of using plants, animals, and minerals as medicine for both internal and external application, the use of food as medicine, dietary counseling, and the administration of medicine. [34]

Pharmacy practice involving the use of medicinal materials derived from plants, animals or minerals as traditional medicines and the art of compounding those ingredients into various dosage forms of TTM recipes.

External medicine - All therapies applied to the external body: (*Th. Gaai-yá-pâap bam-bàt* กายภาพบำบัด), Body (*Th. Gaai-yá-pâap*), Therapy (*Th. Bam-bàt*) including but not limited to:
   Bone setting (indigenous chiropractics)
   Thai cupping
   Thai scraping (a practice similar to Chinese Gua Sha)
   Thai Yoga and Traditional Thai Massage techniques including compression, Thai acupressure, beating, passive stretching and focus on sen channels (pathways of movement in the body such as tendons, ligaments, nerves and circulatory vessels)
   External application of herbs through balms, liniments, compresses and poultices[34]

This branch includes Nuad Thai or Traditional Thai massage. However, it includes many more therapies, including blood-letting, specific point therapy (*Th. sên* เส้น)(channel) therapy, and much more.

Ancient Thai Codex from the Royal Library in Bangkok give insight into the spiritual basis for Thai Ayurveda and related healing arts.

Chapter 6: Samkhya Creation Principles

Cosmos = Numerology Principles of 1, 2, 3, 4, 5, 6 and 7

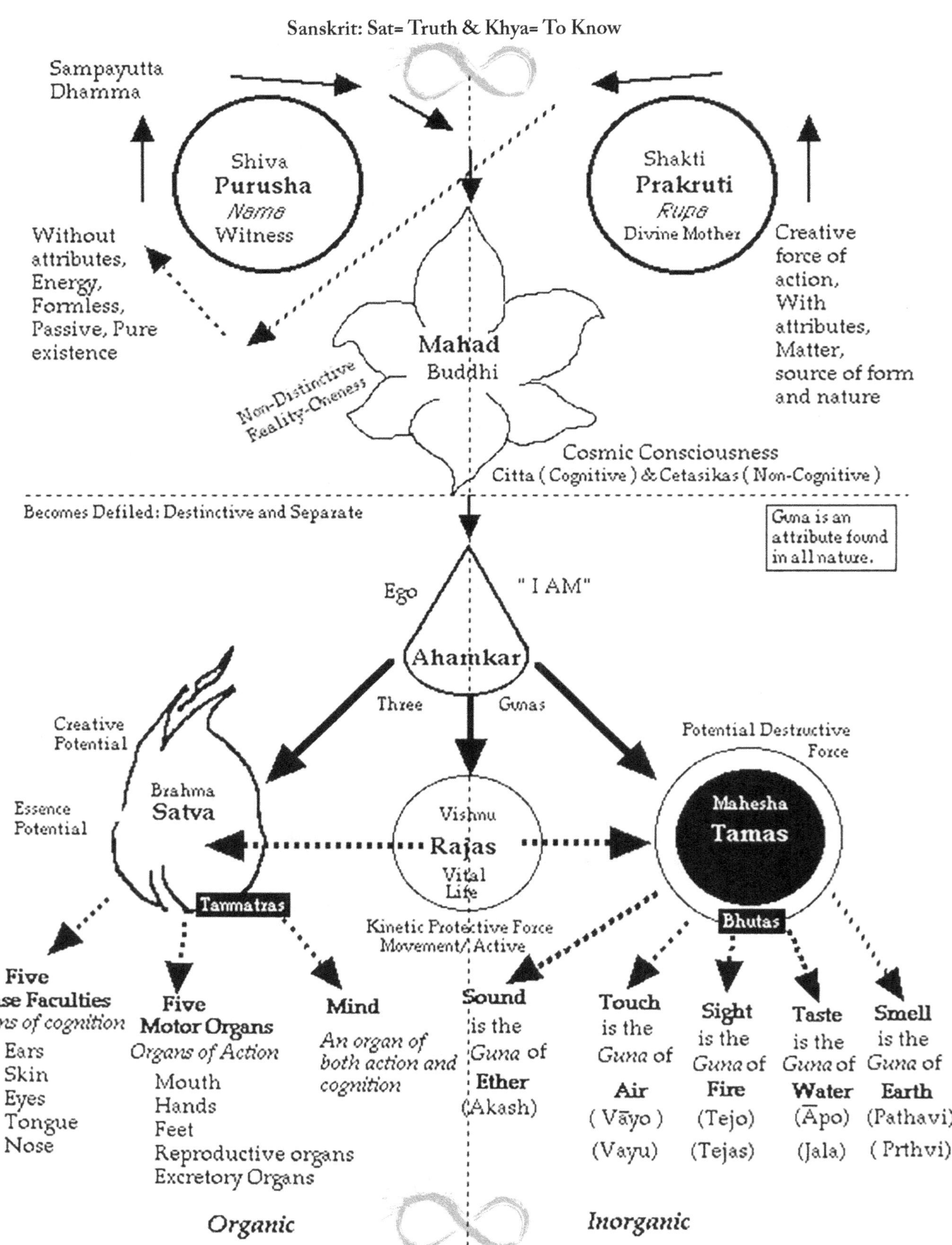

Samkhya Creation Principles: An Ayurvedaic Model of the universe

Every traditional system of medicine has what they call their cosmology. It's usually one simple inclusive model where all the major concepts are placed. It's basically where everything comes from. A map of their universe if you will. This is the cosmology of our Ayurveda. Some aspects of it may take some time and consideration to understand.

The Chart is divided into two parts. It ha a top portion and a bottom one: divided by a dotted line across the middle of the page. Everything above that line is pre-incarnation, primordial. Everything below line that is post incarnation, post-iteration. We'll start at the very top and work our way down the page.

At the very top it says "cosmos equals principles of one, two, three, four, five and six." One of the things that I found helpful for me when I was trying to master various systems, especially traditional Chinese medicine for example, and also in my study of classical Thai and Indian Ayurveda, is that these traditional cosmologies are based on a numbering system, a numerology.

The primary essential concepts have a number that's associated with them. That number gives you a branch of the tree or a place to hang things. For example, if you can count to ten, you can learn everything there is to know about Traditional Chinese Medicine (TCM). Also, for example, in another text I have a chart just like this, which is the complete cosmology of Traditional Chinese Medicine. All you have to do is be able to count to ten, or actually, count to twelve. If you count one, two, three, four, five, six, eight, nine, ten, eleven, twelve you can actually learn all the fundamental principles of Chinese medicine because they are arranged according to a numerological hierarchy.

As I studied the Ayurveda, I saw that Ayurveda also has this kind of organization. It helps with your memory. The title of the chart is "Samkhya Creation Principles". "Samkhya" is a Thai word which is the same as the Sanskrit word "*Satkhya*". If we were doing classic or traditional Ayurveda, we'd say "*Satkhya*" creation principles or in Thai, "*Samkhya*". The word "*Sat*", is the word truth, and "*Kya*" is to know,

So "*Satkhya*" means simply, to know the truth. It means to know the truth about life. In this context: where everything comes from and how everything relates to everything else.

Starting with "zero", on my chart at the very top, I put a little infinity symbol. That infinity symbol represents the origin of the cosmos. The origin is, by definition, as far back as back goes. The origin of things before there are things to originate. It is the same place as just before the big bang. The idea is that reality, consciousness, manifestation, diversity, multiplicity, infinite varietal expression of all of these things, both energetic and material are just not there, there is this place, where they're not there.

In traditional Vedic literature, that space is the clear mind of God. I think of it like this. We have a space where there was this possibility of consciousness, this possibility of manifestation, but nothing's happening for whatever reason. I think of God rumbling around alone in the house of possibility.

One day as God ambles around the house of possibility within the mindless emptiness of God, it's nothingness, but, there is nothing to contemplate at this point.

God walks in front of a mirror, and in the moment that God walks in front of the mirror, something happens, something changes in the universe. Now maybe that mirror was some aspect of undefined God consciousness, but God walks in front of a mirror, in Vedic literature it says, Brahma had a dream. What happens is God becomes self-reflective and in that moment, all the possibility of all that there is becomes manifest. Some might refer to this as the big bang, the big bang is just a theory, I'm just using that as a metaphor.

Because previous to this self-reflective moment, there's nothing to reflect. There's only infinitely none, or infinitely one.

But then something changes and the primordial consciousness becomes self-reflected and in that moment there is now in the universe, God and not God. Or God, and God two, or other God. There's this God and that one. Then there's interaction between the self-reflective consciousness and the original primordial consciousness. The whole possibility of the universe changed the second God walked in front of that mirror or became self-reflective. The next moment those two parts interact with each other and create something further. Something that is different from the original primordial consciousness and something that's different from the reflective self-consciousness, something new. We refer to the primordial consciousness as first force, and that self-reflective consciousness is second force and that, which is the derivative of those two things is the third force. That's "Three", the origin of the law of three.

So first we have the infinity symbol and then we have one. (In Chinese medicine that primordial consciousness is the Tao (Dao), singular.) Essentially, the primordial original "all that there is", becomes self-reflective and then becomes consumed with the reflection. In that moment, generates the third force which is that which is the prodigy of the first two.

First force is male, second force is female, third force is both male and female. You say Mother, Father, child. It's a perfect example of cosmos.

The dictionary definition of a cosmos is something that within itself has everything it needs to replicate and continue its existence in perpetuity. It's all there, everything needed for survival or existence, and then within the context of that, it has everything it needs to continue, infinitely. The family is a cosmos. If you have a male, a female and a child or at least if you have the paternal contribution of sperm and the maternal contribution of egg, you may produce a child. Out of that child, you may produce an infinite number of future generations. This is how the universe is created from one and grows into infinity.

It is the process of how infinite multiplicity and infinite expression, diversity creates infinitum out of energy and all the continuums that exist. When God becomes self-reflective, then you have an active part and you have a receptive part. You have a male part, and you have female part that's were "two" comes in.

In Thai, the male or Yang is called Nama. Purusha is the Sanskrit word. So, the male or the primordial male or primordial patriarchal influence is called Purusha/ Nama. This is also exemplified in the icon of Shiva. If you look on teachings on Vipassana Bhavanna it talks about the reconciliation of Nama and Rupa as an objective on the meditation. That means a balancing, a harmonizing of the male and female parts. Of the light and the dark parts, the extrovert, and the introverted parts, inside and the outside and so on and so forth.

Ayurveda comes from classical Hindu tradition from the Vedantas, and so there are numerous references to deities. Male deities and female deities and gods and goddesses, icons etc. In the past, this has been an impediment for some students. They might say "I don't want to learn about Shiva. I don't want to learn about Shakti or Brahma or Krishna, I'm of this or that religion. I don't believe in that stuff."

Let's just think of it from a cultural, philosophical viewpoint. There's another way that you can look at these deities or icons and that is as an archetype of what they are trying to communicate. Think about the teachers at that time in history when there were no books and no written materials. However, they knew about the archetype of the male, the primordial male, and about the archetype of the primordial female. They knew about the universal archetypes of progeny and of derivatives and hierarchies of energy.

How did they communicate that? The ancient Reishi made a images, that incorporated all of the different aspects that they were trying to communicate. Today we would just write a book, or make a video. In the past when there was no such thing there was still this urge to communicate and pass on to subsequent generations this information. They did however have wood, stone, water and minerals so they could carve and shape and make paint, even forty thousand years ago.

So that's what they did. Some of the archetypes were directly from nature and they were archetypes of animals. The figures of animals are the oldest known indication of organized human art in communication. But there are also body parts there, like hand prints. You can see images of a buffalo and hand print.

We don't necessarily know exactly how to interpret those symbols because they're so proto-civilization. We're not quite sure what context of life the artist was in, but we know that these records exist. Ayurvedic culture is the derivative of the great Sumeran culture.

You want to follow the path of how we get to Indian culture that starts with Sumer, then it goes to Babylon and then you have the derivatives of the Chaldeans, the Aramaics, the Abyssinians etc. Then we have the Babylonians and the Persians and you have divergent branches from the Sumeran, Chaldean, Abyssinians who go north and west until they trail to the Indus Valley and then south into Mesopotamia and out of Mesopotamia to Africa, India and so on. They were great, fabulous, well defined cultures four, five, six thousand years before there ever was an Indian culture.

So, if you look at the time frame of when these cultures existed, they predate the Indus culture by three to six thousand years. They were great cultures, with intact philosophies and whole systems of medicine, social sciences, politics and religion. Sophisticated systems which pre-date the Indian culture.

Their ideals, travel with them and we see these kinds of expressions of this numerology in those cultures. Much like I'm giving it to you now. Father principle number one, Parusha. On the right-hand side, we see "Prakruti" which in Thai is "Rupa". This is the Shakti principle. From now on when you look at a deity, like a statue or an image or picture of Shiva, instead of looking at it as some God to worship or to venerate, read about who was Shiva? What was Shiva's role in creation? Who was Shiva in the cast of celestial players? What was the role, the archetype of Shiva? And then this quality of the latent possibility of manifestation and consciousness that is the Shiva principle or the Purusha principle or Yang principle or male principle would be more clear.

Now the female side of the equation, Prakruti, the feminine Yin or Shakti principle, in Thai, Rupa or the divine mother. The Purusha principle, the divine father is the witness, the Prakruti is the divine mother. They have two different roles or qualities about them. One is latent possibility on the male side and manifest possibility on the female side. We say that the Purusha principle is without attributes, energy, formless, passive and pure existence. It's primordial being without doing. Doing comes in with the Divine Mother which is the creative force of action with attributes. Matter is the source of form and nature. Although distinctive qualitatively one from the other, they are two ways of looking at the same thing. Right from the beginning, from the infinity, there are the origins of the first triad. Male principle, female principle interacting and or relating to each other form the origin of the first triad. They come from infinity and infinity is still within them. Infinity is represented as the dividing line between these two things and that's why there's always going to be challenges of male and female relationships. Infinity is the Ahamkar and infinity is the Rajas Guna after manifestation of consciousness occurs in the realm of life incarnation.

We are archetypes of the universal principle, which are biologic counterparts of these universal principles. We share all the attributes and so between us there is a little divide. This divide is in the infinite expression of our consciousness according to our nature. We're not meant for that divide to keep us in opposition even though there is a polarity here, this is the first polarity.

When you look at a magnet, a common bar magnet, it has a positive pull on one side and a negative pull on the other. You can put the magnet under a sheet of paper and sprinkle some iron filings on top of the paper and it sorts out according to the field lines of the magnet. You get two spheres with radiating circles that broadcast on the ends. Invisible energy shaping matter.

What most people don't realize is right in the middle nothing's happening. There's actually a place on every magnet where there is no magnetic field, a "Null" field. A magnet is completely a magnet, except where the two fields come together. There is a place on every magnet that's neither positive nor negative and it's called "Blocks Wall". That's the electrical or engineering term for the space that occurs between positive and negative polarity, it's the transition space, where one thing, through some mystical process, becomes it's complete opposite.

The only place where one thing can become its opposite is a place of power. It's a place where anything is possible and so that is the infinity space in this first triad. It never goes away. We always have that little place, that Blocks Wall or our equivalent. Many people understand about polarity i.e. Theory of opposites, theory of energy… this is good, this is bad, this is positive, this is negative. There's polarity bodywork. There's polarity energy healing. There's polarity chakra balancing. There's polarity this and that.

But really there is no such thing as positive and negative, if you don't consider the dividing line between the two, the gap or the space or the transition space between the two, where one becomes the other. In Chinese medicine this first part of this chart is shown as the Yin/ Yang symbol.

If you have a circle and on one side you have a paisley fish, that's dark and on the other side you have a paisley fish that's light and in classic symbols there is a white dot in the black field, and there is a black dot in the white field. Taken basically the understanding of the image is Yin and Yang, light and dark, positive and negative, male and female, inside and outside. This and that, this and the other, up and down, here and there. They get the polarity, what is not considered is that the eye plays a trick. I believe the original creators of the symbol knew it was going to happen.

One time in class, before I had the discussion I drew a Yin /Yang symbol on the board and asked everyone in class what it was and how many different things did it signify.

Everyone in the class said two, night and day, Yin and Yang, male and female, hot and cold. Everyone expressed duality. Everyone said it's two things being expressed. I said no, there are three things clearly illustrated in this symbol. There is the Yang principle, there is the Yin principle, and there is a third element … the line between the two. The line is invisible because one field (white or black) becomes the other. The curvilinear interface which demonstrates their inter-influential relationship is seen as a line there. If you extended that line off the circle it then takes on the nature of illustrating a third force in the diagram.

In the symbols that have a dark dot in the light field and a light dot in the dark, the purpose of that little dot of the opposite color is to show you that this is not a static symbol. It is an evolving symbol where one energy becomes the other in turn. There is no Yang without Yin. There is no Yin without Yang. There is no male without female. There is no female without male. There is no such thing as Yang independent of Yin. There's no such thing as male independent of female, that is analog thinking. The symbol is two dimensional, so we have the illusion of a static relationship between the two. Without knowing the key to the symbol it's easy to think they are two entirely different energies or concepts.

The core concept being their relationship is mutual and complementary, not oppositional.

The implied movement or transformation indicated in the symbol is from greater Yang to brighter Yang to lesser Yang and from greater Yin to brighter Yin to lesser Yin. These are the classic phases as seen in Traditional Chinese Medicine. We have to know about these dynamic and changing relationships between Yin and Yang to understand how meridians work, for example.

In Ayurveda there is no male principle without the female. There's no female principle without the male and both of them are defined by the infinity which is their origin. Infinity is the place from which the third force will emanate and which is the bridge for their interaction. In Traditional Chinese Medicine TCM) that place is called the interface. The interface is aligned between Yin and Yang.

First we have the male principle described as without attributes, energy, formless, most passive, pure existence, it is latent possibility i.e. just the possibility of possibilities. Then you have the female principle which is described as manifest creative force. That with attributes but no manifestation. No force of direction. What happens when the two come together is everything that is, becomes. Because now you have energy and matter and matter and energy in an endless revolving dance. In Ayurveda, we say the thing that comes into existence is the Mahat. The original undifferentiated cosmic consciousness.

When the male and female principles in their primordial energetic realm of infinite possibility interact, consciousness is born. In the realm of possibility, when possibility dances with concrescence, when possibility dances with manifestation, consciousness is born. Consciousness is born and the first consciousness is undefiled. It's not fractured or deformed. It's pure and clean and it has an existence outside the limits of time and space. The first corrupting influence is the distortions of time and space or perceptions of time and space. That happens after we're born (incarnated). We have this undifferentiated cosmic consciousness or Mahat and it has two primary qualities. The two primary qualities of the Mahat or in Thai, the Buddhi consciousness are cognitive and non-cognitive. Cognitive is potential conscious faculty and non-cognitive is potential materiality faculty. All simultaneously occurring, without any issues.

Non-distinctive reality or oneness is the primordial conscious state. We have a dotted line across the chart showing the undifferentiating cosmic consciousness becoming incorporated. We are incarnated. We are re-iterated as a new consciousness into the world of the material expression of concreteness and limitation. Suddenly the infinite consciousness of will, soul and spirit is encapsulated in a specific time, a specific place, in a specific form. It's a little bit traumatic. This first manifestation of consciousness into the world is called Ahamkar and it's the source of us, the source of all the "I's". It represents the original generation/ creation of the ego. Whatever says "I am" begins here.

Whatever is within us as a distinctive identity begins here. Remember, previous to being born, previous to being incarnated, we didn't have "I am". We were non-distinctive, undifferentiated cosmic consciousness. After birth we're condensed and separated from the knowledge of who we really are and where we really come from. So much so, that we think that we are it. The world now is all about us. And that's "I am", that's ego and the source of ego.

The Three Gunas: Rajas, Satvas, Tamas

Now classic Ayurveda says that the ego which is manifest when you're born has three principal characters and it has three principal defilements called Gunas. My professors in India referred to them as the three evils. The three egos, three-pernicious influences, three defilements. The three distortions of that which was perfect, that which is not perfect anymore. They also referred to them as the three fractures or the three broken aspects.

Followed by the Dhatu and Dosha which are the further materialization of these qualities. Basically, the concept is defining the nature of our imperfections. It is defining the ultimate origin of all imbalance and disease.

We chose to be here like some kind of group, or class experiment. We were an infinitely diverse, infinitely connected entity of creation and consciousness with a life outside of time and space and were apparently bored. We came up with this idea of let's explore the limitations of self-reflected consciousness and the encapsulation of ego. Let's explore isolation. Because we're Godlike beings, we want to know all that there is about everything that's potentially possible. The only thing that we didn't know very well was isolation, independence, and ego.

We came up with this experiment which we call life. We all incarnated at the same time. This infers the idea that there's not many people (incarnate beings). There's not many souls. You don't have a soul mate for example. If you want to know who you soul mate is, it's every human, every living sentient being on the face of the planet right at this minute. We're all part of the same experiment. In the act of incarnation we set all these criteria in order to make the game of life fair.

In order to make the game fair when we incarnated our self, squeezed our self into the isolation tank called life. We arranged to forget who we are at the moment of birth. Once born you forget where you come from, forget what your possibility is as an expression of consciousness in life. You manifest incarnation as a baby. You're utterly and completely dependent on outside influences for your life support. A state of being which is very different from the godlike being you were before incarnation. A sentient being which had no need of support because there was nothing other than that. To produce support we come into the experiment. We had other conditions on the experiment. These other conditions were nobody gets out until everybody gets out.

All the religions of the world try to handle this equation. This idea that nobody gets out, till everyone gets out. They create all these ideas about afterlife and purgatory and Bardo. All of these different things which are about this idea that just because you die, doesn't mean you're done. You're not done till everybody's done. Why? Because every other person, every other living sentient being, is still on some level a reflection of your consciousness, an aspect of our group's soul, our group consciousness.

The Tibetans are particularly good at expressing this idea of the integrity of soul being of all living things. We're the encapsulated God, Spirit, the undifferentiated cosmic consciousness an infinite being of pure and undefiled expression of pure male and female, infinity of creation and light, and all possible potentials and we're squashed down to a peanut.

And that's us. So we're born and that peanut which is us, the Ahamkar, has three different characteristics of ego. Those three characteristics of ego are called the Satvic, Rajasic and the Tamasic principle. Notice the deities associated with each character or quality. These deities represent the archetypes of these principles.

Satvas/ Satvic Principle:

Satvas expresses lightness, essence, understanding, purity, clarity, compassion and love. It activates the senses and is responsible for the perception of knowledge. If you want to know more about the characteristics or qualities of for example the Satvic principle, read and study Brahma. Look at icons and symbols and pictures and images of Brahma. Explore who was Brahma? What did Brahma do? We also call the Satvic principle, the sun or the solar principle. The sun principle, also absolutely vital. Satvas and Tamas are related as two halves of one coin. The composting, degenerative, deterioration, deconstructing principle of the Tamasic is not possible without the sun's energy.

Satvas relates to the five motor organs, which we call organs of action. They are: mouth, hands, feet, reproductory organs and excretory organs. The organs of action are how we implement our consciousness in the real world. It's how we extend and affect the world without inner consciousness. They enable us to be able to eat, reach, run, reproduce, and evacuate. They facilitate what we can take in, let go, grab or hold and throw. These are the tools that consciousness uses to interact in the environment that we exist in.

Interestingly, the mind is also Satvic. The mind is both an organ of action and cognition. The first thing I want you to notice about the mind, is that in Ayurveda theory, the mind is not special. In fact, it's no different than the excretory organs. Sometimes the mind acts as an excretory organ. The mind is not very different than any of the other organs of action and cognition.

It's not special, it's not superior, and there's nowhere in Ayurveda where it says the mind of the brain is in charge. Its function is like all of the other organs of cognition or action. It's either to act as an interface, to take in information or to direct external action. However, it's not necessarily where consciousness resides. Consciousness is not contained or constrained in or to your brain. We now have science that supports this understanding.

Rajas/ Rajasic principle:

The Rajasic quality is kinetic protective force. It is the active and vital life force (Prana) which drives or directs both the organic and inorganic realms to satvas and tamas. It represents movement, action, stimulation and the vital life force. It can alsoimply aggressivenes and extroversion. Rajas is the most active of the gunas. All desires, wishes, ambitions and imaginations are influenced here.

This is why we're not completely limited. Even though we're born in a finite shell, in a shell which literally begins to deteriorate at the moment of birth in some way or fashion. We have hope. The hope is that by using information that comes to us through our cognitive facilities we can generate, store and accumulate more life force; then the possibility of our expression of our nature changes. This represents the possibility of change. It doesn't guarantee it, it just represents the possibility.

Looking at the Rajas/ Rajasic principle we see the ruling deity is Vishnu. In Thailand located at the National Museum in Sukhothai, Chiang Rai, is one of the oldest and finest Bronze sculptures of Vishnu. It is of unknown origin however most likely dates to the Mon/ Khymer empire, it's just beautiful.

This Vishnu statue it is older and more of a stylized representation of Vishnu than any other similar aged statue in India. Indian people come from India, every year by the bus load to look at the statue. Vishnu is the life force. Vishnu is Prana. Vishnu is the air, the ether, the ground of being, as it manifests in our world today. We have to have all of these things, the life force, the solar principle, the male principle, the female principle. We are in materiality, the reverse or mirror image of the undifferentiated primordial consciousness. We are encapsulated in ego but we are still a perfect model of what came before, following the principle of, "as above, so below".

Now each of these defilements, each of these three evil or self-limiting characteristics has further divisions, further expressions in materiality and manifestation. For example the solar, sun or the Satvic principle representing essence and potential, has three Tanmatras: The five sense faculties, the five motor organs, and the mind.

The five sense faculties which we call organs of cognition are ears, skin, eyes, tongue and nose. Cognition is "the mental action or process of acquiring knowledge and understanding through thought, experience, and the senses." Cognition is the process we're in, we take in information from our environment, make note of it, and then we compare and contrast that information with experience and memory. Our sense faculties are the interface between the external reality and the internal reality. Without these, we're just a ball of goo as far as our understanding of the world. The body parts: ears, skin, eyes, tongue and nose, actually represent Satvic quality and in balances that relate to the ear, skin, eyes, tongue and nose are particularly Satvic. How do I know that? Because that's what's on the chart. That's the traditional listed correlation.

Right side of the chart

Tamas Principle:

Tamas is characterised by ignorance, inertia, heaviness and resistance.It produces disturbances in the process of perception and activities of the mind. Delusion, false knowledge, laziness, apathy, sleep and drowsiness are due to it.

Tamas has two deities primarily, Mahesha and Durga. Durga is sometimes called Kali. You want to learn, about the female principle. What is the defilement or the female destructive principle: "Kali the destroyer." Utterly and completely necessary, in life all composting is the destructive process. The production of soil in Humic elements and minerals that are then biologically available for living systems is a process of decomp/ decomposition. This is the Kali principle, the Tamasic principle. It is absolutely, vitally necessary for life in the physical realm.

Tamas has the equivalent of Tanmatras. They're called Bhutas: sound, touch, sight, taste and smell. Sound is the Guna of Ether element (Akash). Touch is the Guna of Air Element (Vyo). Sight is the Guna of Fire element (Teho). Taste is the Guna of Water element (Apo). Smell is Guna of Earth element (Patavi/ Prythvi) depending on how you say it. Ether, Air, Fire, Water, and Earth of course are the principal elements of Ayurveda.
Notice that before the five elements, we have the sound, touch, sight, taste and smell. The way that we interact with the five elements of the Classical Indian Ayurveda elements or the Thaat Thang Sii which are the four Thai Ayurveda elements, is through our senses.

Notice at the very bottom of the chart [???] we have Vata, Pitta and Kapha. Vata, Pitta and Kapha don't exist in and off themselves. Technically the Tri-Dosha don't exist. They are a shorthand way of describing the composites of two elements. Each Dosha is a composite of two different elements. All of the Dosha are derivative of the defilement of the Satvas, Rajas or Tamas expressions of the ego.

This is why body types are not necessarily a positive thing. They represent imbalance and forms of deterioration. They represent that deterioration quality of Kali. In other words, they're why we are composting, because we have Doshas.

We will eventually die. We will deteriorate because it is the nature of our manifestation in this shell which is ruled by the female to deteriorate, to compost and to become food for worms.

The Two Worlds of Organic and Inorganic

We have the two worlds, the Satvic world is the organic and the Tamasic world is the inorganic. The dividing line is movement. This is the traditional Ayurveda way of separating living things (organic) from the mineral and crystal world (inorganic). The mineral and crystal worlds move but slowly compared to the organic counterpart. The division between the two worlds is the difference between motion and inclination towards motion (kinetic force vs. Latent Kinetic force).

Crystals are alive. Crystals grow. Crystals have organization. They have organized life. They only occur in very specialized places. They have to have the right conditions and they have to have the right support for the right amount of time to form properly. To be clear when speaking of the differences between these two worlds or kingdoms… the distinction is not between alive and not alive! Both kingdoms are alive however, the scale or speed of life if difference between them.

Each one of the numbers in the numerology represents a law or a hierarchy of creation, and or an interaction, so, law three is the male, female, reconciling force, or the Satvas, Rajas, Tamas… Four is ego plus these qualities. Ego was sense faculties, ego with organs, ego with mind. Ego affecting and interacting with elements gives us four. We still have ego as part of the picture, it didn't go away. There are other fours also. Five is the five elements

I'll skip over to seven. Seven for example is the Ray of Creation, seven colors in the rainbow. In one of the oldest symbolic/ iconic representations of the first chakra, the center of the first chakra Yantra (geometric symbol) is an elephant with seven trunks.

Usually we don't see all the depictions of all the traditional characteristics in the icons of the chakras. We don't know what we don't see. But in these older symbols, the center of the first chakra, Muladhara chakra is actually an elephant with seven trunks. All seven primary chakra are represented in the first. Additionally, that is five elements plus two other qualities (Male and Female).

Chapter 7: The Five Bodies: Koshas/ Sheaths (Th. Rangkaai)

The Origin Of The Body

More than just the origin of the body, it's the energetic construction of the body corporate, not necessarily the individual parts which we will get to later such as chakras and energy lines and centers: the corporeal body.

The universe is made up of two things: matter elements and energy elements. We say the matter elements are the universe with attributes and that energy elements are the universe without attributes.

The next statement is an algorithm:
- Matter is the vehicle of energy.
- Energy is consciousness, which manifests.
- When consciousness manifests, it finds a vehicle.
- When consciousness manifests in a human, the vehicle is the mind.
- When the mind manifests, it looks like a body.

Consciousness is fourfold. It has four different aspects:
- It has a mental aspect or "manas", which is the ability to recognize.
- It has an intellectual aspect, which is the "buddhi", the idea of discernment.
- It has identification or is-ness, "ahakara", which is the impulse of attraction and repulsion: I like, I don't like.
- It has a quality of being or "chitta", which is this sense of real, non-temporal, the idea of applying impulses and doing things.

Those four qualities make up the manifestation of consciousness. The ordinary mind is an organ just like your ears, tongue, nose, hands, feet and genitals. The energetic parts of the mind are these qualities of recognition, discernment, attraction and repulsion, attachment and a sense of being or "I am", of being able to do something.

When consciousness assumes physical forms, it exists in five bodies.

The Five Kosha Bodies

In yoga terminology these five bodies are called koshas or sheaths. The word kosha means envelope or sheath like the enclosure or wrapping for a knife or sword. It could also mean a sheath as in a layer like on an onion. Each layer in the onion, which is whole within itself, is distinctive and separate from every other layer. A sword goes into a sheath. The sword is the consciousness. When we talk about the Five Kosha we're talking about the layered way that the egos encapsulate. The three qualities of consciousness which are "sheathed" in the Koshas are Satvas, Rajas, and Tamas.

The five sheaths are from external to internal (outside to inside):

#5	The sheath of MATTER	(*Sans. Annamaya*)	(Physical Medicine) Pressure
#4	The sheath of VITAL AIR	(*Sans. Pranamaya*)	(Energy Medicine) Breath
#3	The sheath of MIND	(*Sans. Manomaya*)	(Education/ Psychology) Intellect
#2	The sheath of KNOWLEDGE	(*Sans.Vijnanamaya*)	(Awareness, Being) Application
#1	The sheath of BLISS	(*Sans. Anandamaya*)	(Spiritual, Ritual Medicine, Devotion and Surrender)

For each of the five bodies, there is a medicine or healing, balancing and compensating art that deals with the manifestation of ego in that particular body. Variations in different medicines are explained by their emphasis on the specific bodies or aggregates / clusters of bodies... i.e.

Matter = purely physical therapy or medicine.
Vital wind= Prana Yama,
Mind = education and visualization/ meditation therapy etc.

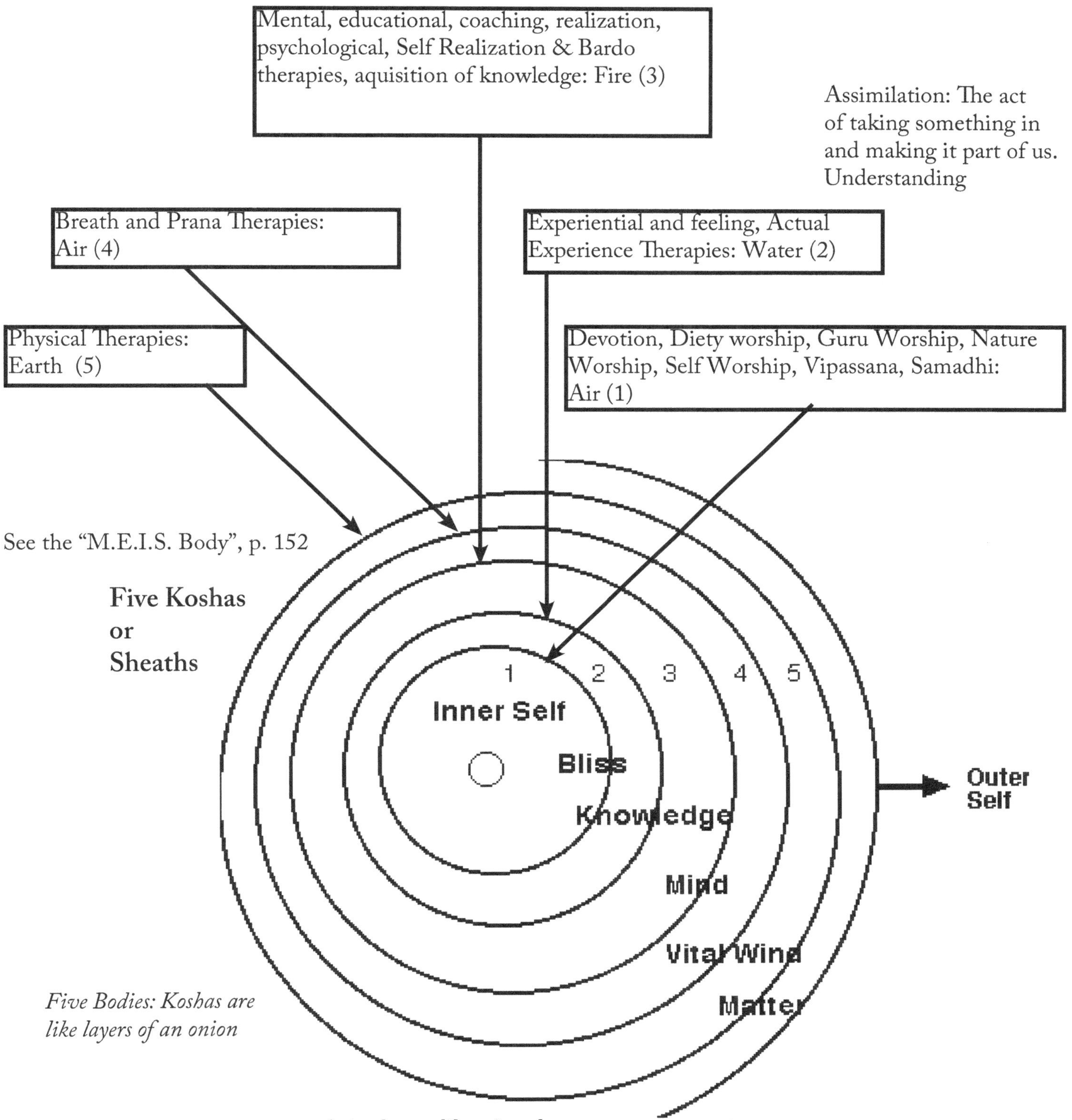

Attitudes are like wires that connect us to events.
To change the events to which we are subject we must first change our attitudes. P.D. Ouspensky

The bodies are encapsulated in the tissue, the envelope of the body. Notice the Koshas are arranged in a sequence of rings from the outside to the inside of the diagram. All of these bodies are simultaneously occurring. They overlap and they all occur in the same place, space, and time. It's an analog illustration, it appears that these bodies are layered or separate, however, they are completely intermingled. The diagram also does not show scale as the biggest of the bodies is the innermost body. The Blissful body is the largest one and the physical body which is on the outside of the diagram is technically the smallest one.

Some of these bodies can affect the whole world. That's how big their area of potential influence is. These are the classic depictions of the Koshas. The statement under the "Origin Of The Body." "The universe is made up of two things, matter elements and energy elements", (this comes from Samkhya Creation Principles), is how we know the universe is created. You have the latent, and you have the manifest, energy with attributes, energy without attributes. Bottom line, the universe is made of two things, matter elements and energy elements.

We say that the matter elements are the universe with attributes and that the energy elements are the universe without attributes. That is an algorithm for how pure energy and latent possibility of manifestation become encapsulated in tissue.

 What affects One Kosha affects All

Each of these five bodies presents a couple of questions. How does it manifest, and how do we treat an imbalance in that body? This also leads us to the very first Vedic assessment. The first Vedic assessment is to look at a person's discomfiture, look at their dis-ease. Try to determine what is the dominant body that's affected.

You have five bodies. You don't have one body. Each of these bodies has a different quality, a different frequency. They're all interacting. Even if the issue is clearly in the physical body such as "I have a thorn in my foot", it's still going to affect me mentally and emotionally. Because the thorn in the foot makes me unhappy. Because it makes me unhappy it's affecting other things than just my physicality.

The thorn might be in an acupuncture point causing a disruption in energy flow. Because I have a thorn, I might miss an important appointment. That will cause me to have some negative emotional consequence. I will now have a negative emotion stored in the tissue relative to the thorn in my foot and so on and so forth.

Because I have a thorn in my foot and I'm cranky, I might have a fight with someone that I care about and love. I might offend them so much that they don't forgive me. They now think I'm a horrible, hateful person. They don't care if I have a thorn in my foot. "There's no excuse to talk to me like that. I won't put up with it, I'm out of here." Now I'm depressed, sad and isolated. I'm embarrassed. I'm taking it to its extreme but that's how it works.

We look at a person and roughly guess what is talking to me. Is it chronic illness? Is the disturbance or imbalance in the Pranic body? Is it fully physical? Is it mental? Is it emotional? What is it? Whatever I see is going to give me direction for the therapy.

Body #5: The Matter Sheath (*Sans. Annamaya Kosha*):

The Tangible Physical Body (TPB): Annamaya Kosha is treated with physical medicine, medicine using pressure. This body is material, therefore it relates to pressure. The physical body is the only body that has a fine demarcation or a line or boundary or border. All the others don't have borders and can expand infinitely.

The Vedas say we are supposed to have balance between all the bodies. We have in our practice physical emphasis. When we look at the therapies, so many are physical. This is any therapy that involves putting pressure on the body, whether it's external or by way of coaching you into creating pressure yourself. For example, Hatha Yoga, Thai Yoga, Yoga Therapy all emphasize and use physical pressure. When you bend, stretch, fold, dangle and balance you're creating internal pressure on the organs, the tissues, the circulatory system and physical tissues.

Food & Right Eating: eliminating toxicities, deficiencies, malnutrition and adding nutritional supplementation are powerful allies in correcting imbalances in Annamaya Kosha.

Sacred Nutrition: Every different body has its food. The physical body requires physical food. We are designed to eat just about anything. You can tell this based on our teeth. When you compare our teeth to all the different animal kingdoms, the incisors of predators and we have the masticators of herbivores. We can eat nuts, chew meat, tear meat off of the bone. Our jaw strength is made to crack and break bone. It's due to life circumstance that we're able to eat such a variety of food. We might have had to in some survival situations. However, is that what we want to do consciously? That's a whole different conversation. The physical body requires physical food. We want the best quality food that we can get. Regardless of the techniques used, we treat and balance the ailments of the physical body using the principles of Chirothesia.

Body #4: The Vital Air Sheath (*Sans. Pranamaya Kosha*) :

The Breath Body (prana body): It is the Pranic body, the breath body, the energy body, the Vibrational body, the body of Chi, Ki and Orgone and Huna. It is whatever you might think of as the energy continuum of the Human Bio field.

Pranic medicine is based on breath. We call energy medicine – breath, prana, Huna, Orgone, or Qi (Chi/ Ki) based healing. Each of the words virtually mean and describe the same thing.

Breath and Prana therapies, could look like Pranayama that have names like Lion's Breath, Mother's Breath, Udjaya breathing. It can look like Kriyas. Breath meditation can also be the recitation of mantras, or singing songs. Because songs require cadence, rhythmic breathing, coordination of diaphragm and abdomen and torso, and the expression of consciousness and the voice. So singing and music for example, can be a great form of Pranayama. Playing a musical instrument can be Pranayama. Breath focus partially creates the high, the euphoria that you get from playing music. What instrument you use to play music is not important. This has been heavily researched. When you play any instrument it changes the way you breathe. People who are masters of any instrument whether it is, a drum, gong, trumpet, organ, piano or a guitar, at some point their breath is completely entrained and in syncopation with the instrument that they're playing. We don't know if it's the breath that drives the instrument, or whether it is the playing of instrument that draws the breath. Either way it is part of why it feels good to make music, the Pranayama. It's why when you sing in a choir you get high, the Pranayama.

Some people are naturally more gifted with their breath than other people. For example, freedivers, they dive as deep as they can without SCUBA tanks. The world record is held by Herbert Nitsch. He has dived over 253 meters or 831'. He can hold a single breath while diving to these depths for over nine minutes! Just a few years ago that this was considered medically, scientifically and physically impossible. The average person begins to lose consciousness at less than 3 minutes. Now we have people who can hold their breath without breathing for 10 minutes and they're not just sitting in the quiet of their meditation chamber holding their breath. They're in the ocean, doing things. They have to do them in the right order at the right time or they could die.

The Pranayama is based on science. It is based on understanding of how to capture the breath and how to organize the breath so it feeds the right parts of the body in order for the machine to function optimally, not wasting any oxygen, any breath. They can tell a certain part of the body to use less oxygen and other parts of the body to have more oxygen. There is a net volume of oxygen that they have. What gives them the capacity to last is the allocation of that resource. They've learned it via practiced discipline cultivated over many years. There is an ancient body of knowledge regarding the breath. You can learn how to hold your breath and actually move it from organ to organ. Anyone can do it. However, we have to know how. That knowledge exists in the body of what I call Kriya Yoga or Pranayama science. If you want to learn more about Pranayama look up Kriya Yoga. That's going to be your gold mine.

There are different ways to accumulate Prana. There are even ways that you can make or craft mechanical devices that will attract more energy. One simple example is a Quartz or other Crystal in the form of a pendant. The crystal is the simplest machine that we can use to attract, focus and concentrate Prana. Crystals have this ability to concentrate energy and to differentiate one frequency from another. The simplest illustration that I can give you is a prism. Look through a prism at ordinary sunlight and you see a rainbow.

You are not imagining these bands of color. The prism refracts the light in such a way that the various frequencies within the spectrum of light that you can see with your eyes are distinctive. A prism is a crystal, it takes the energy and it refracts it or differentiates the various frequencies within the light.

Crystals have some very interesting properties. Aside from how they manipulate light, they actually cause changes in all forms of energy and the electromagnetic frequency. Studying research done by Jaques Pierre Curie and later Woldemar Voigt's discovery of Piezoelectricity, he found out, that you can take an ordinary quartz crystal, and if you hit it, or deform it with pressure it produces electricity.

It produces electricity in a DC electric potential. The crystal produces light, electricity, and it produces a magnetic field. Crystals produce and change light. Crystals change and produce electricity especially when they're stressed, deformed or under pressure. Crystals also produce magnetic fields.

We are said to be crystalline or crystal based organisms. There are crystals in all the tissues of the body. There are crystals in the osseous membranes of the skeletal system. Osseous Crystalline Matrix is described by Dr. Robert O Becker, former chief of medical research of the Veterans Administration. He proved that there was sufficient crystal in the osseous matrix membrane that when you bend, stress or deform a bone, it produces an electric charge.

Body #3: The Sheath of Mind (*Sans. Manomaya Kosha*):

The Mental Body: The only way to treat or cure a deficiency in the mind is with education and mental therapy which facilitates the crafting of intellect. That's why there has to be Jnana yoga. There has to be psychology. We choose to use a holistic psychology that's noninvasive, non-coercive and nonviolent. I can't reject psychology and say all psychology is no good. The Vedas tell me that I have a mental body. They tell me the way for me to treat my mental body is with education and training my mind to work in a particular way.

The mental body. We look at mental education, coaching, psychological realizations, self-realization, Bardo therapies, the acquisition of knowledge and so forth. The mental body underpins the Pranic body. To have more Prana, and be more powerful pranically you must have more understanding, more information. You have to acquire the keys to be able to express it. Innately we can only go so far with natural ability.

Mental education and coaching, this is the Jnana Yoga. Jnana is for the mental body, and the mental body underpins the Pranic and physical body. The mental body is the gatekeeper for the knowledge and the blissful body. When we think of therapies or medicines for the knowledge body we think of anything that we are doing to enhance or correct or gain access to or broaden the capacity of any of these bodies in relation to any other. These therapies are feeling and experiencing based. They represent a balancing which comes out of doing. The act of taking something in and making that something part of us is the crafting of understanding.

This can be tricky, it's not enough that you hear the lecture, take the lab or the class. You have to take that understanding and do something with it to increase your essence or being.

Essence is manufactured. You weren't born with all the essence that you would ever have. Essence is something that we're given a little bit of in the beginning and then all of the quantity of that, that we ever have in our life is completely proportional to the educated doing and being. Essence is something that can grow, that we can increase. Essence is food for the spirit.

Body #2: The sheath of Knowledge (*Sans. Vijnanamaya Kosha*):

The Knowledge Body: We affect the Visjnanamaya Kosha with awareness and focus based applications and therapies. In other words, we do. That body is best treated by exercises and therapeutic processes, which emphasize a concept, "become what you know" or "be what you know". To the degree that you know and have knowledge and truth about yourself and your life and who you are and what you are about and fail to live according to that, becomes a source of friction and creates disharmony in your life including injury in yourself and others.

The knowledge body, the awareness body, the being body. The keyword here is application. The only way you can treat Vijnanamaya Kosha is by doing things. In other words, it changes as the result of direct experience. If you want changes at that level, you must acquire direct personal experience. This is why I try to emphasize for example, the importance of validation, verification and practice. You must acquire your own information, your own deep insight. Doing is what generates the insight. You have to get your hands on as many people as you possibly can. Be happy while you do it. It's doing something and the doing builds the vehicle. You can't be more without doing more. We have to do to be. Amrit Goswami says it succinctly "You have to do, be, do, be , do!"

Knowing this gives you the possibility of doing something with it that you didn't have before. Doing something that may be able to fundamentally change you. For example: doing a physical exercise. Doing Pranayama and Yoga i.e. causing deformation to the body gives you access to certain energies. The trick is you want to be able to direct those energies for health and longevity. You can direct those energies for recovering of injuries, for stimulating the immune system and so on.

The Vijnanamaya Kosha therapy is to become or be what you know through the process of assimilation: The act of taking something in and making it a part of you.

Body #1: The Sheath of Bliss: (*Sans. Anandamaya Kosha*):

The Blissful Body: Therapies and healing exercises to balance this sheath include spiritual medicine, ritual medicine, and practices involving devotion and surrender. Those are considered to be balancing of ego centric or mechanical aspects of this body. Practice devotion. This might include deity worship, guru worship, nature worship, self-worship. However you want to define it.

This is the spiritual heart of us. It is our Atman, our soul, our infinite being. It is the parts of us that have a perspective on our life that's not limited by time, space, events or circumstances.

Consider the concept of reincarnation. Reincarnation is a traditional Vedic idea. Imagine an ordinary deck of playing cards, if you're esoterically minded you can imagine a tarot deck. Each card represents a reincarnation and or reiteration of you manifesting in life. I've got all fifty-two cards. This is a metaphor for all of my reincarnations and all of my conscious reiterations of my eternal spirit.

My consciousness is coming from the space of existence in the undifferentiated cosmic consciousness. This undifferentiated consciousness is existing in a dimension which has no limitation of time or space. That's the perspective of the Atman, the soul. The soul direct, one on one, direct communication with God, maybe is a manifestation of God. Each card represents a separate life encapsulated in body tissue. We call that (each card) a lifetime. Take that deck of cards and hold it in your hand tight on one side and flip the other fanning it. When you do you will feel wind come off those cards. You'll hear the sound. The wind and sound represent the space between the cards. That wind is metaphorically your blissful body. It is evidence of the between place which always exists. The essence part of us that doesn't change.

Even though each card thinks it's unique and different. Each card says "oh I'm the queen of hearts, off with her head", and this card over here says "I'm the, the 10 of clubs, I'm power and prosperity", and this card over here says "I'm the, the jack of diamonds, I am the lower part of the intellectual center and I am unique". Every card thinks that it's life is completely unique, isolated and defined by the borders and the design of the card and its color scheme.

And yet, what the cards are missing is that they are nothing outside of the context of the deck. The only thing that's the same from card to card is the space between them. That's what you feel when you fan the deck. You feel that air, that wind. That wind in a sense is the essence manifesting. In this life, I still have that connection, I still have in the empty space, in the inner empty space, my cord of connectivity to my timeless self, my blissful body. Also note in my metaphor the way you directly experience the space between Lives (the cards) is by fanning them. Only by doing something do I generate the direct experience.

I want to find out how I can get better access to seeing my life from the perspective of the spirit. The Atman, the soul has a different perspective. The timeless part of me sees the deck, sees the limitations of all the reiterations and all the incarnations for what they are. It has a different perspective because it's not limited by time or space, it doesn't see an end to things. It doesn't worry about the ends of things. Because from its perspective there is no end. It doesn't worry about ultimate consequences in every little thing. Because ultimately all of the things that happen in that space, represented by the cards themselves are of no consequence. They're transitory. They will go away. They pass and yet something remains.

We need all these different kinds of medicine i.e. the medicine appropriate for the needs of the Kosha. I, you, we need all of the medicine focuses, even if you're not religious.

I promote devotion, even though it's the science of Ayurveda, and Native American Medicine. You must have some kind of devotional practice to be completely balanced and healthy in life.

We attend the Blissful Body's needs through the organized practice of devotion. Everyone should have some devotional activity that you engage in every single day. If you don't have a devotional practice then I want you to consider that you're practice of becoming a self-realized conscious, enlightened person is like you're a car trying to roll on three wheels. You may be able to drag yourself down the highway, but, you will have some restriction to your progress. These five bodies are important.

If you don't have a devotional practice, you have to find something to be devoted to. You have to find something that when you look at it, when you think about it, when you roll it around in your head, when you meditate on it that it opens up that part of you.

You have to find something. I've heard people say they don't believe in anything, I don't actually believe that for a second. I've heard of Atheists. However it's like what one wise man said, "there are no atheists in fox holes (combat)". Everyone's praying, in the fox hole. There's no such thing as a non-believer, in an ultimately risky situation. Everyone wants to believe that there is some outside agency or influence that is aware of our situation. We suspect, we project it as outside agency.

There's always the inner agency. That's really where that feeling starts. The feeling that I'm more than I think I am. I'm more than I see in the mirror. I'm more than what people tell me I am. I'm more than my role, my positions, my titles, my relatives idea of myself and so on. There's something else about me, not quite sure what that is, but, I want to know that part more. I want to have more of a real-time access to that because having glimpses of a perspective of my life that is not entirely limited by the circumstances of my life gives me hope. We need hope in this situation. We're encapsulated. The Buddhist call this world Samsara, the world of pain and suffering.

That's the world that we live in. So what neighborhood are you from? Oh, I'm from the world of pain and suffering. Wow, that's a rough neighborhood, I heard about that place. It's pretty rough. If you say, "I'm hanging with the Blue Crystal Medicine Buddha where everyone is enlightened". I can't relate. Since we live in Samsara "the world of pain and suffering", one of the things that we need more than anything else is hope. The source of the hope is that blissful place, that inner most body. When you are cut off from that, it's a source of disease. One of my Ayurveda teachers, Dr. Pillai, said that by definition all Ayurveda, all Ayurvedic treatments, all yoga, all the 8 Limbs of Yoga, all the branches of Yoga, all the practical medicines and treatments, exercises and meditations are only to cure one disease. That one disease is separation from the knowledge and direct personal experience of connection to God. Anandamaya Kosha is where that connection resides in the body.

Anandamaya Kosha: Blissful Body is not just one little place. Every cell has all 5 bodies. All these bodies overlap, and they're interdependent, inter-relating to each other. In fact, that Anandamaya Kosha Sheath/ body might be our biggest body. It may also be the one that we have the most difficult time relating to.

If you look on page 8 [Page ????], we have variations and different medicines which are defined by their emphasis on the specific bodies or aggregates or clusters of bodies. These bodies don't work in isolation. They work with each other. The more you meditate on this, the more it will give you some insight into other things that you do.

For example, if you teach Hatha yoga. You can't just teach technique. You cannot and think that you're going to really deeply affect people. You may help their fatigue, they may be more physically fit or aerobically fit, and have better circulation and range of motion. However, you are not affecting the whole person. You have to engage the other bodies. The Pranic body is the most immediate body to the tangible physical body (Pranamaya Kosha). So if you're going to teach yoga, you have to incorporate Pranayama. Prana (vital life force) is what supports the outer body. Think of a balloon. What is a balloon without the air? It's a bag or sack. It's formless and misshapen. However, as soon as you put the breath in it, it takes on form. It takes on particular characteristics and has a fullness about it. It also becomes stronger. The more air inside the larger and more defined the balloon becomes. Up to a point. There's a limit. It's why you can't go crazy with Pranayama.

There are basically 108 Kriya's or Pranic exercises. These are all the different Pranayama exercises coupled with either physical Asana or meditation. They use meditation imagery and or physical yoga, and or Locks and Bandhas or all the above all at the same time. In Kriya yoga, they teach the dangers of over emphasizing

Pranayama. If you overemphasize any of these bodies, it leads to imbalance. If you overemphasize the physical body it leads to in balance in all the other bodies: the Pranic body, the Mental body, the Knowledge body, and the Blissful body.

If you overemphasize the Blissful body, in other words you're just all devotion, all the time, devote, devote, devote. You're so sacred, so spiritual. You're going to forget to go to work. You're going to forget to pay the rent. You're going to end up a homeless person. You can only be so overly devotional if somebody else is going to pay the bills for you. I have a problem with that, Karmically. If my spiritual life is dependent on you paying my bills, don't I owe you something? There's some karmic debt here and if I'm so spiritual I don't put anything back into the system materially am I not creating a debt in some way? If not an energetic debt, an actual physical debt? If you have to pay for my spiritual lifestyle; if you have to support me there's a problem with over emphasis of the blissfulness.

After seeing many clients (unwell), I realized there was a hole in their life in the area of devotion. They had no devotion. They had nothing that they could rely on that was slightly bigger than themselves. I saw that as a loss. So, my teaching to them, my counselling, my therapy was to tell them that they needed to find something to believe in If you don't have anything that you can believe in, in the sense of being devoted to it, then then there is an empty place underpinning all of the other bodies, that is weak and creates a feeling of disconnection.

One of the things that comes out of devotional practice is a feeling or sense of connection. It's feeling a sense of oneness with something greater than yourself. The ancient traditions of Ayurveda and Indigenous Traditional Medicine instructs us that we all need devotion to be able to get through this life. I don't believe people when they say they don't. I think that they're expressing some buffered defense based on past negative experience and that there's some conversation they're not telling as to why they would say such things.

In ordinary life, I think most people need to have devotion. I don't say what I think that should be. Personally, I have many in my life, because of the quirkiness of my character I have many objects of adoration and many ideas of devotion. That means that pretty much any time of the day or night I can find something that I can relate to. I can say a prayer or mantra. I can create a positive visualization. I can do it 6 different ways because that's a discipline I've cultivated, my devotion in life. For you, it might be more simple, just one thing, but if it works, then that's what's important.

On Page 69, there is a rough model of the layers of the onion from the outer self to the inner self. We believe we have an outer and an inner self. We believe that these various bodies interact, are supported by, and dependent upon each other, first those most closely related to them, but to all other bodies overall.

A metaphor to describe their interactions is the picture of a symphony. The symphony is going to play a song, which is your life. In life, you have different instruments playing different parts of the song. You have a rhythm section, a melodic section and other sections that might move between them. You also have a conductor. All of them together are necessary and working together to play this song of life. If any one instrument goes out of tune, gets out of phase or becomes too dominant, it's to the detriment of the whole. If you randomly decided right in the middle of the song, to play a solo of some unrelated music, you might break down the whole symphony and the conductor at some point would start banging on her podium and would call the whole thing to a screeching halt until she could find the offender soloist.

Sometimes the offender soloist is a big deal as in there's an ego problem and you've got the virtuoso pianist who wants to shine inappropriately, not in accordance with the agreed plan, which is the actual performance piece. In this case the virtuoso and conductor will have to have a conversation on who's in charge.

Then you get all the way down to an instrument that just consistently is out of tune. Again the conductor calls the whole thing to a halt to say, 'tune that instrument!'". If that doesn't work then we will replace that function with another person or part that will hold consciously to the theme the orchestra under the guidance of the conductor is trying to portray.

You might have a rhythm section that likes to play a little bit slower than the conductor wants the movement to go. That would make the conductor just crazy. Maybe the rhythm is not predictable. It then throws everybody else off.

Each of our bodies is like a section in a full on orchestra. In order for the body as a whole to manifest its mission, function and purpose in the most beautiful way, all of the parts have to, in their own individual way, be compatible and in sync with all of the other parts. To the degree that is not happening is the difference between the Atlanta Symphony Orchestra and the high school band, where hardly anyone is playing in tune or on tempo. It's more like herding cats, musically. Then you get to another level of being where there is syncopation and a synergistic and dynamic interaction that is all in harmony because all the parts understand the mission. They see the bigger picture and vision of the conductor. Independently they strive to meet the mission. You then have all these different parts moving exceptionally yet with an individual expression. It's still you cranking on your instrument, but you are in a group of others that is a subsection of the orchestra. Altogether there is a point in time where the piece comes out and the vision manifests. It's a beautiful thing.

The greatest impediment to that happening is ego. The ego in my metaphor is the impetus in every member in the orchestra to think or act as if they are more important than the orchestra. At any point if that comes in, there is a degeneration of function. There is a deterioration of function.

This is why we have so many different therapies. Right here we have a model for every kind of medicine and healing art. Every kind of therapy you might imagine or invent will fit into one of these categories and bodies.

Five Medicines for Five Bodies

Let's go back into more specifics of each body's medicine.

There are pros and cons of working on each body. If there is an issue localized to the physical tissue, then that therapy should be very effective for it. The problem is so many things that ail us cross over and source themselves or affect more than one body. That means that any given point, no matter how perfect that physical therapy is, if there is a prana or energy aspect to the imbalance, there is a place where that therapy will no longer be effective and sometimes it might impede the healing process.

1. **Physical:** For the outermost body we use physical therapies such as manipulation therapies, etc.

2. **Breath:** Breath body – acupuncture meridians and acupoints are found here.

You have to go through the physical body, pierce the tissue to get to that energetic body and to affect it directly. There are some therapies that try to skip that intermediate step of piercing the physical body like qi gong. Qi gong therapy and exercise is considered a medical modality for health. It seeks to bypass the physical by cultivating ways of affecting your energy without touching you or with very light touch.

You have pranayama therapies that focus on the movement of the breath.

Breath affects the physical body. When I put pressure on the physical body I do affect energy whether it's intentional or not. I can not not affect energy – in this metaphor they are right next to each other so they will affect each other.

When I do breath-based therapies I cannot help but affect the physical and the mental bodies. That's also why energetic therapies like acupuncture have mental and emotional results. You can treat physical and mental illnesses with an acupuncture needle. The breath body is the bridge between the mind and the physical body. It's the connection vessel. It's how we get there from here.

3. **Mental:** Notice on mental body, I listed some things: education, coaching, realization, psychological, self-realization, bardo therapies, and the acquisition of knowledge.

This was traditionally called satsang. Satsang is where the teacher sits down and espouses the their understanding, sharing knowledge and wisdom with the students. That knowledge and wisdom is a certain kind of energy. The energy is called shakti or shakti pot. In other words, I'm not just espousing facts and numbers, but I am sharing my knowledge and wisdom in an intentional, willful, wholesome way to the best of my ability. That means that I am also enrolling other qualities and information coming from other centers of my own self.

The mental body directly affects the energetic body and the physical body. Practices of meditation and self-realization, productive psychological therapies will also help balance energetic and physical imbalances.

Coaching is important because it teaches you how to hold, carry and regulate, find and cultivate your energy as well as how to project and move it. We do that through an educational process, even though what we are talking about is all energy. The way we learn how to use the energy is through mental coaching. We also use affirmations and other techniques – those two bodies are right next to each other.

4. **Knowledge:** Then we move into the next body where we see the therapies are about experience and feeling. In other words, 'it's about assimilation'. It's about the act of taking something in to generate actual real understanding. In the mental body I learn the concepts, I learn the focus and get the visualization, I learn the affirmation, the posture, the mantra, what pranayama will work for what affect. In the next body, I actually have to do those things. I have to do it because it's based on actual doing.

5. **Bliss:** In the Anandamaya Kosha, the inner-self body, we affect directly through practices of devotion, deity, guru, nature or self worship, Vipassana, Samadhi and various kinds of meditation. You can substitute the deity of your choice. None work better than others. Although some people will say that their experience is that this image, guru, avatar, icon appears to affect them more directly. That is based on how that person, image, or icon resonates with your fractured self in other areas. For example, if the guru that you are practicing
devotion to feeds you more strongly solutions for your mental imbalance then you will be more strongly attracted to devotion that them. If your greatest weakness or your chronic or chief feature – the greatest imbalance you have that you can't see is in the emotions, then you will be attracted to having devotion with a teacher, guru, icon, symbol that has more information and energy in the emotional state.

If your greatest imbalance or inequity is in the moving center and is more physical, then your object of devotion is going to be a teacher that gets you moving more. You will not be similarly attracted to another teacher who is more emotional and sedentary, is more spiritual because you will want one who gets you to jump up and down or the equivalent which might be martial arts or sacred or ecstatic dancing.

You can take this inner-self or blissful body and, as a therapy or situation in life, you will want the heart-on-
Page 80

heart guru, the being guru who stresses being what you know. Next there is the guru who stresses understanding. Then there is the one who stresses energetic understanding and finally you have the teacher who is masterful and speaks to you in the realm of physical action, movement and exercise.

It's quite possible that as you move through these bodies and roles in your life that at one time or another you will be more attracted to one system or teacher or another based on your imbalance. Chief feature is your chronic and most negative attribute or part of your development, it is always the one thing you cannot see. We never see our own worst attribute. We never see our primary ego-centric weakness. We are made in such a way that that part of us is naturally invisible to us but not to others.

The Vampire metaphor:

The vampire, the bloodsucker, un-living living who can tackle you, glamour you, bite you and suck your blood – they are very physical and sensuous and in lore they are above average intelligence and skill and have access to wisdom and knowledge that is very ancient and regularly transmitted to other vampires and yet when they step in front of a mirror they can't see themselves. In lore and literature, a vampire is a powerful creature and creative force however politically incorrect it might be to be a bloodsucking parasite of the undead. The one thing a Vampire can not see or do is to see directly its true nature in the world.

The stories of vampire lore, as they intentionally or otherwise were crafted by people like Mary Shelley, were trying to express this concept of the invisibility of chief negative feature. This concept is quite old in its origins, in fact we don't know it's origin.

This tells me something. It tells me that as I look at this body and myself, I can only hypothetically guess which of my bodies I'm most focused in and which ones I'm most out of balance in. If I want to know, I have to find a person or group of people who can show me that chief negative feature, the greatest ego-centric emphasis of my incarnation in this world. Only other people can show me that.

Why we are attracted to gurus or special teachers – special education teachers, because x,y,z guru may in fact harmonize with us according to our greatest weakness. Now, what comes up immediately about that is that if that doctor, guru, swami, or teacher is successful, there is a point in time where you should no longer be dependent on them. If they have in fact helped balance that chief negative feature in a substantial way, then you should change. If they don't, then there is some other play at work. Maybe their teachings are not being effective and they are not helping you to evolve. There are quite a few teachers who innately know about this idea of weakest feature and they use that as a tool to gain power and authority and prestige over people. It's insidious because their students can not tell that that's what's happening because they don't see why they are attracted to that teacher in the first place.

In classical Ayurveda, the idea is that as a therapist, I can see your greatest imbalance easier than you can. You can't see it at all. I can tell you where your imbalance is. The trick is that I want to craft an educational model to cultivate therapists that are as compassionate, loving, nonjudgmental and objective as possible. Knowledge is power. We want to make discernments about imbalance and what body we are going to treat, for example.

And we want to be able to do so in a compassionate and non-judgmental way. If I can't communicate like that, then you will not subscribe to the therapy. What if, for example, you come to me with a headache and I tell you it's because you're ignorant. You insist that the reason you have the headache is because you don't eat right and you want me to teach you how to eat right. I do an assessment and I say, 'well, it looks to me like you eat just fine. The reason why you have the headache is because you're ignorant. You need education and you need discipline.' The problem is between the mental and the knowledge body. It's not the physical body. It's not about the food, it's about who you are. That's why you're having this issue.

The 'who you are' between the body and the energy shows all of the energy variation that you get with your headaches. If I can not communicate that to you in a loving and un-judging way, you will not listen to me. What you'll do is find another therapist who will agree with you and they will treat you. The problem is that most of the time, you are wrong about what's wrong with you. You have to be. We have to be. By definition, we can not see our chief negative feature. The most wrong things about us, whatever those might be, whatever body they occur in are the ones most invisible to us. That's why the therapy game is a hard one.

Sometimes you have to work at things tangentially. For example, you come to me with a headache and you think it's because of your diet. Where I see the problem is in the mental. Where I will start your treatment is right in the middle meaning energetic and physical therapies with an education emphasis. That will give you enough physical stimulation to think that you are having progress there. You might even have some physical remedy. I really want to focus on the education part to treat the mental body because that is where your main imbalance is.

We get into all sorts of whacky strategies about how to guide our clients in productive ways of being that solve the obvious imbalances. It's as if you were to walk in the room with a big nail sticking out of your head. It looks like someone shot you in the head with a nail gun. It's obvious what's wrong with you but I'm still going through the process right? Your feedback is important to see where you are relating to what body. I will ask you, 'how can I help you? What can I do for you?' you might say, 'oh man! I have really bad heartburn.' I go, 'heartburn? Ok. Is there anything else that might be bothering you?' You answer, "let me think about it…no no everything else is fine.' But I see plainly that you have a big nail in your head. I go, 'let me ask you a question. Does the big nail sticking out of your head cause you any discomfort? It seems like it would.' You grab the nail and go,'what nail?' you smooth your hair around the nail and go, 'nail? I'm not following you. Nothing comes to mind when you say that.' I say, 'okay, well let's focus on the heartburn and how that might relate to nails in the head along the way.'

We try to work at it indirectly until at some point you realize you have a big nail in your head and there might be a reason for that and in fact it might relate to your heartburn. That nail is also affecting the energy body. There is a reason why someone shot you in the head with a nail gun. It might have to do with the way you speak or relate to people. Maybe you are always angry or disrespectful. If you are insulting that is imbalance in the mental and blissful bodies. I might give you some devotional exercises and meditation. "Don't do headstands right now." "oh, ok." I work at it indirectly.

Many times, in cultivation of strategies with people we have to work up to it because you can never see your chief feature but I can.

I have a list of primary imbalances, chief features and their descriptions: what they sound like, smell like, look like, etc. When I see it, smell it, hear it, etc. I make a note. All of that may be invisible to you at first. Over time, I might be able to show you which body is most out of balance and how we can work at it from different sides. We have many different therapies.

In SomaVeda® we have therapies for all the bodies.

That's why when we work sometimes we might have a very devotional attitude. Other times we might be very physical. Still other times we might be very focused on the breath. We coach. Sometimes there is homework for the client. Why? You have to cultivate a discipline to become what you know.

Eventually to have holistic healing, we have to have therapies that address all these bodies.

My first assessment is, that I look at the new client and listen to them and what they're bringing me and I try to have a general idea what body is talking to me.

Understanding these bodies and how they work together, how they support each other will tell me an area of emphasis. That observation will tell me for example if I'm going to do a SomaVeda® Thai yoga session on you. It will tell me if I am going to emphasize a hard-physical session and to think that that's going to give you some benefit. That will tell me for example, a strategy on whether I should have a high Pranayama emphasis in the session and whether that will give you the best benefit. That will tell me how much of the session we're going to spend on learning and education,

I've had clients that what they needed to get well, was not for me to fix anything. There were things that they did not know, that they needed to know. They needed to know things they can do for themselves or have other people do. The primary activity that I engaged in with that client was education and coaching. That's what gave them the most healing response. Counseling, coaching, education are balancing for the respective bodies. Commonly, after doing assessment, listening and looking at them, I realized that the big gap in their life, is that they weren't doing anything useful with what they knew.

They weren't maximizing what they knew. I then had to encourage them to do something, not just to learn something. I've had clients who were sick and my primary recommendation to them was to go back to school. They would say, "but I have a bad back, I have migraine headaches", yeah, I know. However, my assessments, my gut and my educated response tells me that you're deficient in the mental body. The words you use when you speak tell me, that you're a little bit ignorant and that's fixable. You have this Kapha imbalance, this Kapha ignorance, and that's repairable. You find the right situation to get the education that will meet their necessity. My recommendation was that they must do, to actively engage in a learning process.

There is no one therapy for all of the bodies, which can be misleading to some and hard to understand.

There are many ways to bring energy, attention, consciousness, breath and pressure to any of the bodies. For example you can bring energy to the being and mental bodies with art. That is what art is. Art is a bridge between the outer and the inner – the physical expression of life, the energetic underpinning and support of that physical expression and the innermost blissful body. That is why art has the capacity to be deeply disturbing, once you see it you are never the same afterwards. You may see one piece of art one time and you now have different thoughts in your head and it never goes away.

Art has the capacity to cause us to have the deepest feeling of spiritual awareness and loving compassion. It is a physical medium: paint, graphite on paper, clay twisted up in some form or another, a piece of rock hammered out…we look at it and are simultaneously affected in multiple bodies. We might even have shifts that work to heal great imbalances just from one piece of work. That's why some people don't like art. They don't like the stimulation or balancing and unconsciously want to support their chief feature. Art challenges them to think or be different. I want to stay with comfort and familiarity. I want to avoid things that will crack that egg. Great literature has a similar possibility. It does it through the medium of the mental body.

Then we have crafted therapies like hatha yoga exercises. In yoga there are 8 branches. Each of the branches is designed to affect one of the bodies more than the others. For example, Kriya yoga is primarily meant to affect the prana body. Hatha affects the physical body. Jnana yoga affects the mental body. Bhakti yoga affects the blissful body. All of them stress discipline over time, which affects the knowledge body. That explains why we have to have multiple branches of yoga. It is also why it's crazy for those focused on one branch of yoga to take some superior attitude over other branches. The whole system was crafted to be a collection of tools to bring different effects to balancing the ego in these five bodies.

In our practice we want to have awareness of these bodies. This is a first assessment.

You look at the client and use your gut intuition and reaction to relate what their primary issue is to what body it is in, go with it. It could be as obvious as the nail sticking out of the head. It might be more subtle than that. You might have to ask a lot of questions or follow them around for a little bit. You might have to spend time with them to see. We are really good at hiding our chief feature. We are perfect at hiding it from ourselves. We are good at hiding it from other people although it is more likely they can see it. We instinctively know this because we see how they react to us. You start reacting to me in a way that I'm not really comfortable with. You are reacting to my chronic or chief feature, which I am projecting to you. I can't see it but you might even be speaking to it. I don't know what you are talking about. I'm not like that at all. Obviously you misunderstand me and/or you are trying to insult me on purpose – obviously. Then there's a large source of friction in this equation.

As therapists, we want to become aware of this over time. It is heavily involved in the dance we do with our clients and as we grow as people.

Student: Should we also be aware of what we are projecting onto others?

Dr. James: initially no but eventually yes. You cannot be worried about something you can not see. In other words, to learn what your chief negative feature is – the negative sources of negative expressions in your life takes a fair amount of feedback over time. First of all, you have to be open to it. You have to accept the idea that when you see it you will not like it. It is going to tell you that you are a way that you never thought you could be. It will tell you that you have ways of behavior that everything about you might be in opposition to. That is very difficult work. Most people run 'screaming for the woods' long before they get to that point.

That is why it is hard and harsh to do real work with real teachers. As much as everyone wants to flock to a guru, they want the easy one. They don't want the real one. The real one will crack the egg with a hammer and will bring up that chief feature, lay it out in front of you like a buffet and then present you with the idea of working with it or not. There will not be much tolerance for anything else because as far as the real teacher is concerned, until you are making progress with the very most negative parts of yourself, you haven't even started working.

We tend to gravitate towards situations or teachers that give us a lot of information about the parts of us we already know about and not too much information about the parts of us we don't want to know about. We tend to stay with them longer.

That's why we say that becoming a self-realized person is not easy. At some point, in the process of becoming self-realized, we have to actually face our true reflections, which we've never seen before.

There is a metaphor about this in the Bardo Thodol (Tibetan Book of Betweens).

The Vajra Haruka, a great 4 headed, 8 armed, 6 legged demon wearing skulls, crushing bones and gnashing its teeth, sounding like a hundred tornadoes with broken glass and holding in every hand a dire implement of dissection and critical and cruel injury and horrific concepts where everything about it is wrong and evil and unreal. It presents itself to us in such a way that we can't get away from it. The aspirant is instructed to recognize that, that which is before them is nothing more than a perfect reflection of their own perfect luminosity. The aspirant is then instructed to loudly and clearly state "that which is before me is a reflection of my own perfect luminosity." The bardo is telling us that the fearsome Haruka is us. The Haruka becomes the embodiment of our chief negative feature. In the bardo, we are instructed not to run away from it because if we run away from it, then it will catch us. It knows where we live. It then destroys us to create another opportunity
Page 84

to have this conversation again. The only release from that negative, wrathful, violent, horrific expression of self is in fact to own it entirely and to recognize it for what it is – it is your reflection in that mirror.

This is very difficult in a therapeutic process because ideally I don't want you to just be better. I want you to become what you are here to become.

As instructional as suffering is, it can often be an impediment to progress and certainly at different stages in life. We spend a lot of time worrying about our pain when we could be studying, practicing, meditating, or becoming what we know. Instead we chase our pain like a dog chasing its tail. We are caught up in the wheel of suffering. In the Buddhist way we call that the dhamma (Sans. Dharma) wheel. We are trapped on this wheel and it seems perfectly natural as our state of life in our evolutionary position.

The whole point of knowing that there's a dhamma wheel is looking for the exit, the point is to get off the wheel. Yet that somehow gets lost in the shuffle. As we get caught up in this idea of suffering as teaching us lessons – "the reason why I am suffering is that it's the universe's way of teaching me". I think that's true to a point. You can take that lesson swift or slow. You can get locked into a recurring lesson plan. If we never get what we need to be able to get the lesson and see where we are and what are our issues, then we are bound into a repetitious state of recurring lessons called reincarnation. Reincarnation from this perspective is not good because there is no end to it. We are trapped in a cycle of endless creation of varying cycles of suffering. What we want to do is find a way to stop it and get off the wheel. There's another life possible.

One or more bodies are always dominant at any point in time.

All the bodies relate in real time to the action of all the other bodies.

A deficiency in one body or quality might look like excess in another. Excess in one body, activity or energy will look like a deficiency in another. They act as counterbalances to each other within their circle of influence. For example, you might have someone who is too spiritual. They have no practical mind or any conception of the consequences of their actions. They are disconnected with the ordinary realities of their lives. They will have and cause problems because their focus is too spiritual. This is just as much of an imbalance as someone who is not spiritual at all. There is no difference. There is equal imbalance.

People who are too spiritual become fundamentalists or very conservative. What happens is that the philosophies promoted by these people become obtrusive, invasive and burdensome to others.

Yet, if you have no conception, knowledge or respect for education, no understanding of the role of energy and connectedness of all living things by way of the web of energy in life and breath, then you are missing most of life. There is a whole part of life that is invisible to you, if you are only in that physical realm.

Then you have people who are very energetic, but they are not able to take care of themselves physically. They can't feed themselves, clothe themselves or hold a job. They can't keep relationships, but they will be spiritual and energetic people. I wish I could tell you how many very spiritual, intuitive and energetic people I've met, who from the point of view of life, were trainwrecks going from one relationship to the next. We have to have balance and compensation in all of these bodies to be functioning. When I look at you as a client and see that one of these is dominant or missing, I get an indication about the package of disorder that you are bringing to me.

An assessment is looking at a person and deciding in which body their primary issue is occurring.

Once I know that, I then have an idea of the primary one, two or three therapies I can use or therapeutic angles of attack that will help with the client.

Let's say, " your problem is primarily in the prana body." Well, we use some physical therapy and we will get some education and meditation going. We will also do some pranayama, directly related to the imbalance.' I just gave three styles of treatment to emphasize.

Student: If you have a client and work with them according to that and then it shifts by the next session or a couple sessions later and then is there a reassessment process that needs to be…

Dr J: There can be. It might but doesn't necessarily shift. All five bodies are always present at every moment in everything we do. As you balance one, you may just see the imbalance in the next, it didn't shift. It was always there.

We say that imbalances show themselves in three ways: inner, outer, and secret.

The outer is the part of the imbalance that I can see from across the street, down the road and around the bend as you walk across the parking lot. It has to do with the way you express yourself, your posture, your voice are all examples of the outer manifestation of our imbalance.
It is obvious to both you and I.

Then we have the inner aspect to the imbalance. That's the part that you can see more readily than someone outside of you you can see with a little investigation.

Then there is the secret aspect to your imbalance, which is the part that you don't know and I can't see either. It may always be secret. There is always an element in a client's healing, which I may never be a part of. It will always be secret to me. Why is that? Well, your life is about you, not the therapist. No matter what, there may be an element in your indication of certain kinds of imbalance that will never be shared and may even be secret to you.

We always start with general assessments based on the outer imbalance.

When I see you come in as a client and listen to your complaints, looking at you, making a determination is all dealing with the outer. It is observations that are readily discernible from the outside like the nail sticking out of your head or heartburn. That's not really the issue, but you don't know what it is. I might be able to find out with a little further investigation. Even if we are successful in getting the nail out and getting rid of the heartburn, there will probably still be some unresolved issues that will remain secret.

That is the way we are made and we have to be okay with that.

My self-image as a healer is not tied up in fixing everything about you. My self-respect as a healer deals more with the outer and inner than the secret imbalances. I allow that there is a secret part of every imbalance that maybe is between you and your innate or spirit. That has nothing to do with me and never will. It's not about me.

As a therapist, you really need to learn what's not about you and be okay with that. Your position in this paradigm may be just to get them to a certain degree of resolution so they can do the rest or someone else needs to take them further.

Student: You mentioned earlier about Jnana, Bhakti and Kriya yoga…what about the second experiential body – what yoga would be associated with that?

Dr J: All of the bodies are experiential. All of the primary 8 branches of yoga have an experiential aspect. There is crossover between the bodies. In Kriya Yoga, you have to learn about the energy body—that's mental. You have to practice pranayama in yoga asanas. In just that there is mind, breath and physical bodies being activated. The primary emphasis is somewhere between the breath and the mind. Some advanced Kriya Yogis only do one or two asanas either sitting or lying down.

The knowledge part is activated with the instruction and learning what a Kriya is, and learning the Kriyas; "Here's what they are. Here's how they work. Here's the anatomy of that Kriya. This is what chakra it emphasizes. This is what Srotas and nadis it balances." This process is part of the practice of Jnana Yoga. Within the context of Kriya Yoga is Jnana yoga.

We teach and practice in Indigenous Traditional Thai Yoga Therapy Hatha Yoga disciplines. The practice of Hatha Yoga is a devotional practice. Quite a few teachers teach breath and pranayama practices. Some teachers instruct in principles and theories of Ayurveda, the doshas and chakras.

The mental part is an example of Jnana yoga. We are doing a class right now in jnana yoga. When we do Puja (*Th. Buch*a) we are doing Bhakti yoga with incense, projections of healing to the client, acknowledging the lineage, it is all part of it.

As I know more, I may choose to specialize in one or more forms. Eventually that is why you have yogis like Swami Vivikenanda who specialized almost exclusively in Jnana yoga. He led no hatha yoga whatsoever. Then you have yogis like Swami Satchidananda who really emphasizes hatha yoga and pranayama but doesn't teach much Jnana yoga. Then there are many variations. Iyengar instructed heavily on the hatha yoga but not so much on Bhakti and Jnana yoga. It doesn't mean it's not there. Even Iyengar will teach Puja (Th. Bucha). They won't do Puja (Th. Bucha) all day because people want to do something. If you went to Swami Satchidinanda that wouldn't be tolerated. In that school, there are some ceremonies where they do ritual and Puja (Th. Bucha) all day and sometimes all night long. If every hour, you wondered when you were going to do yoga, "I'm tired of all this praying, visualization, affirmation and all that. I'm ready to get moving." They would just toss you out. As far as they are concerned they are doing yoga from the first minute to the last minute.

Student: how can you tell what a person's Chief Negative Feature is?

Dr J: I can't answer that until you've been in class about a year because you learn what they are – the common expressions. If you see it and it is obvious and they can't see it. That's one of the things – we have these aspects to our ego centric nature that will hide us from our most negative features. The proof is when I ask you about things I see that are very obvious and you have no idea what I'm talking about. 'nothing comes to mind' you might say.

Chapter 8: Thaat Thang Sii
Four Traditional Elements in Thai Ayurveda

There is a color plate here that's titled, [*Th. Thaat Thang Sii*], the four traditional elements of Thai Ayurveda. This diagram is from a codex which is a like of book made in the form of panels of which are sewn together and would usually have a wooden plate on the top and the bottom, they're quite durable. But this particular codex is in color; it was commissioned by the King of Thailand. Without this codex we wouldn't know it, we would not know that in the 11th century in Thailand that they were practicing a sophisticated derivative form of Ayurveda. We wouldn't know that definitively. We would know it by way of an oral tradition but this is an 11th century manuscript that was part of a training course for Reishi doctors. And this shows a chart which looks a little bit like labyrinth; you see the four elements coming in from four directions.

A chart like this one is a whole book, not just a picture, or a graphic. In the past a diagram or painting, like this would have been used to teach both entry level and very advanced concepts about medicine and also of the philosophy that's behind the medicine. In this one chart we have geometric constituents, we have circles, we have indication of four directions. As soon as the four directions cross that circle that gives you quadrants, quadrants defined by triangles. So we have various kinds of geometries which are hinted at or which are overtly implied. Indigenous people everywhere in the world have the four direction medicine concepts, this knowledge or idea of the importance of the four directions which are both compass settings, stages of life as well as represent the interaction of the various elements to make up all that there is.

In classical Hindu, classical Indian Ayurveda there are five elements: ether, air, fire, water, earth. In Thai tradition there are only four, Thaat Thang Sii, because they combine the influences of ether and air into one element called Lom. So the Thai say: Lom (ether/air), Fai (fire), Din (earth), Nam (water).

They combine the classic Ayurvedic elements of ether and air as one comprehensive element called Lom. That's why in Thai there are only four indicated, but in classical Indian Ayurveda we talk about the five elements. They're exactly the same thing and the meaning is exactly the same there's no difference whatsoever.

This color plate is interesting because each of the elements is depicted as it occurs in nature: water is waves, earth is mountain, fire is fiery, air looks like clouds. All four of these elements in their respective quadrants comes spiraling into the center where they all come together to make the world. This is what we call a cosmology because it is actually showing a worldview and showing what are considered the representation of all that there is. This cosmology gives us the big picture, the macroscopic viewpoint at least in reference to the elements. You can discern by looking at this picture that everything is made up of some combination of these elements.

Everything there is, is a combination of these elements one way or the other according to it's nature. Mountain is relatively more earthy than sky or clouds, but clouds have substance. Clouds have water. Condensation or heat is what makes clouds. Mountains are relatively more solid with a dominance of the earth element but all mountains also have all the other elements. For example, if that mountain was the result of a volcanic explosion then at the heart of that mountain is fire. Mountains have springs throughout them, water. There's no such thing as a dry mountain or a mountain without water. It's the air element in the mountain reaching for the sky that make the mountain taller, that makes it high. You could say that's an expression of air element. Mountains move; mountains are not stagnant. A mountain seems stagnant and still and we'll say things like quiet as a mountain or still as a mountain or strong as a mountain, but mountains are in constant evolution. Their shape is changing, their character is changing, their height is either increasing or decreasing, it may be slowly over time or suddenly like an earthquake.

The Four "Thatu" (Dhatu) or Elements of Thai Ayurveda: Thaat Thang Sii

1) Akat/ Lom = Air   (*Sans. Vayudhatu*)
2) Fai = Fire   (*Sans. Tecudhatu*)
3) Naam = Water   (*Sans. Apodhatu*)
4) Din = Earth)   (*Sans. Pathavidhatu*)

Thaat Thang Sii:
Ancient chart depicting the
Four Elements of Traditional
Thai Medicine

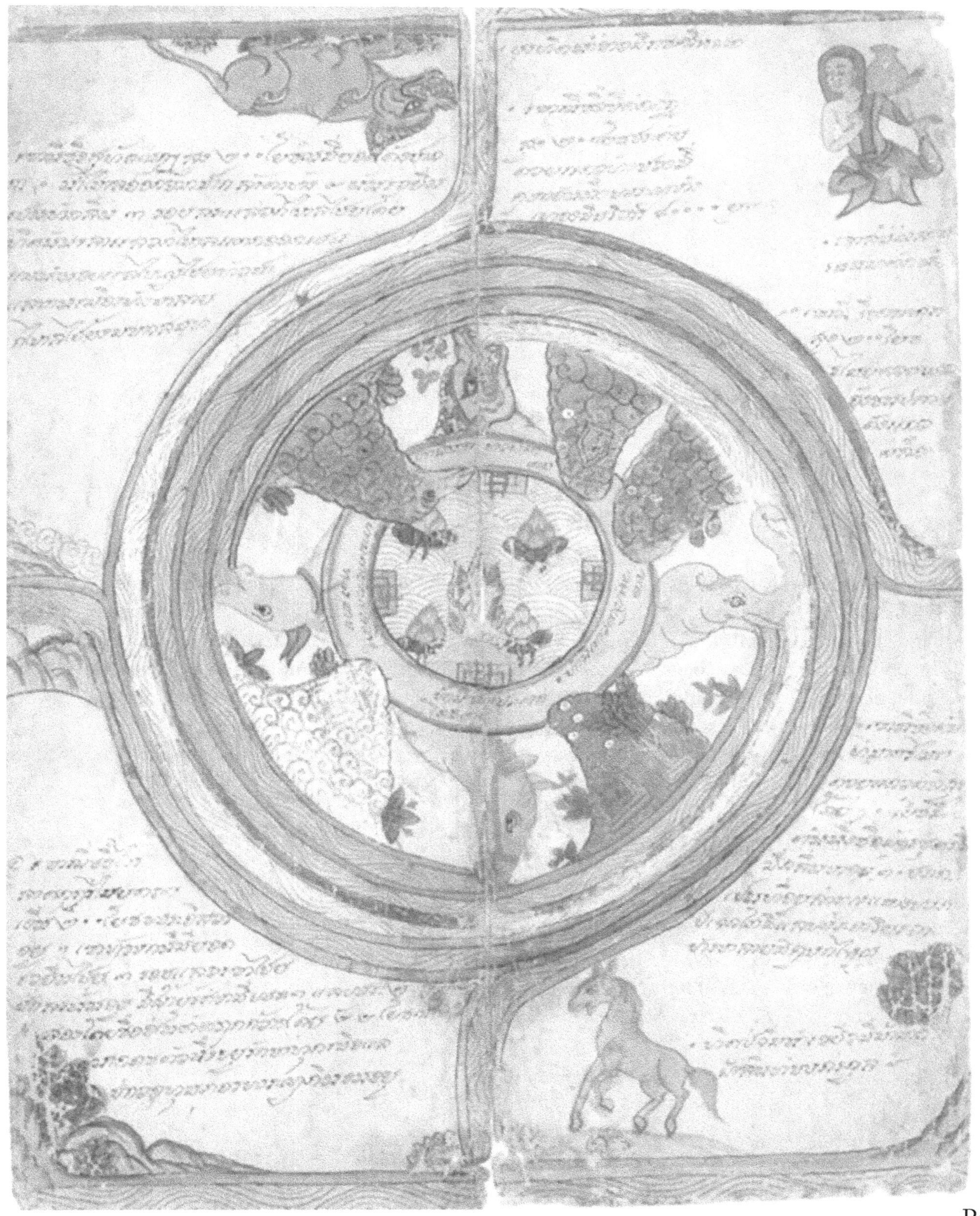

Chapter 9: Five Elements of Traditional Indian Ayurveda

The Five Elements in the body (*Sans. Pancha Mahabbhutus/ Panchabhuta*), are the idea of the macrocosm of universal principles of the Five Elements (the five *Panchabhutas: Akashadhatu, Vayudhatu, Tejasdhatu, Apodhatu, Prthvidhatu*) and the three constitutional elements or Gunas of Satvas, Rajas and Tamas. How they actually manifest in the body is our primary focus. We're a microcosm of nature. A combination of interactions between the celestial influences and the terrestrial influences of heaven, and earth. The difference between us and these grand influences is one of scale. All of the various energies which can be found in the larger universe are also found on a somewhat smaller scale within us. It's easy to see the presence of the five universal elements in the human body.

Pancha Mahabhutus/ Panchabhuta

ETHER Element: (*Th. Akat/Aagaasathaat/ Lom*) (*Sans. Akashadhatu*)
AIR Element: (*Th. Lom/ Prana*) (*Sans. Vayudhatu*)
Fire Element: (*Th. Fai*) (*Sans. Tejasdhatu*)
Water Element: (*Th. Naam*) (*Sans. Apodhatu/ Apasdhatu*)
Earth Element: (*Th. Din*) (*Sans. Prthvidhatu*)

Originating out of the original Cosmic Consciousness, the primordial sound OM (AUM) appears as the first soundless vibration. Out of this vibration comes all of the elemental constituents of the material or manifested universe: So first is Om. First is this manifestation of vibration and consciousness. Ether (*Akat- Lom*), Air (*Lom/ Prana*), Fire (*Fai*), Water (*Naam*), Earth (*Din*).

The first of these manifested vibrations is Ether or space. In other words, the primordial "Om".

Om and If There Was a Big Bang:

If there was a big bang, if there was a time when there was nothing in the universe except for one thing, that one thing was called "The Singularity". The singularity was one point of infinite density and infinite energy, but unexpressed. It was just the one point. It was less than one molecule big. Astrophysicist, Mathematicians, Astronomers theorize that we can't even define how small this singularity was. And yet, in that one point, whatever the origin of that singularity, all possible expression of all possible energy and motion and consciousness and space was compressed into infinite density in that point. And then for some reason, that point divided, exploded. We call that point, that time, that place "the beginning of time". All time is relative to that point dividing, to the present time for us. That's our timeline.

That dividing is called, the big bang, because it created an explosion that was so big, that it is still going on. It created an outward push of propellant motion, of various kinds of matter, and energy. This was 15 trillion years ago. It was so big that debris from that explosion is still expanding away from it. While the debris is expanding it's not passive. It's interacting with other debris. We call that the formative process in the universe. The formation of cloud clusters and birthing rooms of stars, galaxies and solar systems. The debris interacting and mingling, attracting, repelling and coalescing in all the different processes.

It was a very big explosion, it made a big noise. Imagine how loud that explosion would have been. In fact, it was so loud that you can still hear it. It's the base resonant frequency of the whole universe. In the absence of every kind of distortion or every other sound that can be identified, there is a sound that stands out. Using specific telescopes which are tuned specifically to ultra-low sound frequencies scientist have isolated approximately what the frequency of the Big Bang sound is. If you point that telescope in any direction of the sky, you get this reverberation, this echo. If you hear this sound amplified over a speaker, what you hear is a frequency of the "Om" mantra tone or sound.

The Vedas state, "originating out of the cosmic consciousness the primordial sound Om appears as the first soundless vibration". Why is it a soundless vibration? It's like in the science fiction books "no one can hear you scream in space". It doesn't mean that the vibration isn't there, it's that what we define as audible sound is based on vibrations travelling through air. You have to be in an environment that has air in order to hear things. If you are in an environment which is a vacuum or a near vacuum, the vibrations in space do not manifest as audible sound. Audible sound is an artifact of cochleal-tympanic auditory nerve interpretations of variations of pressure waves of energy moving through air. So no air, no ear- no sound. The first and the loudest primordial vibration was the carrier wave for creation.

What is driving everything out from the center? The carrier wave (voice of God). The ancient Reishis said there was such a thing, they could hear it, they knew what it was. They said it is "Underpinning everything." If everything is consciousness and vibration affecting material, then what drives it? What is the uniform code or pattern that drives this organizing of the universe? The ancient Yoga Reishis said that it was Om.

This is why we chant Om mantras. It is to remind us, to bring us more in sync with the primordial fundamental rhythm which has always been part of creation. A music, a song of creation which has always been part of the life of the universe. Therefore, it's always been a part of every other thing. When we're out of sorts with the universe, then one of the tools that we were given to bring us into harmony is this mantra, the sacred Om. Mantra is a word. Although OM is used as a mantra Om is not a word. Om is a tone. In Vedic literature it's referred to as a seed syllable (Bija).

Where do the five elements come from?

Where do five elements come from? Where does the theory of the Thaat Thang Sii (*Sans. Dhatu-* Five Elements) come from? Why would people ever have thought that matter can exist in five different states? Ancient people were logical, and paid attention to their environment. There are many observable natural phenomena that actually mimic all of these stages. Ancient people did not separate their ideas of themselves as separate and distinctive from the natural world around them or which they found themselves living in.

The life cycle volcanos is one example. Ancient people were familiar with volcanoes. Volcanoes have several distinctive states which correlate with five elements transforming. They have a gaseous state where they exude many different kinds of gasses some visible some invisible. Carbon dioxide is invisible. Sulfur is visible. What appeared to be solid one minute ago became something less than solid. If one of the largest things on the planet can in a moment become less than solid, as far as an ancient people might be concerned, they may have thought that everything has that capacity. If the mountain can turn into gas, fire and liquid, what cannot turn into gas, fire and liquid? If the earth can become fluid and then become solid again. What cannot become fluid and solid again? If solid cold earth can become fiery, fluid and run about, what cannot? What does not have a fiery element?

The Eight Constituents which make up the Body

The physical body is composed of eight ingredients. Three of them (Gunas) are constitutional. The Three Constitutional constituents are: Satvas, Tamas and Rajas or Sun, Moon and Life/Shen. They also correlate with three Forces: First Force or Active principle, Second Force or Receptive Principle and Third Force or Reconciling Principle. The three Gunas are qualities of Ahamkar the ego manifested in a person.

Five constituents are elemental: Ether (*Th. Aagaasathaat/ Thaad Lom*), Air (*Th. Thaad Prana*), Fire (*Th. Thaad Fai)*, Water (*Th. Thaad Naam*) and Earth (*Th. Thaad Din*). That is a similar concept as found in Traditional Chinese Medicine (TCM Five Elements). And yes the names of the elements are slightly different. Chinese medicine's elements are: Fire, Earth, Metal, Water and Wood.

The three constitutional elements (*Satvas, Rajas, Tamas*) go with the five elements (Dhatu) which gives us 8 different constituents that make up the body. The numerology of the cosmology (Samkhya Creation Principles… Page. 58) is again similar to that of TCM.

This concept is similar to that of the Chinese medicine Ba Gua or Eight Trigram theory in Traditional Chinese Medicine. Historically, there was always commerce between China and India. The largest religion of China for many years and to the present is Buddhism which was brought to China by an Ayurvedic Physician of Indian origin, a monk named Boddhi Dharma. His name means: The knowledgeable person who brought the teachings. There are many paintings and illustrations of him. He founded the temple of Shaolin Buddhism on Wodang mountain, Szechuan (Sichuan) China. Buddhism allegedly spread from there to the whole country.

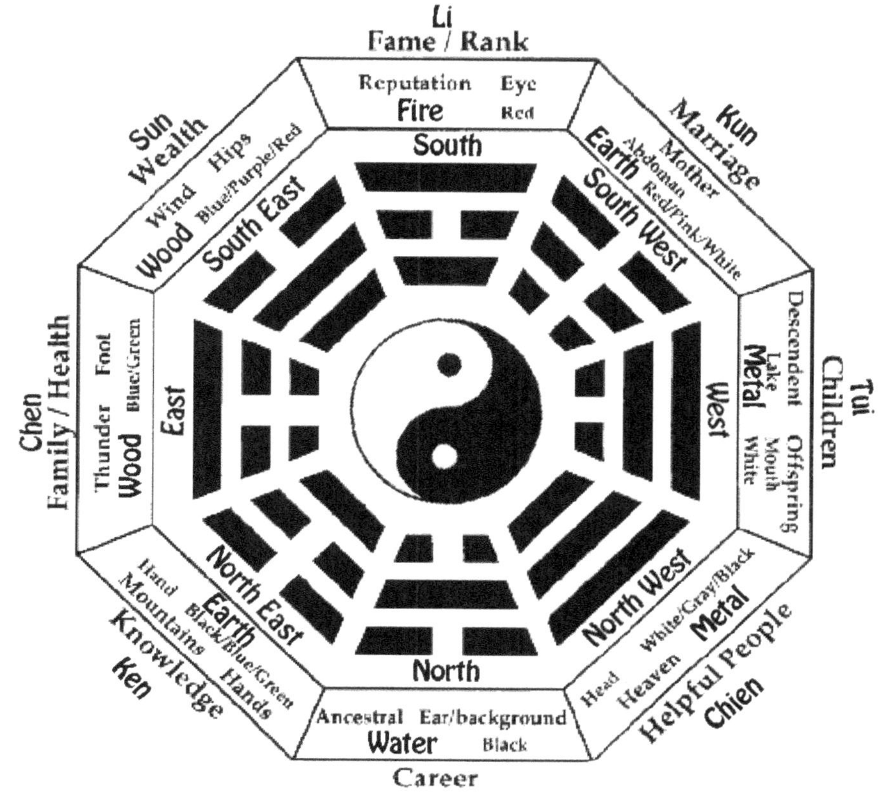

There was heavy influence from Indian Ayurveda in Chinese culture. What we call Classical/ Traditional Chinese Medicine (TCM) has much in common with Ayurveda. Because of language and cultural differences, terms and language make them seem quite different. However, conceptually there are many similarities.

Traditional Chinese Medicine Eight Sided figure: BaGua

As Above, So Below: The Five Elements In The Body (Macrocosm / Microcosm)

Each of the five elements manifests in the operation of the physical body as a sense, or as a faculty of cognition as well as certain physical functions. All matter is composed from the interaction of all five of these elements. Since all five elements originated in the realm of energy or vibration emanating from consciousness, then all five are present in all matter in the manifested universe. Energy and matter are seen as variations and distinctions on the same continuum. Energy elements and matter elements are two halves of the same coin.

The cosmic Algorithm: Cosmic consciousness preceding manifestation leads us to a formula: past actions or original inclinations in Thai called Kama or karma precede energy elements and energy elements precede physiology or matter elements. Another way of saying this is "Acknowledgment precedes intention. Intention precedes extension. Affirmation precedes action and action leads to manifestation."

If we understand the origin of the elements correctly. If we understand their relationship to primordial consciousness and the continuum of primordial consciousness' formation of elements with qualities leading to manifestation of all that there is, then we understand that consciousness rules all.

There is a continuum of manifestation from primordial original to relatively final or complete manifestation. All forms of traditional medicine know this. This is why Puja (Th. Bucha) is so important. Puja (*Th. Bucha*) represents the origination of consciousness and conscious acting or manifesting of that which is envisioned. Puja (*Th. Bucha*) is most important. Everything else that we do in the middle i.e. between Puja and Puja is support for the manifestation of our intention; our life intention, the patient's intention, the patient's family's intention, our treatment intention which we made in the first Puja (Th. Bucha). The Dhatu, our elements of Thai Ayurveda or Thaat Thang Sii, are called Lom, Fai, Naam, Din. (Sans. Pathavidhatu, Apodhatu, Tecudhatu and Vayudhatu).

Each of the five elements manifests in the operation of the physical body as a sense or faculty of cognition, as well as certain physical functions.

All matter is composed from the interaction of all five of these elements. Water is the easiest to use as an example. When cold and solid it demonstrates Earth principle. When heat or light causes it to melt it becomes a liquid. More heat raises its vibration to that of steam, an expression of the Air principle. The steam eventually dissipates into the atmosphere, space or Ether.

Since all five elements originate in the realm of energy (or vibration emanating from Cosmic Consciousness), then all five are present in all matter in the manifested universe. Energy and matter are seen as variations and distinctions on the same continuum. Energy elements and matter elements are two halves of the same whole.

We are a microcosm of all nature. A combination of interactions between the celestial influences and the terrestrial influences. The differences between us are one of scale. All of the various energies which can be found in the larger universe are also found on a somewhat smaller scale within us. By examining the Dhatu, the presence of the five universal elements in the human body not only do we learn more of ourselves, but we learn something more of the universe we are a part of.

Ether Element: (*Th. Akat/ Aagaasathaat/ Lom*) (*Sans. Akashadhatu*):

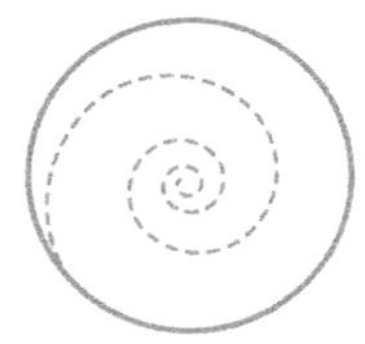

The principle of pervasiveness. The first of these manifested vibrations is Ether or space. So visualize space as empty space for the purposes of getting the hierarchy. Before there was anything, there was nothing. However, obviously, nothing is something or there couldn't be anything in it. So Ether is space, but it's not empty space. Because even the singularity that formed the origin of the universe and the big bang theory was in something, it occurred in something. According to Ayurvedic theory, it was in the Ether, the pure undefiled Ether.

Ether may be the dark matter of the universe. A well thought-out recent theory from quantum physics is identifying dark matter, previously unknown but representing 99% of the material in the universe and is completely invisible. They're now referring to it as plasma. Plasma is a substance which has a virtually infinite capacity to carry and communicate energy. We've identified this substance now called plasma and the current speculation in quantum physics is it is plasma that actually underpins or is the 99% of the universe that we cannot see. Previously called dark matter, now plasma.

Ether is the undifferentiated matter or consciousness which is the support of all. Ether is the clear mind of God or the absolute possibility of all that there is. Ether is the mind of God. It is the underpinning of everything that was, is or ever will be. There is nothing that does not occur in Ether. Consider that when teachers and sages make these statements, "Everything is God. Everything is from God, God in everything" that they are talking about Ether element in a material sense. This is not talking about Ether in a philosophical sense.

It is the hidden element behind everything that ever was, is, or will be. Meditation on emptiness or Zen meditation of Mushin or Vipassana can be valuable. When we do these Zen or emptiness types meditations
Page 94

such as Mushin (empty mind) and Vipassana (insight), we're meditating on all the things that we don't know, don't see, all the things that are between or behind or above all of the other stuff. All of the other stuff occurs in something. It occurs in a field of consciousness which is ruled by past association cognition and intellect, and yet it occurs in a field of something which we call The clear mind or The true mind. The true mind is not subject to interference. It is that which abides no matter what comes across the screen.

These meditations are good for cultivating a clear mind. Doing Oms gives us a moment to resonate with something greater than us. Emptiness is greater than us. This is why chanting Oms is balancing for the Chakras. The oldest Chakra balancing treatment I know of is simply sitting and chanting Om while breathing. The Om represents a greater field of influence. We take our little distortion patterns and subject them to a greater field of influence and it has a balancing effect. That balancing effect has been always the same at all times, it doesn't change. What a perfect therapy. Aside from the fact that I just like to do Oms because they make me happy. I like how they make me feel.

In the absence of all other Dhatu there is always Ether element. There is Ether or Lom. Then is the Ether a characteristic of God? If you subtract from the equation all of the non-elements, what's left over is Ether and Air. In the absence of everything, that which abides, can we not say is a quality of God? "

Physical and process correlations of Ether element: Ether or space is found throughout the body in all the various cavities and passages. These include the open areas in the mouth, sinuses, nose, gastrointestinal tract, respiratory tract including the esophagus, and bronchial passages in both lungs. Also included are the abdomen, diaphragm, thorax, as well as the interior network of capillaries, the lymphatic ducts, vessels and any empty space in any tissue or cell body. There is a connection between the Lom (wind) and the blood.

In food, the bitter taste contains the most Ether, although Ether by itself is tasteless. The bitter taste is composed of both Ether and Air, and it is Air that provides the specific qualities of the taste. A good way to increase the influence of the ether element is to consume bitter foods, especially if a person is overly driven and regimented by their routines (compulsion). However, an excess of Ether in the diet, especially the diet of the individual with a Vata constitution, can result in the dosha becoming too dominant. This increased Ether stimulates creativity, however, it also leads to becoming ungrounded.

Air Element: (*Th. Lom/ Prana*) (*Sans. Tejas/ Agni/ Vayudhatu*):

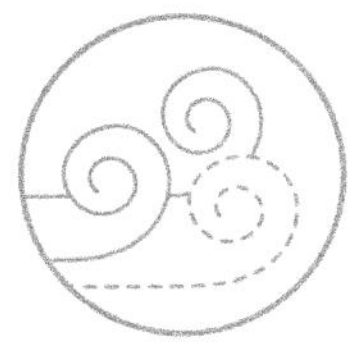

The principle of vibration. The movement or action, of this ethereal element creates the second element of Air. Air is something that moves.

The origin of air is Phassa (*Pali . samphassa/ Sans. sparsha*). Phassa is the Tanmatra--primordial, unmanifested form--of touch [See Samkhya Creation Principles Page???]. Phassa is the potential of the touch and contact experience expressed in its most subtle form.

The Atthasalini (Expositor, Part IV, chapter I, 108) states about contact: Contact means "it touches". It has touching as its salient characteristic, impact as its function, "coinciding" (of the physical base, object and consciousness) as its manifestation, and the object which has entered the avenue (of awareness) as proximate cause.

Touch and air are inseparable. Because of their intimate relationship, the skin (through which we receive touch) is considered the associated sense organ of the element air. The hands (through which we reach out and touch the world) are its associated organ of action. Hence, disorders of tactile perception and those of grasping are the result of disturbances in the functions of the air element. However, in consideration of the concept of Phassa, we understand that Air Element is also the means or vehicle for how the consciousness interfaces with the world.

Phassa is manifested by coinciding or concurrence, namely, by the coinciding of three factors:
1. The physical base (vatthu) i.e. the sense, the experience or impression,
2. The object i.e. that which is experienced and
3. The consciousness i.e. that which perceives the experience.

When Ether is in motion and or there is motion in the Ether, the element Air is manifested. Within the body, the moving element of Air is seen as any movement or even any inclination to move. This refers to the movement of the muscles and tissues including all pluses and rhythms such as of the heart, lungs, and peristalsis, as well as the energetically based pulses such as that of the meridians and organs. The movement of the stomach wall and the angulations of individual tissues as well as any discharge, drainage or elimination. The circulation of nervous impulses, the blinking of the eyes and we would also include any unintentional movement, palsy, twitches, ticks, jerks, spasms and trigger points. There is a connection between the Lom (wind) and the blood (th. lyad). The blood is considered a vehicle for transporting the wind throughout the body.

From an Ayurvedic point of view if there is such a thing as a trigger point, it would be an area of excess Air element. A trigger point or a spasm is an area of localized spasm or high neurologic activity, excess activity coupled with a deficiency of oxygen (ischemia). The innervation point in the muscle tissue which we call the trigger point is actually an excess or an imbalance in the Air element. Whereas, in some conventional physical therapy, the therapy to fix or cure the trigger point is with direct digital compression on the motor nerve to actually interfere with or distract or control the signal to reduce the spasm.

In Ayurvedic based therapies, yoga therapies and so on, we may use a number of additional methods than solely compression or vibration, for example, detox protocols and herbal therapies. We believe that by having a more balanced equilibrium in the element Air you will have fewer trigger points.

Think of the classroom and the open space of the classroom as the Ether. When the air conditioner is on, it's moving something in the space, we say what's moving in the space is Air element. The air conditioner comes on, you feel the breeze. The breeze that's in motion is Air element. The reason why you can feel it is because of the contrast between no air and air. Because when you feel the movement in the air you are affected by it and feel it. Air, wind, humor, vapor are all Air element. Air is Ether in action. When ether is mobile or has motility or has a mobile quality, then we call that Air.

Fire Element: (*Th. Fai*) (*Sans. Tejasdhatu*):

The principle of radiance. When we say Fire element in the body we're referring to the process of maintaining homeo-dynamic stasis or metabolism. Fire is the motive force behind every process in the body. It's the foundation of digestion or Agni. It is also the spark of intelligence. Fire activates the retina, allowing us to perceive light through the eyes. Body temperature, metabolism, eyesight, mental function, and the action of enzymes are all Fire element. Metabolism, anabolism, catabolism are all fire element.

The origin of the Fire element is the Tanmatra of vision called Rupa. [*See Samkhya Creation Principle's Page 58*]

This demonstrates why with focus, we can consciously alter metabolism, temperature and bodily functions normally considered to not be under conscious control like the heart rate. There are certain processes in the body called autonomic nervous processes such as blinking, the beating of the heart, peristalsis or angulations of walls of the small and large intestine and others. These autonomic responses are not considered to be under conscious control; however, through intention and focus on the elements, meditation and regulation of the breathing it's possible to control all of them. There is an interface elementally that gives us access to all of these processes.

The Five Types of Fire / Pitta

Because fire has a destructive quality, in the body it is always mixed with a small amount of water to keep it from destroying the tissues. The vessel or container of fire and water elements is Pitta.

1) The fire that provides our body with the capacity to digest food is called Pachaka Agni.
2) The fire that ignites the intellect, digests ideas, and allows for understanding is Sadhaka Agni.
3) The fire of perception that that digests visual impression into recognizable images is called Alocaka Agni.
4) The fire that energizes and invigorates the body, adding color to the body is called Ranjaka Agni.
5) The fire that digests touch and sunlight and gives off the radiance associated with healthy skin is the light provided by Bhrajaka Agni.

Fire which manifests as heat and light give rise to the sensing and perception of light and color vision. The eyes are the organ of fire.

The feet are the organ of action associated with the fire element. It is through the feet that we react to what we see. Use of the feet allows a person to change direction based upon perception. Not only may the direction be changed, but also the intensity of progress. The choice of direction and the intensity of action are functions of the fire element.

The eyes govern, or oversee the action of walking and are thus related to the feet. Whether you have standard eyesight or not you still have the function of eyes. That function which perceives and which interprets the environment that you find yourself in. Whether you're physically blind or not makes no difference.

Blind people have the function of eyes, they can see things. They just may not "see" them in exactly the same way as someone who's not blind. If I took you to my friend and master teacher, Aachan Tawee of Sawankhalok, Thailand, you would very quickly come to the understanding that just because he's been blind since birth, it is irrelevant to his ability to see what's going on, to perceive. The blindness has not impeded his ability to perceive. It's an elemental function, it's there whether you can see or not. Biologically we equate the eyes to seeing however, we "see" whether or not we have eyes.

The connection between the eyes and the feet is pretty obvious. I see what I want therefore I go toward it. The feet provide motility. The feet provide mobility for the inclination to run toward or away from that which we perceive as good or bad for us. The intermediary in that process is the action of the feet. We can relate podiatry issues in this example as a Fire Element imbalance as well. Consider issues of the feet. Examples such as: having pain in your feet, not being able to walk properly, having fallen arches, your feet are constantly injured or feet have other chronic issues, these are all fire imbalance.

How about you don't like your feet? There are people who think they have ugly feet. Some clients have emotional issues about their feet such as they don't want people to see their feet or touch their feet. Having done thousands of sessions, I regularly have clients who really want a SomaVeda® Thai yoga session with the condition that I don't touch their feet, they'll keep their socks on. They don't want to show me their feet, they don't want me to touch their feet, or to pull or touch their toes.

If I was doing an elemental assessment, looking at the overview of the person, the profile of their symptoms, I would pick out what elements are more active, more prominent. These foot issues are something I would consider in the Fire category. Earlier I mentioned the correlation of Fire and the immune system. There is a correlation between the immune system and the feet.

It has to do with motility and mobility. If you are near or about to be exposed to something which is going to compromise your immunity, you move away from it. If we were in tune with ourselves, when we were in the presence of or near enough to see things that would stimulate our immune system we would walk toward them. This explains some of your inclinations, for example wanting to take a yoga class. You might think that the reason you want to take a yoga class is because it looks cool.

There may be another reason, that when you see certain kinds of activity in your environment that the immune system recognizes as something that would be directly beneficial, it has the capacity to get the feet moving. The mind moves much slower than the immune system, in some estimates up to 36,000 times slower. The immune system is not only smart, it's quick and smart, it makes these decisions fast.

The mind is slower, so here we are moving toward the yoga class, moving toward the "Googling" of where is the yoga class in my neighborhood. I'm getting the car keys and heading off that way. I've never done this before … however it comes about. On the way, you come up with a story to justify the activity. The mind begins to concoct the story as to why you're attracted to the yoga class. It will cherry pick from whatever is available. However, the initial incentive to move toward that direction was not a conscious decision in the sense of a mental activity. It may have been an instinctive inclination being driven by the immune system.

Every organ, every system in your body has the capacity to take over and run the whole machine at any time depending on circumstance. Every system in your body has a voice in the cooperative orchestra of all voices put together. These inner voices, corporately described as the innate, have opinions on which direction you go and what you do in your life.

90% of the time it's reactions in response to conversations and influences which are coming from organs and systems which are driving the machine, all of the mental processes are after the fact. After the fact, there is a judgment, an explanation, coughing up a story of why I did what I did. Why I do what I do. Why I like what I like. The gods of the body's universe are the organs or the individual constituents of the body and they all have voices.

Think of the elements as the character or characteristic of the voice. We can learn to see the elements. We can then learn to hear the different voices. We can learn to see when one voice is more dominant than another voice and what voice that is.

If I was a more conscious person, I could actually hear what my liver is trying to tell me today. I could hear what my immune system is trying to tell me today. I could hear what my stomach, spleen, gallbladder, pancreas, endocrine system and so on are trying to tell me today individually. Then out of a sense of knowledge of the world and knowledge of myself I could make decisions based on what is good for the community. I would make different choices. I might make better choices. All choices that are contrary to the inner voice, expression of the organs and the elements that drive those organs are, from the body's point of view, irresponsible.
Page 98

There will be a consequence for not listening.

Another reason we call someone "not well" is that they don't act in accordance with the nature of the body's communications. When I act in harmony with the body politic, the elemental inclinations, the voices of the organs, tissues and the different constructs of my body, from the body politic's point of view, I am considered to be a more intelligent person. I'm rewarded with a sense of well-being, sense of wellness, a sense of integration of my parts. My parts aren't having a fist fight trying to get their way. All the parts are essentially getting along. Why? Because I'm the captain, I am in charge of navigation or certain aspects of flying the plane, but I work for the airline. The airline gives me the route. I do have some leeway, some variability according to circumstances as they arise.

In rare emergency situations, I can override airline policy and go a different direction. I can land where I'm not supposed to land at all. Because of the exigency of an emergency circumstance I may temporarily override the operating system or rules. For example: I was once on a flight from China. A woman experienced a ruptured appendix while we were over the Pacific ocean and the pilot detoured to Japan. We weren't going to Japan. In that emergency circumstance the passengers and the crew commended the pilot, "Good on you captain, you sorted it out, you got us to the nearest safest place where this woman can get emergency medical treatment and it saved her life. Good on you." If he had just woefully stuck to his flight plan as per airline protocol the woman may have died. Would everyone on the plane have blamed the airline? No! They would have blamed the pilot.

I'm the pilot of my body's life but I still operate in a community of other agencies' agendas and other voices. I'm not absolutely in charge. When I act like I am, often because I'm not listening, I'm not seeing what's evident. I will make decisions that are counter-intuitive to the survival of my machine and I will not be well as a result of it. The Panchabhutas give us information (insight) which indicate more clearly what is going on inside of us.

Physical and process correlations of Fire element: When we say Fire element in the body we are referring to the process of maintaining homeodynamic stasis or metabolism. Fire is the motive force behind every process in the body. It is the foundation of digestion. It is also the spark of intelligence. Fire also activates the retina allowing us to perceive light into the body through the eyes. So, body temperature, metabolism, eyesight, mental function, and action of enzymes are all Fire element. (Metabolism, Anabolism, Catabolism). This demonstrates why with focus, we can consciously alter metabolism, temperature and body functions normally considered to NOT be under conscious control, i.e. heart rate etc.

Water Element: (*Th. Naam*) (*Sans. Apodhatu/ Apasdhatu*):

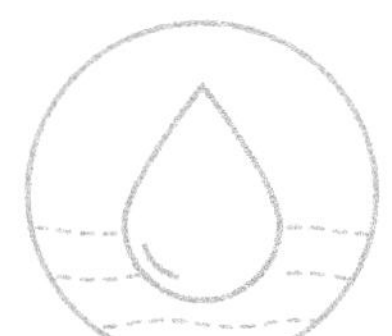

The principle of cohesion. When you make a fire it doesn't create light. It liberates light that was already in the material. As a result of this intense light and heat certain particles of the Ether dissolved (changed state/ transformed) and became Water element. We call this dissolving the process of transmutation. Fire becomes as a liquid.

As the material elements move further from the source, there is this process of transmutation. Another word that could be used is condensation or condensing. As the original elements expanded and then as pressure for the expansion ceased to be quite as heavy, various elements were then attracted to themselves, to each other and began a process of coalescing into proximity.

As this occurred it produced a condensing effect. Out of this condensation, this cooling, we have Water. It's one of those fundamental elements of the universe. Hydrogen is one; oxygen is one...there's oxygen everywhere in the universe. There's hydrogen everywhere in the universe. There's water everywhere in the universe, maybe not as much as here, but there is. One of the primary technologies used to look for habitable, possible earth-like planets by astronomers is to look for water using it's light frequency.

This is the origin of the element water. Water cooled and in solid form became the foundation of earth. Water became the foundation of earth. Metaphorically think lava runs when hot and when it cools it becomes solid earth. Ancient people were familiar with volcanoes.

Our planet is sometimes called the Water Planet. The single greatest influence elementally that we can point to as a justification for the presence and variety of life on our planet is the predominance of water. We come from water. We carry the water that we come from within us. Eventually we are composted by the bacteria and viruses which will put us back into the ground and the water that's within us is released back into the body of the planet. It will re-circulate, become rain again and become oceans and rivers and ponds. It's one continuous cycle, the cycle of Water Element.

The Five Types of Water

In the human body, water is expressed in five distinct ways, known as the five types of kapha.

> *1) Bodhaka Kapha:* The water that protects the mouth against the actions of chewing and against the enzyme that begins the breakdown of carbohydrate (salivary amylase). Bodhaka kapha is the salivary fluid, and also the mucous membrane secretions of the lips, cheeks, and pharynx.

> *2) Kledaka Kapha:* The water that protects the mucous membranes of our stomach against the acids that aid digestion.

> *3) Tarpaka Kapha:* The water that stabilizes the flow of neurological impulses and protects the nerves of the brain.

> *4) Sleshaka Kapha:* The water that protects the joints from the friction of motion. We find Sleshaka kapha in the synovial fluid that moistens joint surfaces, and in the bursae that allow tendons to glide smoothly over each other.

> *5) Avalambaka Kapha:* The water that protects the respiratory system from the movement of breath (a drying process). Avalambaka kapha keeps the mucous membranes of the bronchi and lungs healthy and also provides the fluids that support the pleura and pericardium.

Water is the medium of taste. The tongue cannot discriminate between tastes without water. We use our tongue the same way a lizard does when it sticks out it's tongue and collects molecules of pheromones and aromatics to discern what is in it's environment. Telling the lizard whether there is danger, whether there is food. The tongue is closely related to the function of the clitoris and penis. The penis and clitoris are considered to be littler or lower tongues. The tongue in the mouth is the upper tongue and it is said that the person who can control the upper can control the lower. So biologically we have more than one tongue, more than one structure in our body that has essentially the same structure as taste buds and innervation with similar numbers of nerve endings such as the tongue has. The function is to provide another way that we sample our environment.

These two little organs, the penis and clitoris, have the same functions, but they're sampling different information. Part of a miscommunication that people have sexually, is that they do not understand this. We do not understand and have limited knowledge and consciousness as to what the role is of those body parts.

Page 100

Another good example is, what is the role of your appendix? How much does the average person know about the role of their appendix or the adenoids in the sinus? So how much does the average person understand about the clitoris as an organ? It's a vital body part. It has functions that are not simply about being rubbed or stimulated. It has other functions.

In Ayurveda part of the function or dysfunction relates to Water element. When we talk about sexual dysfunction in Ayurveda we may talk about the emotional aspect. We may talk about relationship dynamics. However, if it's an organic dysfunction, if it's really coming from the system, then what we're looking at is Water element. If you have problems with sexual performance, sexual identity or identity and connection or correlation between you and your parts, if there's a disconnect between you and your parts, balancing Water Element would be part of my treatment strategy.

There's an epidemic of what's called erectile dysfunction. The number one by volume of dollar sales, most financially lucrative drug (medicine) sold today is Viagra. If you believe that there is any benefit at all to drugs, I want you to consider for a second that the king of the drugs is a sexual performance enhancing drug. Most other drugs sales pale in comparison. You might think the highest dollar volume sales of drugs would be for drugs that save lives. It would be a reasonable assumption, but could not be further from the truth.

Consider the idea of erectile dysfunction. In Ayurveda erectile dysfunction, inability of the penis organ to achieve turgidity under stimulation is actually an imbalance in water metabolism. ED is often correlated with atherosclerosis and hypertensive disease. Both of which also relate to water metabolism or have water metabolism as an issue. Examples being: retention of fluids, edema, congestion etc.

Part of the cause of ED is chronic dehydration. Consider that to maintain a proper water balance, you need to consume everyday about one-half your bodyweight in ounces. Of whatever percentage of fluids you do intake, a percentage is often coffee, tea, soda or some non-water substance, some non-pure water substance. I looked at some research provided to me by Doctor Charles McWilliams where he showed that as far as the body's metabolism is concerned, tea is not water. The body does not respond the same to tea as it does to pure water. Only pure water causes the metabolic responses that water creates in the body.

Teas and coffees have long been considered diuretics. Consider that if all the volumes of fluids you take in are coffee, tea or some other diuretic, that even though you're consuming a volume of water, it's not reaching the cells and it's being passed through. Contemporary studies now indicate that coffee may have less diuretic properties than previously thought. Regardless, pure water is the origin of life. You have to drink clean pure water and the proper volume of water. One of the first things to recommend if there's a sexual performance issue and the inability to achieve the turgid state of the penis, is to drink more water.

If you're chronically dehydrated the beneficial effect from drinking water may not be immediate, as you have to reconstitute the water base metabolism. The damage from the chronic dehydration has to be repaired. For example: if you were in the desert and were dehydrated, no water to the point of near death. Then you're rescued and you're given water orally, you're bathed and perhaps have an IV hydration. How long do you think it takes to recuperate from that dehydration, the cellular damage, tissue damage, metabolic damage, system damage of just that period of dehydration? A period which might have been only 3 or 4 days.

How long do you think it actually takes for all of the effects of that near fatal trauma to resolve? It will be however long it takes until every individual system that was affected to completely regenerate new cells to recuperate the damaged cells. Some systems, maybe the lining of your stomach replaces itself approximately every 14 days. Some cells in the liver might take 3 months. Some cells in other tissues like osseous membranes, bones and so on could take up to 6 to 9 months.

So hypothetically a three-day traumatic event of dehydration, enough to put you near the brink of death, could actually not be fully recuperated if you were properly rehydrated the day after for 6 to 9 months. When you have chronic dehydration over time, you have chronic damage. You have chronic cellular malfunction. You have chronic deficiencies, excesses of toxins which are not being washed away and incomplete delivery of nutrients among other things.

In Water properties we see examples of all five elements!

We know for example people have been boiling water for a long time. They're all kinds of ways to boil water without a pot. For example, you can take an animal skin, literally, just any kind of hide, fill it water, put it over a fire and the animal skin won't burn. It will boil the water as if it was in a pot. You can find a shallow place in a rock, fill it with rain water, you can heat up stones in the fire and throw them in the little pocket of rainwater and that water will boil.

People have been boiling water for a long time, for cooking and it's really useful in making tools that require animal sinew and glue extracted from the animals and things like that. It's helpful in making certain kinds of wood crafts, being able to steam the wood. Steaming makes the wood pliable for making it into different shapes which hold after the wood cools. The ancients would have been familiar with this idea that water is stable as a liquid, but when you stimulate it with heat, the water develops a life of movement on its own. If water is in a crucible it completely conforms to the shape of the vessel.

Water's first transformation is it's ductility and malleability of shape. It's one of the elemental substances that does that completely. It's part of its memory function. But then when I add heat or friction to it the water in and of itself, by itself starts to move. We call that a rolling boil. Then just after it starts to move (boil), the water seeks to escape the container and run away. We call that steam. Once a certain amount of the water has escaped from the heat, light, and fire, it turns into vapor and disappears (diffuses) and becomes Air. If we did this practice in part of the world that's a little bit more northern i.e. where things occasionally freeze, we know that water has one additional state, the state where water becomes hard as earth (ice).

Physical and process correlations of Water element: Water is the maintenance and support of the liquids and secretions in the body, the digestive juices and salivary glands, mucous membranes, blood plasma, cytoplasm. No organ or tissue can survive without water for long. It is immediately vital to the function of all of the organs and body systems. This is why you could be constipated for years but diarrhea can become fatal or life threatening within a matter of a few days. Diarrhea affects water metabolism. Water metabolism is absolutely critically vital to the maintenance of life.

Earth Element: (*Th. Din*) (*Sans. Prthvidhatu*):

The principle of inertia. The water cooled and in solid form became the foundation of earth. From the earth, all of the organic and living beings receive their substance. This includes all organic life of man and women, to the realms of animals, as well as the kingdoms of plants and herbs. Earth is also the source or the origin of the inorganic substances found in nature and the mineral world. So in this fashion all of the five elements Ether, Air, Fire Water and Earth became manifest.

Earth element is what we sense when we smell. The sense of smell is the function of Earth in the body. The nose is the sensory organ of smell. It shares function with the anus in the process of excretion. We know the relationship between the unclean colon and bad breath smell for example. The treatment for severe halitosis or clinically diagnosed bad breath is actually cleansing the colon. It's either an issue of pathologic bacteria or gut dysbiosis which aren't properly populating the gut. It is a matter of unresolved or fermenting, auto-intoxicating waste that is being maintained in the colon that produces bad odor.

That's the first tactic. The sense of smell is the intermediate facility between us and the dirt. The sense of smell is constant and active and is a primary sense faculty. Even though most of the day it is sublimated to other activities: visual, auditory, cognitive or what have you. The sense of smell is never not active. It is constantly judging and weighing the information from the environment in real time. We actually do have the facility of a bloodhound to make fine distinctions in volatile organic solids which we take in through our nose and our sinuses. Although we don't have the cognitive process to discern and to differentiate all those smells to the degree of a Blood hound. However, you can differentiate millions of different sense impressions. It's literally infinite. You don't really get a sense of the variety of possible smell sense impressions you're capable of until you're taking up a practice for example of aromatherapy.

You start to learn that specific kinds of things have smells which affect you in specific ways. Some smells make you happy. Some smells make you sad. Some smells make your eyes work better. Some smells make you wider awake. While some smells put you to sleep and everything in between. This is all information coming in from each other and from our environment. It's also a useful red flag of course. Because if our environment is full of toxic volatile gases and elements and we're taking those in, they are having a potentially harmful effect. These effects are predictable for the toxin. We just don't know what the toxins are.

We breathe in a complex soup of toxins which generate hormones and pheromones changing chemical states in the body which cause organic changes in the body. All of our systems physically, mentally and spiritually must contend and defend against this onslaught of toxicity coming from the environment. We don't know that the reason we feel the way we do is because it's something we smell. The reason I feel the way I feel right now is because of something I smell. I don't rationalize it. I don't know this in real time. However, according to our understanding of Earth element, it's a primary influence.

Physical and process correlations of Earth element: Earth element is the glue that binds us together. All solid structures in the body are earth: bones, cartilage, nails, hair, teeth, muscles, viscera, skin, tendons, cartilage, connective tissue and fascia.

> **Five elements example: Lymphatic System**
> - Capillaries are Ether
> - Movement of fluid is Air, the fluid itself is Water
> - Discrimination is selective. T-cells and active constituents and dynamism and strength of the Immune function is Fire
> - The substance and materials that actually make up the nodes and vessels them selves is Earth.

Five Elements and Five Senses

Correlate the five elements to the five senses. Ether is the medium through which sound travels so that we can hear. The ear is the organ of hearing and expresses action through the organ of speech. Air moving or moving through air stimulates the sense of touch. The sensory organ of Air element is the skin; the integumentary s ystem. The skin on the hands is especially sensitive. They are responsible for holding, giving and receiving.

For example, a psychological pattern that we might describe as hoarding. The hoarding represents a distortion of the proper functioning of the psyche that is a mental aberration or illness. Hoarding is a symptom of a mental illness. One of the keys to help the hoarder is to help the patient become more stable mentally and emotionally. Almost always, this phenomenon, this aberration of personality which the hoarding is a symptom of is a result of unresolved negative emotional trauma. Air is responsible for holding, giving and receiving. What if you can't let go of something. What if you just can't let go. You can't let go of an idea, feeling, a thing? What is that an imbalance of, from an Ayurvedic point of view? There is a correlation to the sense organ of Air, the skin.

I'm looking at the possessiveness as a symptom. Let's take the opposite of holding. What if you can't hold on to anything? Hoarding is less socially acceptable than not being able to hold on to anything. However, from a Vedic point of view, they're equally imbalanced. One is just more socially acceptable. The letting go and giving away of the selfless doormat of a person who takes no responsibility and holds on to nothing; who gives in the face of everything. Helpless is more socially acceptable. We can look at that person and say "Oh they're just a giver."

The client might justify it by saying "I'm practicing non-attachment." Practicing non-attachment is not the same thing psychologically as not being able to hold on to anything. We need to be somewhere in the middle. Yes, we want to practice non-attachment to things we don't need, to things which don't have any benefit for us, for our life or for our family. We want to let that stuff go. We want to come to finer and finer gradations of trying to understand what those things might be. However, if you're healthy and you're balanced you should also have the capacity to acquire what you need. If you can't there's an imbalance. Something's not working. Equally we would say that's an imbalance in the Air element.

Ether is the medium through which sound travels so we can Hear. The Ear is the organ of hearing and expresses action through the organ of Speech.

Air moving, or moving through Air stimulates sense of touch. The Sensory organ of Air is the Skin. The skin of the hands is especially sensitive and the hands are responsible for holding, giving and receiving.

Fire which manifests as heat and light gives rise to the sensing of perception of light and color, vision. The eyes are the organ of Fire. The eyes govern or "oversee" the action of walking and are thus related to the feet.

Water is the medium of taste. The tongue cannot discriminate between tastes without water. The tongue is closely related in function to the Clitoris and to the Penis. The Penis and Clitoris are considered to be little or lower tongues. The tongue in the mouth is the upper tongue. It is said that the person who can control the upper can control the lower.

Earth is what we sense when we smell. The sense of smell is a functioning of Earth in the body. The Nose is the sensory organ of Smell and shares function with the anus and the process of excretion. We know the relationship between an unclean colon and bad breath smell for example.

Assessment of MahaPanchabhutas by:
Quality, Sense organ, Action, Organ of action and and Tamas attributes

We see in the first row across the top. The correlation is on the left. It says the element Ether, Air, Fire, Water, Earth.

Now we go down. What are the senses that correlate with those five elements? They are hearing, touch, vision, taste and smell. What are the sense organs that relates to those elements? They are ear, skin, eyes, tongue, and nose. What is the actions of those elements? They are speech, holding, walking, procreation and excretion. What are the organs of action? They are the organs of speech, hands, feet, genitals, anus/ rectum. What are their Tamas attribute? They are sound, pressure, temperature, moisture and odor.

ELEMENT:	ETHER (Akat)	AIR (Lom)	FIRE (Fai)	WATER (Naam)	EARTH (Din)
SENSES:	Hearing	Touch	Vision	Taste	Smell
SENSE ORGAN	Ear	Skin	Eyes	Tongue	Nose
ACTION	Speech	Holding	Walking	Procreation	Excretion
ORGAN OF ACTION	Speech	Hand	Feet	Genitals	Anus
TAMAS/ ATTRIBUTE	Sound	Pressure	Temperature	Moisture	Odor

If you learn and memorize this chart you will be able to look and assess a person very simply. You start with simple questions: Where is the imbalance? Where is the symptom? The client might answer "I have a problem, you know my hand it tingles and I have numbness in my fingers and trouble holding onto things."

The first thing you do is look at the chart and ask "Hand, is there a hand on here?" Yes, hand is listed. It says the hand is an organ of action, the element Air rules it. It's VATA. Already I know something about the strategy that I might recommend for you to help you with this issue that you have with your hand. Does that mean there might not be other things. No, It's likely there are more or other issues going on with the client.

What if it's not something listed? This is where it gets a little tricky. There are other lists. This is why the Charaka Samhita is seven volumes. If their issue is not listed you can go Sherlock Holmes on them. What I mean when I say that is to use the process of deduction, the processes of correlation and deduction.

Mahapanchabhutas (elements) Relationship To Tri-Dosha and Dhatu/Tissues

Elements	Dosha	Dhatu	Upadhatu
Water	Kapha	Rasa (plasma, interstitial fluids)	Breast-milk, menstrual fluid
Fire	Pitta	Rakta (blood)	Tendons, blood vessels
Earth	Kapha	Mamsa (connective tissue)	Ligaments and skin
Earth + Water	Kapha	Meda (fat, mucin)	Sweat
Air + Space	Vata	Asthi (bones, skeleton)	Teeth
Water	Kapha	Majja/ Shukra (bone marrow, nervous tissue, sperm, egg)	None

Chapter 10: The Three Processes: Malas, Agni and Amas

MALA: Metabolic End Products

In Ayurveda Malas are described as waste products (excreta, waste substances, metabolic wastes).

Normally when we think of waste products we have in mind urine and feces. These are waste products for sure, however, it is more accurate to think of the end byproducts of all biologic, organ, tissue including down to the cellular level.

Waste and end products in the body are important and play important roles while still in the body. Just because they are made does not magically make them to then disappear. For example, the feces facilitates, stimulates the function of the colon. Urine sets the stage and influences via hormone systems, the balance of fluids and electrolytes in the tissues.

The concept of what Malas are is not restricted to waste products. You could also say that also production of chemicals, enzymes, hormones, pheromones, neuro-transmitters etc. are all Malas which in turn influence the dhatus which generate them.

Malas are a good news, bad news event for the body. For example oxygen metabolism derived free radicals are end products or Malas of the cells. These free radicals are initially directed to kill pathogenic bacteria to prevent infection… Good News! When there are not enough pathogenic bacteria for the free radicals to "scavenge", they then can attack healthy tissue causing degradation and disease… Bad News! Ayurveda indicates this balance of healthy directed function and unhealthy disease process is in turn ruled by the Dosha.

The body derives its fuel in the form of nutrition which we provide to it on a constant basis through the food, liquids and air we consume. The metabolic processes in the body convert these food substances into minute and micro-components so as to suit the needs of the body and also to get compatible with body elements, tissues and organs. As a result of these processes 3 types of elements are formed which are needed for the body mechanics to run on a constant basis. These are the waste products of metabolism which are formed on daily basis and at the same time should be expelled out consistently so as to balance and maintain the body mechanics.

Malas are 3 in number i.e. Stools/ Feces (Sans. Pureesha/ Shakrut), Urine (Sans. Mutra) and Sweat (Sans. Sweda), (Ashtanga Hrudaya Sutrasthana 1st chapter).

When they are expelled in proper time and proper quantity, the body will be free from unwanted materials and toxins which could disturb the smooth functioning of the body.

Body shows some signals in terms of urges or reflexes when these are produced (except sweating which occurs spontaneously as and when needed) and the malas are accumulated and ready to be voided. Excess or deficit elimination of these malas can lead to serious pathology and cause many diseases.

AGNI: Fire of Life

The Charka Samhita has many references to Agni. It states "Life, complexion, strength, enthusiasm, glow (lustre) of skin, structure, immunity, tissue, metabolic fires and the life force- are all good if the Agni is good"

"Agni – is a word which is used very frequently in Ayurveda. Since Ayurveda preaches that Mandagni or 'Low strength of the core or interior fire of the body' is the root cause of many diseases, the mainstay of treatment of many psychosomatic disorders too lays in correcting the fire. Good health and good immunity depends on how well the Agni is balanced inside us.

Be it the fire in the outer world or the fire in the interior world of our body, if it is used skilfully it proves to be constructive and on the other side an ineffectively maintained or improperly managed fire is definitely destructive in nature. If discovery of fire is the key factor of evolution of mankind, well managed interior fire will surely be the key factor for evolution of good health in successive generations." (Dr Raghuram Y.S. MD (Ay))

Fire is the primary evidense of life. No fire = no life. The presence of fire is the witness and proof of our life, the proof that we are alive. When we live, we feel the heat and temperature of the body. After we die, the warmth, heat or temperature of the body goes away. When Agni is balanced it is referred to as "Sama Agni."[67]

The broad types of Agni (Macro-Fire) are: Jataragni and Kayagni. These 2 Agnis are once again sub-classified into 13 types.

"Jataragni" is a term made up of 2 words, Jatara which means gut or belly (the digestion zone) and Agni (Fire). Thus Jataragni means 'Fire in the belly' which depicts the physiological components of digestion and metabolism which takes place in the stomach and intestines.

"Kayagni" is a term made up of 2 words, "Sans. Kaya" and Agni (Fire). The word Kaya carries below meanings in different contexts –

Deha – Human Body
Kayagni – Fire in the body
Manas – Mind
Hridaya – Heart
Sakala Shareera – full body

There is some debate as to whether these divisions are substantial or not. Depending on the Ayurvedic text and or commentater speaking, they are either vary different or virtually the same! The bottom line regarding the divisions of Agni (Jataragni and Kayagni) is that they are both considered to be Pitta Metabolic fire. It seems the bulk of commentaries sum up all Agni functions in descriptions of Kayagni regardless of where it might be situated in the body or the individual cell..

Agni is the fire which governs the preliminary process of digestion before the food is converted into a form in which it could be absorbed, assimilated and utilized in various body functions in the form of nutrition and energy. It functions independently and helps in primary digestion.

Agni is the fire which governs the preliminary process of digestion before the food is converted into a form in which it could be absorbed, assimilated and utilized in various body functions in the form of nutrition and energy. It functions independently and helps in primary digestion.
Balancing Agni is the same as balancing Pitta Dosha.

AMA: Toxic Waste/ Toxicity

Ama is a Sanskrit word that translates to words like "unripe," "uncooked," "raw," "immature," or "undigested."1 (1 Pole, Sebastian. Ayurvedic Medicine: The Principles of Traditional Practice. London: Churchill Livingston, 2006. Print. 44-46, 103-105.)

Essentially, it is a form of un-metabolized waste that cannot be utilized by the body.1 (1 Pole, Sebastian. Ayurvedic Medicine: The Principles of Traditional Practice. London: Churchill Livingston, 2006. Print. 44-46, 103-105.)

To some degree, the formation of small amounts of ama is a normal part of the digestive process, provided it is efficiently removed. But when it is not regularly cleared and eliminated, ama becomes hugely problematic. In fact, ama is said to be the root cause of all disease, and amaya, a Sanskrit word for disease literally means "that which is born out of ama."2 (Lad, Vasant. Textbook of Ayurveda, Volume II: A Complete Guide to Clinical Assessment. Albuquerque: The Ayurvedic Press, 2006. Print. 190, 199-202.)

The connection between ama and the disease process makes perfect sense because the qualities of ama are in direct opposition to those of agni. And remember, strong agni is essential to the maintenance of proper health. In other words, when agni is compromised and when ama accumulates, our health suffers, and the two situations are mutually reinforcing.

Causes or support of accumulating Ama

1) Faulty and or inappropriate diet i.e. eating habits:
    Overeating or emotional eating
    Improper food combinations
    Especially heavy food
    Fried food
    Excess amounts of cold or raw foods
    Highly processed or sugary foods
    An excess of the sweet, sour, or salty tastes

2) Counterproductive or Harmful Lifestyle
    Irregular eating habits
    High Stress
    Excessive or inadequate sleep
    Unpredictable or irregular life schedule
    Sleeping or eating before food is digested
    Sleeping during the day (for some constitutions)
    Lack of exercise
    Excessive exercise
    Repressed or unresolved emotions

General Support for Digesting & Eliminating Ama

There are ways to support and encourage the body to digest ama and eliminate it from the body. The strategies support the whole person's innate and natural, physiological detoxification process. The idea is to support and improve if possible the digestive capacity, improve tissue nutrition, and help to eliminate ama via the urine, feces, and sweat.

Probiotics: Categorize as good food which has beneficial pre and probiotic bacteria. Probiotics these days are necessary supplements to prevent gut dysbiosis, incomplete digestion and a whole host of Mala related illnesses.

Therapeutic Herbs: Bitter and astringent tastes are a powerful combination. The bitter taste dries and drains ama, while the pungent taste destroys and digests it.

Special care should be taken in cases of high pitta or severe inflammatory conditions (e.g. ulcers). Herbs that reduce or control Ama also tend to be quite hot and if used too much can aggravate the Pitta. Many of these herbs can be found right in your kitchen. Look for spices like fresh and dried ginger, cinnamon, nutmeg, mustard seed, garlic, cumin, black pepper, fennel, and coriander.

> Sweating
> Pranayama and Therapies emphasizing Prana
> Yoga and Yoga Therapy
> Diet
> Fasting
> Cleansing Therapies:
> SomaVeda® Therapeutic Day Program with adjunct therapy such as a Pancha Karma and or Complex Decongestive Therapy Program. These support the elimination of Ama among many other beneficial things.

> **Dealing with Negative emotional issues:**
> Support more positive mental states by reducing and or eliminating the unresolved old negative emotional issues (NEMOs) which interfere with them. Preferred therapy is SomaVeda B.E.T/ EFT and or similar.

Chapter 11: Tri-Dosha, The Three Constitutions

(Law of 3 in the Mind/ Body Continuum)

Vata (*Th. Lom*)	Pitta (*Th. Di*)	Kapha (*Th. Salet*)
or Three Defilements		
Desire (Non- attachment)	Aversion (Like and dislike) (Tolerance, Compassion, Discretion)	Ignorance (Education)
or Three combinations of Elements		
Ether + Air	**Fire + Water**	**Water + Earth**
or Three Humors (Winds)		
Air, Prana, Breath	Bile, Acid	Phlegm, Alkaline, Mucus
or Three Correlations		
Subtle Essence/ Prana	Catabolism/ Metabolism/ Anabolism	Sen Lines/ Meridians, Channels
or Three Forces		
First Force: Active/ generative	Third Force: Reconciling	Second Force: Passive/ Receptive

The three doshas originate on a spiritual plane from the basic mental confusion that produces subject object dualism. The main concept of "what is health" is seen as one of balance, balance within the physical body and balance between it and its corresponding aspects in the outer world. This balance is seen and expressed in the harmonious relationship of and between the three doshas. This subject /object dualism produces the karmic force necessary to manifest life and the perceived universe.

"The science of understanding our nature or our constitution is the science of Tridosha. Tridosha defines the three fundamental energies or principles which govern the function of our bodies on the physical and emotional level… Each individual has a unique balance of all three of these energies. Some people will be predominant in one while others are a mixture of two or more." (Tridosha: The Science Of Ayurveda and the three doshas (vata, pitta, kapha): (Dr. Mark Halpern of the California College of Ayurveda: http://www.ayurvedacollege.com/articles/drhalpern/Tridosha_Science_Ayurveda)

The literal translation of the word Dosha can be a constitution. According to Ayurvedic physician Dr. Sharadini Dahanukar in his book "Ayurveda Unveiled", states "The word dosha is derived from the root dus, similar to the English prefix "dys" (as in dysfunctiona, dysmeorrhoea). If directly translated, the word dosha would mean fault, stain, transgression against the cosmic rhythm or an inaccuracy that leads to chaos. However, in the context of Ayurvedic philosophy, doshas are not per se harmful. Rather, they seem to be called doshas for they have the capacity to cause chaos or disease under certain circumstances… It is this intricate relationship between the troika - dosha - dhatu - mala that constitutes the foundation for the principles of Ayurvedic physiology, pathology and therapeutics." (Ayurveda Unveiled, Dr. Dr. Sharadini Dahanukar & Urmilla Thatte, National Book Trust, India, 1996, p. 14)

It can also be wind, thus making your Dosha your Humor (Wind) type or how the elements manifest as wind in you. The ultimate origin of the dosha being the encapsulated ego or the Ahamkar manifesting as three personalities, personality inclinations or ego constructs. The dominance of these elements determines literally our mechanical faults or our literal inclination towards strength or weakness.

The three humors: air, bile, and phlegm also correspond to subtle essences, energies, channels and three Dhatu. (Vata, Pitta, Kapha)

The Five Elements, *Thaat Thang Sii* (*Sans. Maha Panchabhuta*) interacting create the Gunas: Tri-Dosha or Three Doshas, humors, winds or body types. The Three Doshas of yogi body types are Vata, Pitta and Kapha.

Across the top (Page 109) I've got VATA, PITTA and KAPHA. They are placed there in such a way so that you would be reminded that VATA is the two elements of Ether and Air, PITTA is the elements of Fire and Water and KAPHA is the elements of Water and Earth. When we're talking about the Doshas i.e. when I say your Dosha, you're Vata Dosha, you're Pitta Dosha, what I'm actually doing is a shorthand. If I say your Vata Dosha is imbalanced, what I'm saying is your Ether and Air elements are imbalanced in comparison with your Fire, Water and Earth elements.

When I say your Pitta is imbalanced, I'm referring to your Vikruti. Pitta doesn't mean anything it is the shorthand for me saying that your Fire and Water element is out of balance. When I say your KAPHA is out of balance, your Vikruti is KAPHA, KAPHA doesn't mean anything, I'm saying that your Water and Earth elements are out of balance. The term KAPHA is a shorthand for the elements. If you really want to understand the Doshas, you have to understand the Panchabhutas/ elements because that's what Dosha are.

Relationship between Dosha: Vata, Pitta, Kapha and Dhatu: 5 Elements

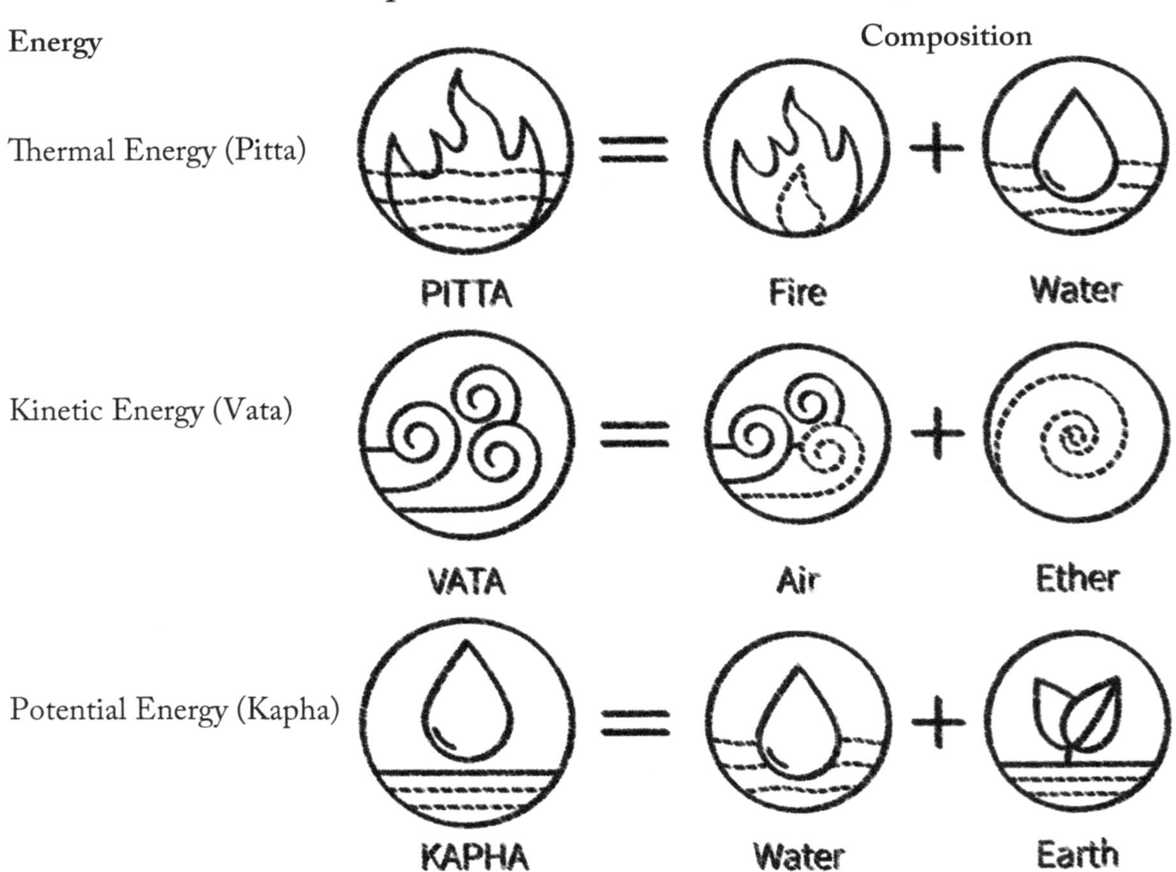

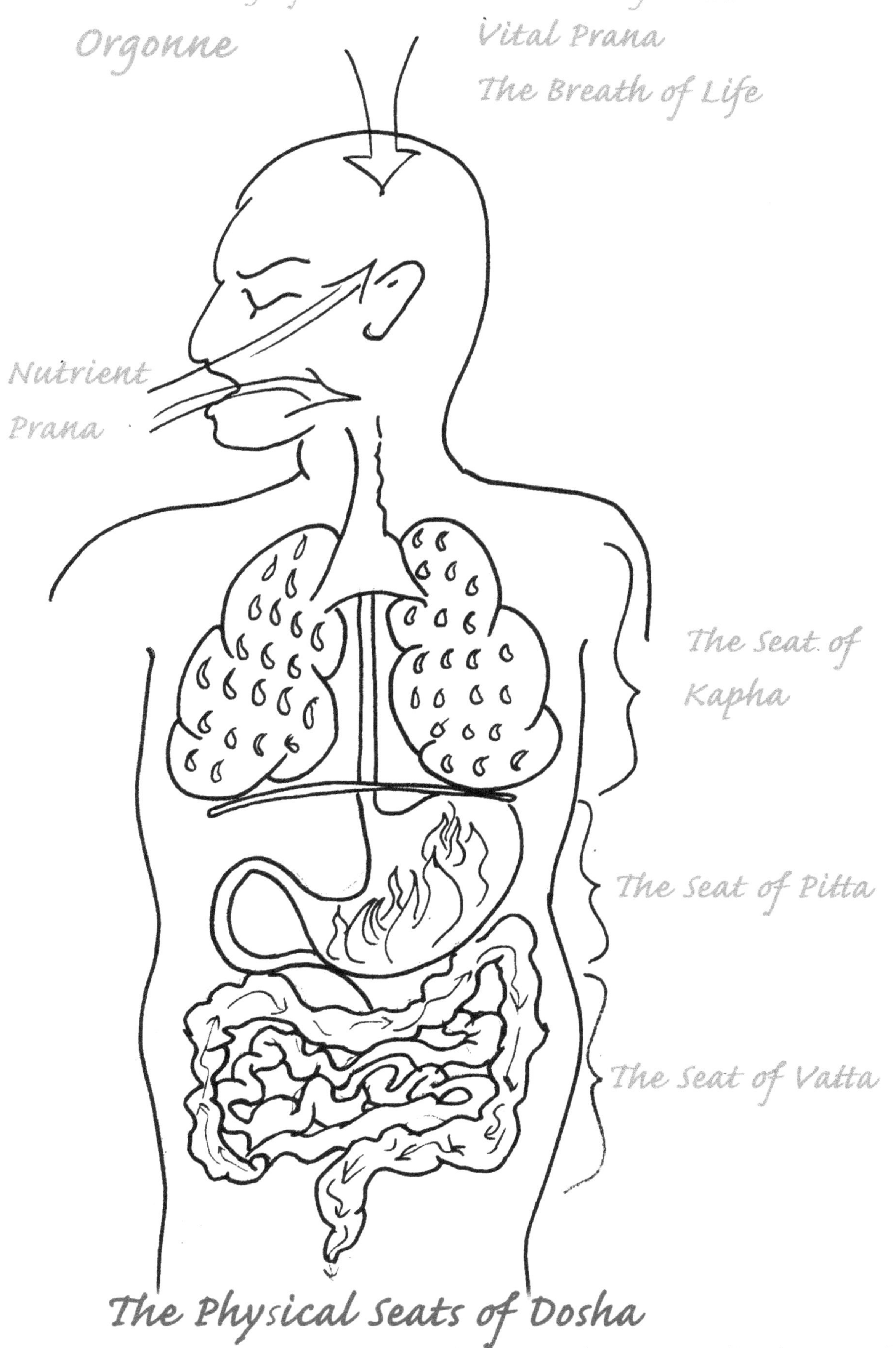

SomaVeda College of Natural Medicine: Thai Yoga Center
Orgonne
Vital Prana
The Breath of Life
Nutrient Prana
The Seat of Kapha
The Seat of Pitta
The Seat of Vatta
The Physical Seats of Dosha

VATA DOSHA

Vata Dosha is the combined influences of the elements Ether and Air (Akat + Lom = Prana) and the chakra energies of fifth and fourth chakras. Vata Dosha is the kinetic energy, that which moves. It is the initiator of all forms of activity. Vata relates to air and prana and breath. If air or prana and breath are not working, then that's a Vata problem.

The primary fault (defilement) associated with Vata is "desire", which you can define as "I want". All the "I wants". How many "I wants" are there? It's many. Somethings I want are good and something's I want are not good. When I want more of the things that are not good than the things that are good then that would be an indication of a Vata imbalance. It's the quality of expression of life. If your life is defined by desire then that is a Vata correlation. This is an indication of the strength of Vata.

The chakra influence determines the field of influence more than the location of the doshas seat. The Tibetan and Thai use the term Air (Akat Lom), Humor or Wind as synonymous with Vata Dosha, meaning all movement, breathing, spitting, muscular activity, speech, menstruation, urination and relaying sensory input. It is related to the mind and is always involved in any mental or emotional illness. It is wind, air, pressure, force and is said to control the other two doshas. It is neutral polarity, the others are not.

      Psychology: Vata is indicated in many feelings and emotions such as freshness, nervousness, fear, anxiety, pain, tremors and spasms.

      Seats of Vata: The large intestine, pelvic cavity, bones, skin, ears, brain, nervous system, bladder, thighs and organs of touch are seats of Vata and any excess will accumulate in these areas. Vata is more active or noticeable in old age as we see the natural catabolism as the body begins to deteriorate.

      Fault: (Defilement) of Desire produces air element.

      Energetic Correlattion: The energetic correlation with Vata Dosha is subtle essence or prana. Any imbalance in the flow of prana. Similarly in Chinese medicine they would say deficient Chi, the deficiency of circulation of specific Chi. In Ayurvedic terms we don't say Meridians we say Prana Nadis. If the Nadis are not open and the prana is not flowing freely through the Nadis, that's a Vata imbalance.

Five Types of Vata (Prana)

Charaka wrote in the Charaka Samhita that there are five types of Vata which seem to be based on both anatomy (structure) and physiology (function). *They are:*

      1) **Prana:** Relates to chest and respiration

      2) **Vyanna:** Pertains to the chest, though more to cardiac functions

      3) **Udana:** Concerns the upper gut. This may be important in emesis and other motility disorders of the upper digestive tract.

      4) **Samana:** refers to the intestines. This controls the churning movement required for digestion of food and formation of stools.

      5) **Apana:** relates to the rectum and genito-urinary system. This controls evacuation, elimination of stools, ejaculation of sperm and parturition (delivery of child).

Five Types of Prana

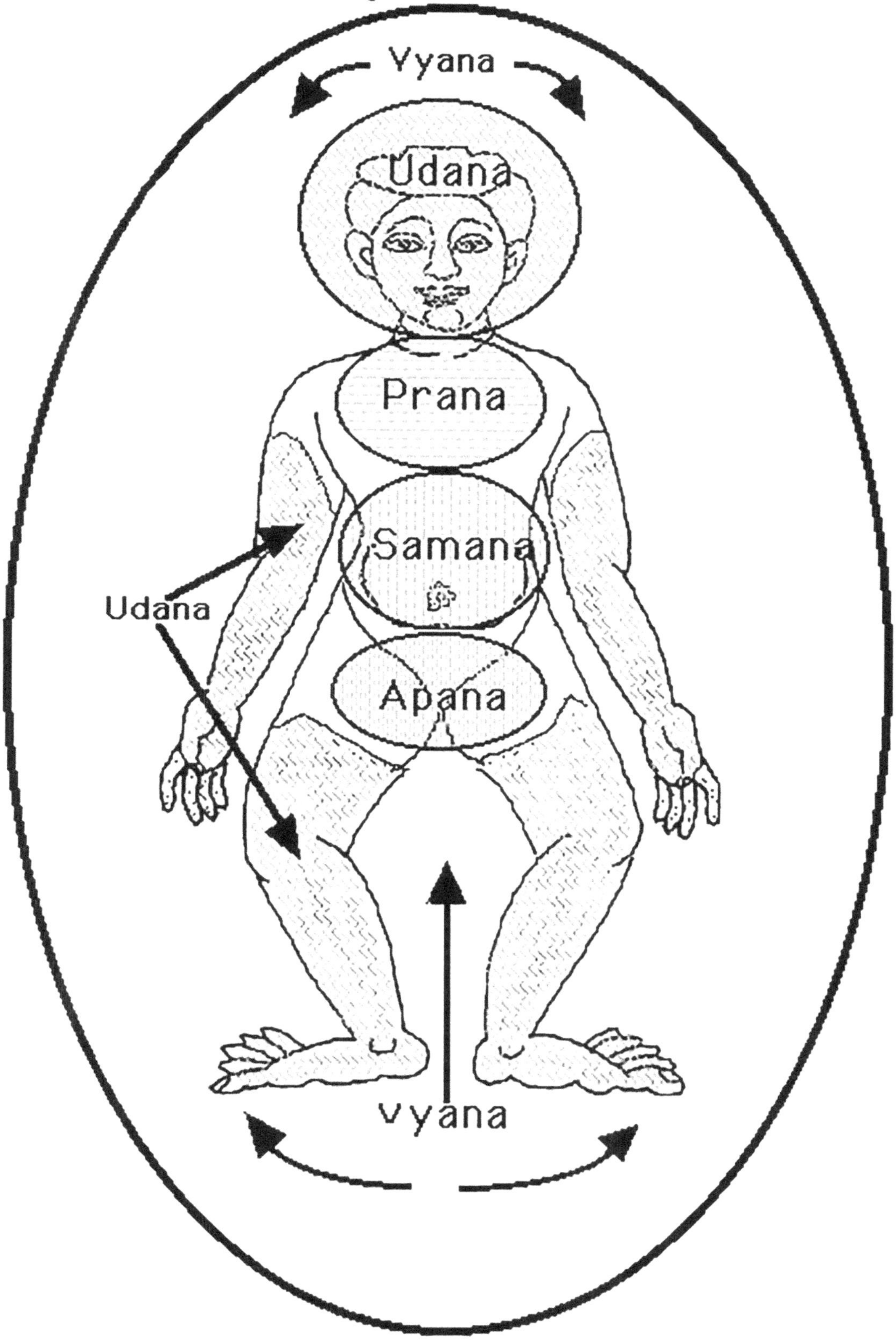

PITTA DOSHA

Pitta is translated as fire (Fai). More accurately, Pitta is resulting from the combined influences of Fire and Water elements, and the chakra influences of second and third chakra, governs processes, actions and reactions within the metabolism of the person. Included in this would be: digestion, absorption, assimilation, nutrition, body temperature, skin coloration, general luster and shine (or healthy appearance of the body), intelligence and understanding.

The primary fault (defilement) of Pitta is aversion, which is like and dislike. Another way of saying aversion is opinions i.e. I'm attracted to this or I'm not attracted to that. How much of your thought life is based on a qualification that happens in your head. You like something or you don't like something? How much of your inner thought life is that kind of thinking? Keep in mind that most of the thinking (cognitive processing) that we do has nothing at all to do with our consciousness. It has nothing to do with our true mind. This mental processing is the expression of organs. It's the expression of elements. All of the thinking process that is characterized by "I like this. I don't like that," is comparison and contrast. It's constant and automatic weighing and measuring. I'm drawn to this. I'm not drawn to this. I like this and I don't like that etc. This is an indication of Pitta activity. If that's the dominant thinking that you have, then you have a Pitta imbalance and or Pitta is dominant.

What is the cure for that polarity of contrast and comparison, the "I like this and I don't like that, I'm attracted to this and I'm not attracted to that"? The constant chatter of that conversation, what is the cure for that? Being fair and open-minded, in other words, it's not black and white. It's not this or that. It's a continuum. I approve this. I don't approve that. Is there no middle ground? Fairness is an antidote for aversion. Others are cultivation of an open mind. Considering other people's opinions even when you disagree with them. Because I disagree with you, I'm going to consider your opinion. Practicing not having opinions about things is a treatment. It's compulsive to have an opinion about everything. That comes from the Pitta Dosha. Practicing, even though my first inclination is to have an opinion, I don't always express them. That's a starting place.

Maybe I can't stop myself from having opinions because it's mechanical. But knowing that it's mechanical, allowing some other part of me to have the say so in whether or not I should actually express it is balancing. Consider adding time into the equation. For example, I have a like or dislike, an attraction or repulsion, but instead of expressing it as I'm having it, I wait. How many times have you had a very definite opinion about something, but when you waited just a little bit it changed. We received new information. We developed a different perspective. What about looking, seeking out and requiring a different perspective? That will have an impact on your thinking.

Acid/ Alkaline Balance

Pitta relates to the acid-alkaline balance in bile. We listen to Doctor Gary Tunsky talking about the importance of pH. We listen to Doctor Tulio Simoncini, an Italian scientist and MD, who has been treating cancer based on a theory that most cancers relate to proliferation of Candida fungus. The Candida only proliferates in an improperly acid environment. He and other researchers state that the way to solve the Candida infection is by regulating the pH (percentage of Hydrogen), buffering the acid balance in the body which then has a beneficial effect on treating the cancer.

For 35 years Dr. Simoncini has been curing people of cancer predictably, reliably and conscientiously with a treatment program that is solely based on balancing acid pH. From our point of view Dr. Simoncini is saying in his therapeutic approach that most cancers are a Pitta imbalance. From a western biomedical point of view that may seem new and novel. However, in classical and traditional Ayurveda diagnosis, cancers tend to proliferate in Pitta imbalance. They relate to the bile in the acid balance in the liver and the blood. In traditional Ayurvedic treatments, if you look at the herbs that are recommended, and treatment programs created for people who have cancer, you could actually see from a whole different perspective. You could say that most of the treatments including Pancha Karma balance pH, acid balance, alkaline versus acid in the body.

The most powerful way to reduce acidosis and to regulate pH. in the body is with a healthy balanced plant based diet. Of course we now have to futher specify Non-GMO and as unadulterated, unprocessed as possible!

Psychology: Pitta is indicated in anger, hate and feelings of jealousy.

Seats of Vata: The small intestines, stomach, sweat glands, blood, fat, eyes, lymph and also skin. In the mature healthy adult there should be more Pitta, as the state of the body is full, mature and stable s howing balanced metabolism. Pitta is positive polarity (+) and 1st. Force active.

Therapies involving both fire and water element as generative or balancing are the basis of "Pancha Karma". More balancing ideas on P. 17 & 18. Avoid "I Like" and "I Dislike". Move towards the center. Follow the middle way or path. Practice temperance, moderation in all things.

Fault: (Defilement) Aversion produces bile.

Energetic Correlation: The energetic correlation with Pitta has to do with metabolism i.e. the three types of metabolism: anabolism, metabolism, catabolism. If you're catabolic when you should be anabolic or you're metabolic when you should be catabolic or you're catabolic when you should be metabolic. Those would all be defined as an imbalance in Pitta.

KAPHA DOSHA:

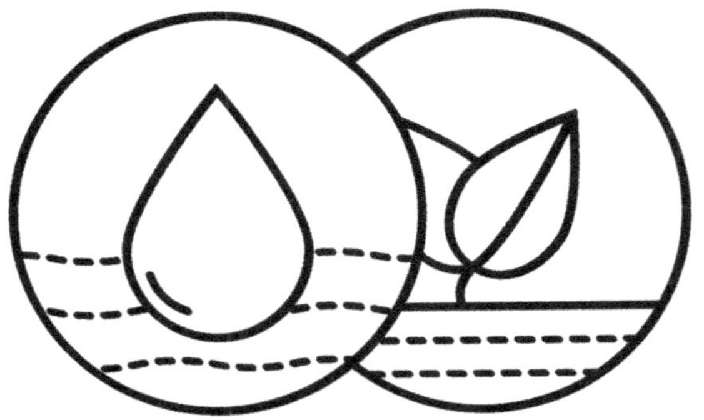

Kapha is the liquid and fluid principle of the body. It is the result of the combined influences of Water and Earth element and the chakra influences of second and first chakra. It lubricates, cements, and supports all bodily functions. It provides strength by directing moisture to expedite healing of wounds and bruising. It fills all of the between places. It carries nutrients and wastes to their appropriate site of use or elimination. Kapha is negative polarity (-) and 2nd. Force active.

We have phlegm, alkaline and mucus. It's just as bad if the pH goes the other way. Being too alkaline is rarer in the population. This is why we say there're more Pittas and Vatas than there are Kaphas. It's the process of a thickening of the interstitial fluids. Interstitial fluids should have a specific gravity and a certain viscosity in order to function properly. Part of their function is circulatory. Interstitial fluids are a secondary system of the circulatory system of fluids in the body, separate from the blood.

When the interstitial fluids become concentrated and too dense, they tend to become stagnant. The fluid doesn't circulate as freely, It stays a little bit too long here or there and eventually may even solidify. Lymphatic fluid, interstitial fluid which has become so dense that it's literally a semi-solid is virtually impossible to move. So what does it do? It accumulates. What does that accumulation look like? Swelling and inflammation. It looks like a rheumatic condition, or like obesity.

The primary fluid, the interstitial fluid, and obese tissue... if you have someone who's morbidly, grossly obese when they wave at you, the hand goes this way and the bottom of the arm goes that way. We call those "bat wings". If you biopsy the excess under arm fleshy tissue you find a substance, a viscous, white semi-liquid, semi-solid substance called mucin. Mucin is mucus. It's interstitial fluid which has become so stagnant and dense that it's in a semi-solid form. Very typical to find in a severe Kapha imbalance.

There must be balance and equilibrium between the all of humors for there to be health. This balance is in constant flux.

Seats of Kapha: Kapha seats are in the brain, chest, throat, head, sinuses, nose, tongue and mouth, stomach, joints, and all liquid fluids and secretions of the body such as blood, mucus, phlegm, plasma, lymph, fat, though primarily it is found in the chest.

Psychology: Kapha is indicated in the emotions of attachment, greed, envy as well as the more positive aspects of calmness, forgiveness and love. Kapha is naturally more discernible in children as their natural anabolism lends itself to the incredible growth they are going through. Become what you know! More balancing ideas on P. 22.

Fault: The primary fault (defilement) of Kapha is ignorance. I define ignorance as willfully, intentionally not knowing. In other words, not understanding, not knowing on purpose. Willfully refusing to acquire that which is
necessary for education. Willfully and purposefully refusing to engage in the process of acquiring wisdom. This is the process of ignorance. You can weigh how much of your thought life is defined by avoiding understanding. How much of your thought life is a circuitry of ignorance and trying to rationalize things that don't make sense?

How much of your life do you spend trying to defend thoughts, actions and deeds that really have no merit, no value? If you have a predominance of this kind of activity in your psyche, in your head, then you have a Kapha imbalance.

Ignorance produces phlegm, excess mucus, chronic sinus drainage, persistent cough etc. Your persistent excess of phlegm and mucous is a reflection of ignorance. What is the cure for ignorance? Reduce the gap between knowledge and being. Always the antidote to ignorance is more knowledge and being. If you have more information and you have more essence with which to compare that information, you will be less ignorant.

Maybe it's not PC to refer to people as being ignorant, but we are all ignorant in some way and at some times. Think about those people or that person, when they're displaying their ignorance, and consider that the solution is "If they only knew the truth"; If they only knew the consequences of their actions; If they only knew the consequences of their words or the actual meaning of the words that they use; If they only knew what motivates the people they hate and why they hate them, they would be happier, healthier, and wiser.

Do they have love in their life? I consider love to be an antidote for ignorance also. Much ignorance is displayed in qualities that are not very loving i.e. violence, racism, bigotry. Where is the love in violence, racism, bigotry and lack of empathy? Another thing that is helpful in ignorance is cultivating empathy. How do you cultivate empathy? For me to be more empathetic with you, I have to know you better. I have to know more about you. I think that's part of the process, education and love. There is always this acquisition of knowledge, understanding or new information that's a part of the treatment, the balancing for Kapha imbalance.

Furthermore, the three Doshas individually have three Gunas or qualities of mental inclination. In this system, each individual Dosha and Guna combination is looked at as an entirely different body type. Positive and negative inclination same as "Defilements" and cure/ remedy.[Page ????] (*See Korosot Chakra Astrology: Meta Journal Press, by the author.*)

Energetic Correlation: The energetic correlation with Kapha is lines (Sen), meridians and channels (Prana Nadi). Vata is that which flows through lines, meridians and channels. Kapha is the lines, meridians and channels themselves.

Example of a Kapha Treatment strategy

How might a line, meridian or channel have an issue? How might a line or conduit of pranic force have an imbalance? For example: An injury or trauma to a specific part of the body that the channel flows through. You could see an impediment of scar tissue. You might have a dislocation of tissue, a burn, cut or broken bone. You could have similar interference or impediment to free flow of energy that's nutritional in origin. You could see a hypersensitivity histamine based allergic reaction of swelling and edema. You could have a low-grade chronic infection which is causing damage to the tissue and inflammation on the energy line. These types of disturbances and the effects that those disturbances cause would be considered a Kapha imbalance.

Your strategy of treating that would be, no matter what else you did, to add a Kapha balancing element. It's based on the location of the symptom, the inflammation, the discoloration etc. Once you know where the lines are, if something's broken on the line such as an area of scar tissue, then you want to ameliorate (soften, make better, mitigate) and open up the communication through that line.

Relationship of Dosha and Metabolism

The Dosha also present as the three metabolisms.

> Vata controls Catabolism (Using Resources)

> When Vata is out of balance metabolism will also be out of balance resulting in excess catabolism. A wasting of the resources of the person which looks like a breakdown and deterioration.

> Pitta controls Metabolism (Distributing Resources)
> Excess pitta disturbs metabolism. There is no middle ground, no rest for the person.

> Kapha controls Anabolism (Storing or Increasing Resources)
> Excess kapha increases the rate of anabolism produces more activity and growth than necessary.

We are all three doshas all the time.

Sometimes we are little more of one than anothers.

First thing I want to do is take a wild guess. If there are 6.5 billion people in the world, and we are relatively evenly distributed between the three types. We have 2 billion Vatas, 2 billion pittas, and 2 billion Kaphas, I guarantee within that range there are a bunch of short round Vatas, and there are some tall skinny Kaphas and there are short round tall skinny Pittas, within some range there are dark Vatas and dark Kaphas and Pittas. There are light Pittas, Kaphas and Vatas. The possible range of expression of that dominant type is virtually infinite. On the one hand, doshas are better than nothing, because we are at least dividing 6.5 billion by three. That's a little more specific. Now you just have to worry about the problems of the two billion I'm looking at.

We have to get to a point where we can assess an individual. Being able to discern someone's dosha is about discerning which group of 2 billion they are part of. It's not very personal or specific. That's why all recommendations of generic type for balancing are wrong in a sense.

If you have a Vata balancing diet, and I've seen books like this. It might work for you but there are 2 billion of you and in an infinite variety of expression. If you fed that brown rice and kale Vata balancing diet to all 2 billion people, some would thrive and become very vibrant and healthy. Some people would become anemic and die. They would lose weight and have wounds that wouldn't heal. There is such a grade of difference even in one type as far as the metabolic expression of that type. Same thing for Pitta.

Pittas like to exercise and have a generally balanced metabolism where they don't gain weight faster than they lose weight and vice versa. They tend to stay the same weight once they mature for like thirty years. That's very Pitta. If I put all of us on a Pitta balancing diet, some of us would gain weight until we ballooned up and some of us would waste away and die on the same diet.

That's why diets don't work. Just because it's an Ayurvedic diet doesn't mean it works better than the Atkins diet. I know if that gets out someone might come and stone me in my front yard one day.

A generic diet of any kind is inappropriate for everybody. It might be completely appropriate for someone and completely inappropriate for everyone else. There's no way to tell. When you write a book and promote a generic diet that's very narrowly defined, you are saying that you know everybody that is going to read that, what his or her type is, and how their body and life situation is going to respond to that diet. Nobody knows that. To say in a book that this is a definitely healthy diet and x,y,z should only eat this is irresponsible. You will cause harm. Why would you do that? The only reason you might do that is to make money or because you are delusional.

We want to learn to identify the types but we also always want to understand there is no such thing as a type. That's why I can't give you the Vata or Pitta balancing diet, because you are not just Vata or Pitta. You are Pitta Kapha Vata. I need to know the % of that. Where's the greatest difference of imbalance in your types. Where are the greatest inequities and the weakest parts of your type profile? Now, once I know that, now I can start to composite some recommendations on what you should be eating, maybe. It's on an individual basis.

Ayurveda diet plans and programs and prescriptions were always meant to be done one on one. Person to person. There never was a generic Ayurveda that you passed out to people. It was all about the relationship between the Vidia, healer, therapist or yogi and the person they were counseling with. It was eyeball to eyeball. That's why the prescriptions worked so fabulously well. They were always personal to the person being treated. There was never a shotgun approach.

When we do SomaVeda® Thai yoga and we physically work the lines, eventually you get to know the lines very well. You learn to spot when there's a problem on the line pretty easily. That's a traditional way in Thai Yoga Therapy of developing a treatment strategy. This is based literally on "Where does is the problem? What line is that on?" We then would correlate that line and symptom to a specific Dosha. By doing so there is a Dosha balancing influence even though we started with a physical symptom correlating to an energy line.

Functions and Qualities of Tri Dosha

These are not all of the qualities that define or indicate any particular Dosha. You'll also notice that some of the qualities seem similar. That's because there is crossover between the Tri-Dosha. There're not three Doshas, Vata, Pitta and Kapha. There's Vata, Vata-Pitta, Pitta, Pitta-Kapha, Kapha, Kapha-Vata and Vata-Pitta-Kapha all three. There're seven.

For example, consider the crossover between Pitta and Kapha elements. The element (*Sans. Bhuta*) of water is shared by Kapha and Pitta. That means that a water imbalance can look more Pitta or can look more Kapha. Sometimes it's hard to tell if it is Pitta or Kapha predominantly. You then have do more assessments, look deeper. You have to look at more qualities to clarify if this water imbalance is a Pitta or Kapha imbalance.

We recognize the presence or dominance of the Dosha by qualities. If you see more of these qualities or these then you know that dosha is more dominant.

Vata Qualities: An excess or deficiency of any of these qualities could indicate the action of a dosha. It could be either way. It could be too much or too little. It's either too much communication or too little communication. Those are equally indicative of a Vata imbalance.

Pitta Qualities: I want you to understand that these are qualities. These come off of lists from Ayurvedic texts as traditional functions. It's more about the quality. We don't get into big debate as to exactly how is generosity different from compassion for example. It's just a rough impression, a first impression often times.

Kapha Qualities: An unction is an oil or salve that you apply to the skin. It's an old English word. You look at some people and they just look kind of slimy. That's unctuousness. You shake someone's hand and you realize that his or her hand is a little wet, clammy and oily…that's unctuousness. You're like, 'nice to meet you' as you wipe your hand down the side of your leg.

Functions of TriDosha Chart

VATA	PITTA	KAPHA
Movement	Body Heat	Stability
Breathing	Temperature	Energy
Natural Urges	Digestion	Lubrication
Transformation of Tissue	Perception	Unctuousness
Motor Function	Understanding	Forgiveness
Sensory Functions	Hunger	Greed
Ungroundedness	Thirst	Attachment
Secretions	Intelligence	Accumulation
Excretions	Anger	Holding
Fear	Hate	Possessiveness
Emptiness	Jealousy	Ignorance
Anxiety	Aversion	Learning
Desire	Tolerance	Knowledge
Non-attachment	Compassion	Phlegm/ Mucous
Generosity	Discretion	Physical/ Organic Energy
Air/ Breath	Bile	Physiology
Subtle Essence	Distribution of Energy	Calmness
Neutralizing	Metabolism	Love
Reconciling	Active	Receptive
Communication	Energy	Structure
Sweet, Sour, Salty	Sweet, Bitter, Astringent	

How the Six Tastes Balance the Dosha

Dosha	Tastes That Increases Dosha	Tastes That Decreases Dosha
Vata	Pungent, Bitter, Astringent	Sweet, Sour, Salty
Pitta	Pungent, Sour, Salty	Sweet, Bitter, Astringent
Kapha	Sweet, Sour, Salty	Sweet, Sour, Salty

Shared Attributes of Tri-Dosha

Look at these shared attributes. Here's where there is oft times confusion in discerning which Dosha is dominant and out of balance.

Vata	Pitta	Kapha
	Oily	Oily
Lightness	Lightness	
Mobile	Mobile	
Cold		Cold
Pungent	Pungent	
	Sour	Sour
	Salty	Salty

PITTA/ KAPHA Share Oiliness, Sour, Salty

PITTA/ VATTA Share Lightness, Mobile, Pungent

VATA/ KAPHA Share Cold

Chapter 12: Dosha Assessments and Management

Prakruti is Important to know

Who am I? (On the basis of my vata, pitta, kapha constitution)
What should I eat?
What should I avoid?
What should I eat in moderation?
What should I eat occasionally?
What should I follow in my life style?

According to Ayurvedic texts prakruti tells us about the susceptibility of an individual to develop particular types of diseases throughout his lifetime. There is a beautiful example that if a vata type person develops a vata disorder then its prognosis is difficult. If a kapha type or pitta type person develops similar vata disease then the prognosis is better and the disease is likely to be cured easily.

Prakruti analysis by means of assessing Tridosha or elemental balance of the body, plays a very important role in diagnosis and treatment of disease. This Diagnostic tool may additionally help in discerning particular dietary regimens, herbs, to avoid or prefer. Prakruti analysis helps us to maintain healthy lifestyle as well.

The Difference between Prakruti and Vikruti

Prakruti is "Constitution", Vikruti is the Nature of the Imbalance.

According to Ayurveda, Prakruti means the physical constitution of a person which is determined at birth. Vikruti means the state of imbalance or disease. Prakruti never changes and could be thought of as the sum of your genetic and biologic predispositions. Vikruti can be thought of as the deviation from what would be considered healthy for the individual based on what they were designed to be like from birth. Vikruti is the difference, whatever difference there might be from nominal function and health.

Prakruti is the science of nature which determines the innate character, physical constitution or disposition of a person. It helps in deciding the ideal lifestyle and therapeutic regimen for an individual. Depending on the predominance of a single dosha, or different permutations and combinations, Prakruti could be of seven types out of which the three main types are Vata, Pitta and Kapha whereas Vikruti has several types and can be determined only through thorough examinations. [

Directions for Using Prakruti/ Constitution Chart for Assessment

First I have to give credit where credit is due. On page 19 at the bottom chart constitution types courtesy of Ayurveda Science of Self-healing by Doctor Vasant Lad, second edition 1985. I wrote to Doctor Lad and I asked his permission to use this chart in my book, that's why I want to make sure that I give credit for this.

They're many versions of this chart. In some Ayurvedic clinics their constitution assessment chart for determining Prakruti could have 200-300 questions. You'll notice that some of the questions are kind of odd. Faith, for example is, changeable, fanatic or steady. How's that an indication of Dosha? What about financial status? Because it's referring to possible imbalance in the Doshas, you might have great financial status because you're a hoarder of money, of pallets, or widgets.

There are four columns, the first column on the left is the correlation for the dosha and then we have Vata, Pitta and Kapha in turn.

The first example is highlighted: frame, when you think of yourself and the word frame what's the first thing that comes to mind? Thin frame, moderate to medium frame, or thick or large frame? If you think you're one specific of these more than another circle that or put a checkmark by it. What if you're somewhere between the thin and moderate or between moderate and large? You check or circle both of them. What if you think you have thin fingers, you have medium frame for your torso but your legs and feet are thick and large, now what do you do? Because you can't tell, circle all three or none. In other words, if you can't tell, if you can't come up with an instant association with one or two of these three, then treat this as the same thing as saying that you don't have one and leave it blank.

Do this with each one in turn. It's always the closest first guess as far as whether it fits or not. Once you've gone through all of these, then you'll have a number at the bottom of each column. Go down each column and add up the checks or circles. Write that number down, you'll have your Vata number, a Kapha number and a Pitta number. We will use those numbers to do a Vedic Prakruti assessment that we call the triangle assessment.

Determining Basic Constitution Or Humoral Type by Chart   (Prakruti)

Aspect of
Constitution   VATA   PITTA   KAPHA

Aspect of Constitution	VATA	PITTA	KAPHA
Frame	Thin	Moderate, Medium	Thick, Large
Body Weight	Low, Thin, Hard to gain	Hard to gain	Overweight, Easy to gain
Skin	Dry, Rough, Cool, Brown, Black	Soft, Oily, Warm, Fair, Red, Yellowish	Red, Yellowish, Cool, Pale, Moist, White
Amount of Hair	Average	Thinning	Thick
Color of Hair	Black, Kinky, Light Brown	Soft, Oily, Yellow, Early Gray, Reddish	Light, Oily, Wavy, Dark Brown, Black
Teeth	Protruded, Overly Large or Small, GumS emaciated	Moderate in size, Soft Gums, Yellowish	Strong, White, Medium to Large
Eyes	Small, Dull, Dry Brown, Black, Yellow, Medium	Sharp, Penetrating, Green, Gray, Large	Big, Attractive, Blue, Thick
Appetite	Variable, Irregular	Good, Excessive, Unbearable, Sharp, needs food	Slow but Scanty, Steady, easily misses meals
Food & Drink	Prefer Warm	Prefer Cold	Prefer Warm and Dry
Taste	Sweet, Sour, Saline	Sweet, Bitter, Astringent	Pungent, Bitter, Astringent
Thirst	Variable	Excessive	Scanty
Eats	Quickly	Medium Speed	Slowly
Elimination	Dry, Hard, Constipated	Soft, Oily, Loose	Thick, Oily, Heavy, Slow
Physical Activity	Very Active	Moderate	Lethargic
Exercise Tolerance	Low	Medium	High

Endurance	Poor	Good	Excellent
Walk	Fast, Quickly	Average	Slow and Steady
Mind	Restless, Active	Aggressive, Intelligent	Calm, Slow, Stable
Emotions	Fearful, Insecure	Aggressive	Calm, Greedy
Temperament	Unpredictable	Irritable, Jealous	Attached
Moods	Changes Quickly	Slow Changing	Non-Changing
React to Stress	Excite Quickly, Quick Temper	Anger Easily	Slow to get irritated
Weather	Aversion to Cold	Aversion to Hot	Aversion to Damp, Cool
Faith	Changeable	Fanatic	Steady
Memory	Recent Memory good, Past memory poor	Sharp, Good, General	Slow but Prolonged
Dreams	Fearful, Flying, Jumping, Running	Fiery, Anger, Violence, War	Watery, River, Ocean, Lake, Swimming, Romantic
Sleep	Scanty, Interrupted	Medium length, Sound	Heavy, Sound, Prolonged
Speech	Fast	Sharp & Cutting	Slow, Monotonous
Financial Status	Poor, Spends money quickly on trifles	Moderate, Spends on Luxuries	Rich, Money saver, Spends on food
Pulse	Thready, Feeble	Moderate	Broad, Slow
Pulse Animal	Moves like a Snake	Jumping like a Frog	Moves like a Swan
Total Each Column:			

Make a mark or underline and highlight whichever of these qualities most closely describes yourself. Total each category and note which of the three Doshas Vata, Pitta or Kapha is prevalent. Root word of Dosha is "Dus" as is disfunction. When not in harmony dysfunction occurs.

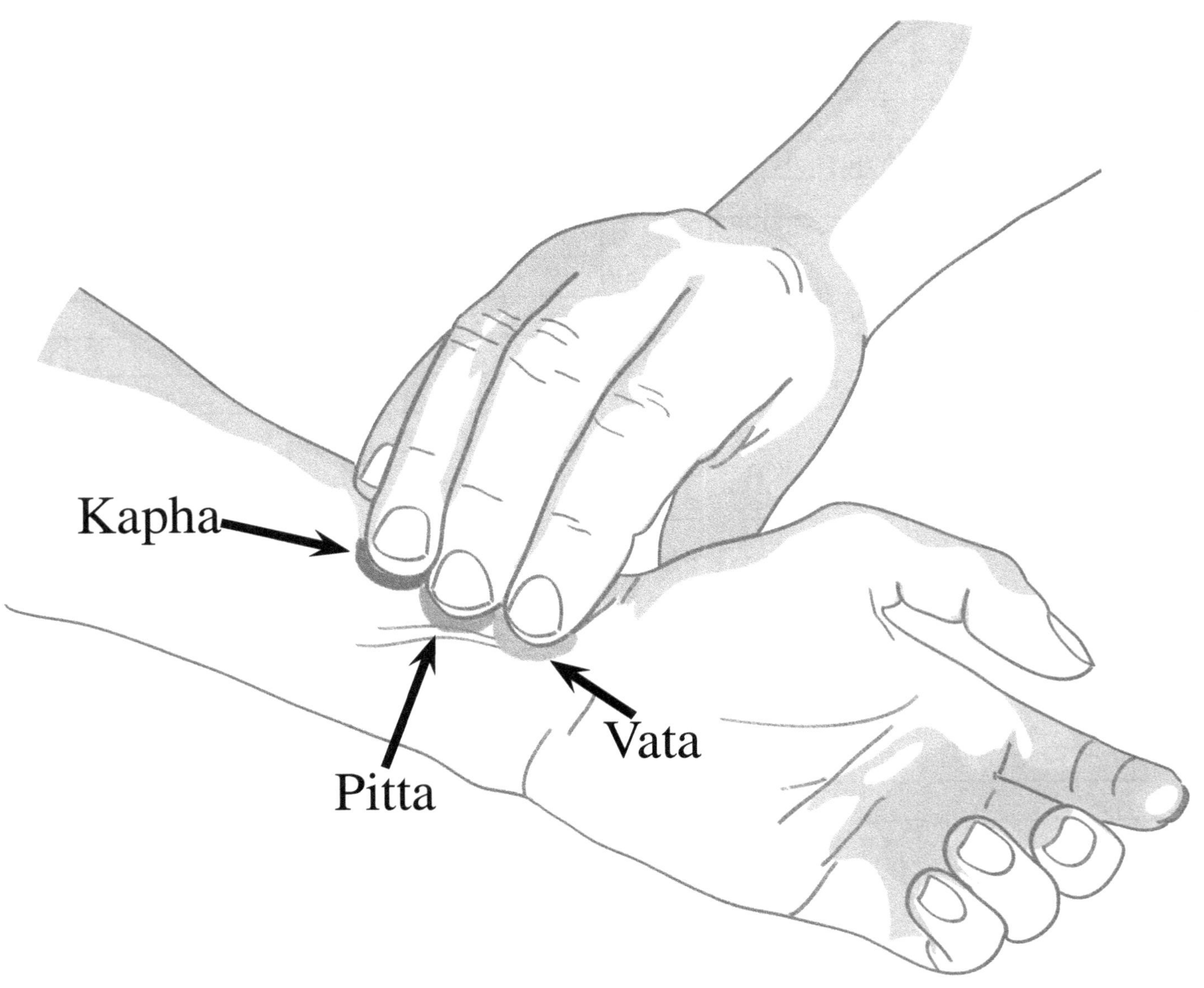

Taking the pulse (*Sans. Nadi Pareeksha*) is the Raja or King of Vedic assessments. Correctly place the fingers on the wrist of the client's arm (Right wrist for man, Left wrist for woman), with the fingers close to the client's thumb. Gentle, uniform pressure is applied with the fingertips over the pulse. Apply and release pressure repeatedly to determine under which finger the pulse is found to be more evident.

Index	=	Vata
Middle	=	Pitta
Ring	=	Kapha

Simple Vedic Tongue Assessment

Have the client extend their tongue and in good natural light examine it.

VATA	Cold, rough to the touch, with cracks.
PITTA	Red and blue-ish in color.
KAPHA	White and exceedingly slimy.
All Three	Blackish with eruptions all over the surface.

We are doing the simple tongue evaluation. You could go much more in depth, you could make determinations by what parts of the tongue have what colors and so on. There's a whole book on Ayurvedic tongue analysis that Dr. Lad published that goes into every little zone and indication. You could spend a good several months just studying that alone. The same goes for pulse, the eyes, and all the others evaluations. We are doing the short-hand version. We have basically four combinations of styles of tongue.

Vata tongue, remember these are qualities: cold, rough to the touch, cracked or has cracks or fissures. Vata tongue looks cold though it may not be cold. It is rough to the touch. We don't really wipe our hand over someone's tongue, it looks rough like a cat's tongue. Fissures, you can probably all think back over your life and you might have looked at yourself in the mirror and noticed a crack in your tongue, you might have felt it before looking at it. Or you've seen other people's tongues that have cracks.

A Pitta tongue is primarily red and bluish in color. It is very definite red and blue.

A Kapha tongue is white and is exceedingly slimy. It's white with a slimy coating.

If you see all three, vata-pitta-kapha, that's a black tongue with eruptions like pimples all over it. That's very bad. Recommend that person go to an emergency room ASAP and be checked out. If you ever have a client and their tongue is blackish and has eruptions, that's the end of your session right there. Eruptions are like large pustules on the surface of the tongue, like ant bites. Be sure to tell them to go to the ER. Quite often that indicates some type of organ failure is occurring, imminent, has occurred. It's usually something major. That's the opposite of a healthy tongue. I've only seen something like that in the hospice. I've never actually seen a tongue like that in a client who was walking around.

We were also told that person was going to die shortly. That's what that meant. They had a fatal problem and they needed attention right away.

It's always this comparison. After you've asked 1000 people to stick their tongue out, you'll know which is which. It pops out at you.

We are looking on the top surface of the tongue. Things like cracks and fissures look like the Grand Canyon. It looks like the tongue is about to split in half. Dramatic cracks run down the middle of the tongue, not just a little of the taste buds. Taste buds are in fact further apart on the side of the tongue. They are larger and full of blood. That's not what we are talking about. Fissures look like the tongue could be in pieces, sometimes the cracking/ fissuring can be so bad in some imbalances that it would actually bleed.

What we are determining is what is the dominant Dosha based on what the tongue shows. However, qualities of the tongue will change dramatically, depending on the balance between the doshas. That's why the tongue is used as an assessment because it gives you a lot of information about the inner and the secret doshas. Technically all we are doing now is the assessment of the dosha.

Simple Vedic Touch Assessment

Yes, actually touch their skin!

VATA   Skin is dry and cold
PITTA   Skin is hot.
KAPHA   Skin is moist, wet, clammy.

You can do this on either arm. I take hold of the arm and relax in the same manner as if I was going to take the pulse. Take the fingertips of my hand and just brush up and down on the inside of the clients forearm. I'm looking for resistance or drag, a sense of dryness or oiliness or slide. There's a certain point where it's so dry that the skin exfoliates so easily that the sloughing skin acts as a lubricant. You'll see the white powdery residue. There's also the dry quality where it literally grabs and feels rough. There's the oily where it slides pretty easy but then there's a point to where it could actually feel like I'm dragging in the oil.

Does it feel dry? Is it warm or cool? Does it feel oily? Does it feel wet?

Clammy means cold and damp feeling. There's a coolness as a shared quality between Vata and Kapha. For Kapha there's moisture and a sense of wetness.
You have to take into consideration if they just doused themselves with some moisturizer like oil or cream. Are they a goo girl?
What you want to evaluate is clean, dry skin. Does it feel wet and clammy when it's clean and dry? Does it feel dry? Does it feel hot or cooler?

Selecting Time of Day & Depth of Pressure

There is good time for specific types and imbalance... Not always standard business hours!
There's actually a better time to do Dosha balancing when you know ahead of time the dosha you are trying to balance. This comes in handy when scheduling.

If I'm working to correct a Vata imbalance, I will try to schedule the client as late in the day as the two of us can negotiate. In the afternoon or evening is best for Vata. The Pitta is afternoon or midday and the Kapha is morning. If I'm balancing Kapha, you need to be the first session of the day and Vata will be the last session. Pitta can be in the middle of the day.

VATA   Evening and light pressure
PITTA   Afternoon and deep pressure
KAPHA   Morning and medium pressure.

Selecting Oil Base For Dosha Balancing

If you are going to use oils, there's an oil that is appropriate for the specific dosha.
Either use as a base or additive to bring this quality into play.

VATA   Sesame Oil: To calm and balance.
PITTA   Sunflower Oil or Sandalwood: to cool.
KAPHA   Corn, Canola or Calamus root or No Oil: to warm.

You can use these oils as you would an essential oil. When I say for balancing the Vata, use sesame oil to calm and balance. I'm not saying than it has to be a full body massage with sesame oil. I might take a drop of sesame oil and touch it to the key points I think are relevant to their condition or take some and rub my hands with it to aromatize the oil and carry on with my regular session. I might burn or take a little in a diffuser. I might put some on a piece of fabric and have it in the room as an essence. That's what that means. It doesn't mean to take a gallon of sesame oil and do a full body massage. It just means to incorporate the essence of sesame for balancing Vata.

Pitta is sunflower or sandalwood.

Kapha is corn, canola or calamus root. Calamus is in the lily family, it's the root of the lily. You can get calamus oil or dried root. Again, when you use something like that all you do is use a little bit. That's all you need. It's more about the vibrational essence. It's not about quantity.

Relationship Between Orifice and Sen

	Orifice	Left	Right
Vyana Prana			
Ether	Ears	#7 Lawusang	#8 Ulanka
Earth	Nose	#2 Ittha	#3 Pingkala
Fire	Eyes	#5 Sahatsarangsi	#6 Thawari
Water	Mouth	#1 Sumana	
Earth	Rectum	#9 Nanthakrawat / Sukhumang	→ Fecal Elimination
	Penis	#9 Nanthakrawat Sikhini (Urethra)	#10 Khitchanna Itaken → Spermatoza
	Vagina	#9 Nanthakrawat Sikhini (Urethra)	#10 Khitchanna Kitcha → To Uterus

(Left margin groupings: UDANA — Ether, Earth, Fire; PRANA — Water; APANA — Earth and below.)

the treatment. In this assessment process, I keep going until I have enough information to be able to devise a concrete strategy on what is the best thing that I can do for the client today, tomorrow or the next day. I may base a whole program based on the Dosha assessment.

Example Vata Dosha: Look at "Seats of Vata" (P. 112), under the different parts of the body that could be aflicted. Also lok at the different types of imbalances that relate to Vata Dosha seeing that they're a composite of those for the elements Ether and Air (P. 92 & 93). Previously I stated that the primary fault or literal fault of the Vata imbalance was desire (P. 112) , there is also a traditional cure for that fault. The traditional cure for the defilement of desire is non-attachment or the cultivation non-attachment.

The client who's thought life and activities of life are primarily defined by desire "I want" have a recommended therapy. The recommended therapy is to engage in some kind of learning process. They need to learn to practice non-attachment and then to actually do a practice based on that. They are recommended to start to have some activities in life that are exemplary of non-attachment. A practical idea in that regard is to cultivate an attitude of generosity. The only way that you can be generous is if you are not completely overcome by desire.

If everything is not "mine-mine-mine" then there's a possibility that I might be able to give something away. I can let go off something.

If my problem has to do with grasping, holding, collecting and saving, from a chakra point of view it is a first chakra issue as well. Do therapy which cultivates acts of generosity. Practice generosity and make generosity a big part of your life. That is an antidote to a Vata imbalance of excess desire. Notice that in the Sanayasin Yoga disciplines that these cures are essentially what the vows of the disciples and monks are about.

If I know that I have Vata imbalance, I will take a vow of poverty. Not only will I take a vow to not make the accumulation of money and wealth my primary ambition in life, I would make a value of the opposite. I would value poverty. I will exemplify that poverty, "even though I don't have anything I'm going to give you everything I have anyway".

There are many examples of people who come out of a situation of "I want, mine-mine-mine," life, based on desire and accumulation of wealth becoming more spiritually inclined people and literally divesting themselves of vast wealth. They then had more balanced and healthy lives.

Differential Assessment

The concept of differential Assessment is to do a series of several different assessments. Each one give a separate and distinctive insight into the nature of the clients imbalance. A treatment strategy is formualted as a result of the combined insight. This gives a more objective analysis of the over pattern of Dosha imbalance if there is one.

* Direct Observation (Your gut sense of Prakruti and Vikruti)
* Assess what Kosha or Body is indicated or dominant in imbalance. (p. 68)
* Assess by Quality: Sense, Sense Organ, Action, Organ of Action and Tamas Attribute (p. 103)
* Questionaire (Constitution Questionaire) (p. 124)
* Simple Pulse (p. 126)
* Simple Tongue (p. 127)
* Simple Touch (p. 128)
* Sen Line (Does the issue relate directly to a specific Sen Line?) (See "*Ayurveda of Thailand*" p.104- 116)
* Orifice of the Body (p. 129)
* Chakra (See correlations between Chakra and Dosha) (See "*Korosot Astrology*")
* Intuitive assessment: Use Radiesthesia method using pendulum/ charts and or Radionic instrument. Dowse for any and all qualities being determined including Kosha, Ray of creation which imbalance is manifesting on or from, Past life relationship or origin, Organ, Element, Sen, Chakra, Dosha, body system, region of body or Marma to emphasize, what additional therapies to include, directional orientation to use in session, allergies, conjunctive therapies and remedies which might   support wellness etc.

The greatest differentiation between Dosha indicates target for balancing. Each individual or "different" assessment adds (+) or subtracts (-) from total assessment indice. Balance greatest difference or deviation from net zero.

Some Ideas regarding Dosha Balancing

The triad of Dosha- Dhatu (tissue), Mala (Metabolic by products) along with Agni (fire of life) form the basis for the human organism. The final component is the mind. What is seen, is your constitutional type. What needs emphasis or balance is the greatest differentiation between outer, inner and secret. What shows, what supports, what controls or modifies... Balance equals reconciliation of the greatest difference between the Dosha either by process of Generating or Controlling. General balancing of Dosha, stimulate and balances the Dhatu stimulating a release of malas (waste products produced from body systems i.e. feces, urine & sweat etc.). The recommendations for balancing individual Dosha are actually the same in certain ways. For example under management of a person with a Vata imbalance [Page ????].

It says if a Vata type of person is exposed to influences which aggravate Vata then the Vata in his or her person is upset right away. The remaining other doshas will not be affected the same way. Aggravated Vata looks like diseases or imbalances resulting in the impairment of strength complexion, happiness, and longevity.

See management of a person with Pitta imbalance [page ????] and see it's exactly the same. It's the same recommendation again for management of a Kapha imbalance.

In Ayurveda, in the Vedic strategies, it's basically the same strategy for balancing Doshas. Any Dosha that's out of balance causes a problem for all of the other Doshas. How do we tell, how can we identify what dosha and what are the issues that the imbalance, the Vikruti, is causing? We look at their strength, complexion, happiness and longevity. That's where the signs and symptoms are found.

An assessment in Ayurveda is based on objectively observing signs and symptoms of imbalance primarily.

What is strength? Strength is physical strength, strength of character, strength of mind, the strength of organs to do their job, the strength of the circulatory system, the strength of the immune system, the structural strength of the bones, osteoporosis, easily fractured and broken bones etc. Would easily broken or damaged bones not be an impairment of strength? MS (Multiple Sclerosis), would that not be an impairment of strength? Fibromyalgia, would that not be an impairment of strength? It's all based on perspective.

What is Complexion? The appearance of the skin. The skin, the epidermis, the integumentary system is the largest excretory/ elimination organ. It is the single largest organ in the body, it's the only organ we can see. So it's no mistake, accident or coincidence that by looking at the complexion, which is the color, the temperature, the texture, the density, the sensitivity of the skin that it tells us significant information about the health of the person.

What is Happiness? What is the happiness of a person? What do I learn by looking at a person and assessing whether or not they're happy or how happy are they? Happiness has to do with enjoyment and satisfaction of life. So what kinds of factors are important? If you have eaten bad food and you have food poisoning and you are vomiting and projectile vomiting have projectile diarrhea are you happy? Are you as happy as when you don't have the symptoms of food poisoning? That's a rhetorical question. I had food poisoning one trip on my way back from working in Ecuador. It hit me in the waiting room. Then on the airplane it became more severe. Knocked me right down. If you'd assessed my imbalance at any time after the first symptom, which was explosive diarrhea in the airport, how happy I was with my life, you would have immediately known something was not right. No question, you would immediately know "He is not very happy right now."

But the happiness quotient will show in inequities in biology, in chemistry, in issues with the autoimmune system. Happiness will show issues with neurology, with emotional well-being, and unresolved negative emotional issues.

Just asking the question regarding "happiness" can give a world of insight into the nature of the client's imbalance.

What is Longevity: Looking at the client and being able to assess do they look like they're here? Are they coming or going? I've had clients walk in the door, that when I looked at them and if I asked myself the question, "do they look like they're coming or going?" Everything that was in me said they look like they're out of here, not long for this life. I look at them and say "Longevity is deficient, this person doesn't look like they're here for very long, in fact they look like they're on the way out." That looks very different from healthy and well.

Here we have it so simple: Appearance of strength, complexion, happiness and longevity. "A Dosha imbalance will cause an issue with strength, happiness, and longevity of the person." That's what you're assessing.

Balancing the Tri-Dosha

Management of a person with a Vata imbalance:

If a Vata type of person is exposed to influences which aggravate Vata, then the Vata in his or her person is upset right away. The remaining other doshas will not be affected the same way. Aggravated Vata looks like diseases or imbalances resulting in the impairment of strength, complexion, happiness and longevity.

Vata is hot, lom means to hold = windy, medium means light, easy on the lines, steam, herbs, tapping, hitting, breath, pranayama, colonics, hip, pelvis, shoulders, music and the oil for balancing Vata is sesame.

Emphasize Lines: 1, 2, 3, 4, 7, 8, ... Not Lines: 5, 9 & 10)

1. Open the Wind! Bput Bpa To Lom! (See Shavayatra) Use light easy pressure over the lines with emphasis on the breath. Hold all Lom for longer periods of time.. 30 to 60 seconds (The exception to this is if the client is diagnosed with acute hypertensive type of disorders.) Especially bring energy, attention and awareness to the hips, pelvis and shoulders (anterior). Use abdominal work to release and to stimulate the proper functioning of the colon. Colonic irrigation, colonics and therapeutic enemas with steam. Steamed herbal compress massage, "Nuad Prakhop Samunprai" is balancing for Vata and Kapha but should not normally be used for Pitta. Steam may be pleasant for Pitta imbalanced person but it is not considered balancing and may cause imbalance! Hot and light, accelerate with hitting and tapping.
2. Proper administration of oleation and fomentation. (Hot Oil and Prakhop Samunprai)
3. Mild purgatives prepared by the addition of fat, hot things, and substances having sweet, sour and saline tastes.
4. Food having the above mentioned ingredients.
5. Massage, poultice, bandage, kneading, affusion bath, Samavahana
6. (Vedic Massage: pressing and kneading by hand.)
7. Use of wine and fermented drinks.
8. Fats and oils used internal and external with massage.
9. (Ghee and herbal essential oil or herbal infusion based)
10. Medicated enema. (Use of oils and herbal infusion)
11. In hands on practice, emphasize asana where you can release wind, bring energy and consciousness to the Lom and adding tapping techniques.
    (Emphasize the windgates during Reishi Hand Yoga "Reusi Dottan" or Hatha Yoga)

For Self Balance: Practice of Vipassana/ Insight Meditation, Cultivation of generosity and gifting added to daily life practice. Engage in visual and or performing arts including dance and music. It is balancing to express or to communicate the feelings and emotions. Allow the Vata person to do this. It is not necessary for you to respond or to even understand, but listening encourages the balancing activity for the Vata client. Ask them "How, are you? What are you feeling or how are you feeling? Walk on the legs and arms to "Bend the Bones". Percussion on the lines... Think "I am doing Chi-gung to you" as you work. This brings the Prana and Chi up and is strengthening and toning for the kidneys. Hit, tap, smack! Make the lines hot and turn red. Let them cough, spit, get up to pee etc. if necessary. All are wind!

Management of a person with a Pitta imbalance:

If a Pitta type of person is exposed to influences which aggravate Pitta, then the Pitta in his or her person is upset right away. The remaining other doshas will not be affected the same way. Aggravated Pitta looks like diseases or imbalances resulting in the impairment of strength, complexion, happiness and longevity.

Pitta treatment emphasis for balancing sessions is cool, slow, deep, work on the lines, alternating with rocking, hold asana, breath emphasis or pranayama, lymphatic emphasis, an abdominal emphasis and the oil is sunflower or sandalwood.

Emphasize Lines: 1, 2, 3, 4, 5, 6 ... Not Lines: 7- 10)

Add visualization to session, coach, engage, follow, use "Hollow Tube" guided imagery, bring the Pitta client into partnership and a state of active engagement during their session.

Use deep slow pressure. Alternate rocking and deep pressure emphasis. Hold each Asana longer but with a comfortable pressure. Of course, if you're holding postures longer and with deeper pressure that means the therapist must be doubly conscious of his/her own body mechanics, positioning, breath and mental focus as well. Alternate during sessions techniques with lymphatic focus... light josseling and rocking with attention to abdominal points. Use cool or alternate with cool by using cold packs, towels or ice. Look for swellings to cool and the like. Release any apparent edema if possible.

1. Intake of Ghee.
2. Oleation with Ghee. (Soak or Massage)
3. Purgation.
4. Use of drugs, herbs or medicants with the diet having sweet, bitter and astringent tastes with cooling properties.
5. Use of scents which are mild, sweet, fragrant, cooling and cordial.
6. Use of pearls, jewels, crystals, stones, rocks and garlands which are kept in cold water.
7. Frequent sprinkling of cold water and air.
8. Hearing of songs and music which are pleasing to the ears, mild, sweet and agreeable.
9. Hearing information regarding prosperity.
10. Keeping company with friends.
11. Company of agreeable men and women attractively dressed.
12. Residence in building cooled by moon rays and open to breeze on all sides.
13. Residence in cold places, in mountains and near river banks, use of cold and fans.
14. Beautiful gardens.
15. Many beautiful flowers around.
16. Adoption of other regiments soothing in nature.

For Self Balance: Practice of Vipassana/ Insight Meditation, Cultivation of generosity and gifting added to daily life practice. Engage in visual and or performing arts including dance and music.

The Pitta needs to cultivate qualities of tolerance, compassion and discretion... to reach outside of themselves. Volunteerism, adoption... the making of relatives, helping widows, orphans, the weak and the sick.

Management of a person with a Kapha imbalance:

If a Kapha type of person is exposed to influences which aggravate Kapha, then the Kapha in his or her person is upset right away. The remaining other doshas will not be affected the same way. Aggravated Kapha looks like diseases or imbalances resulting in the impairment of strength, complexion, happiness and longevity.

Hands on hot massage! Hot room, hot oil and steam. Fast and light with enough pressure to create some friction effect. Make the client warm, sweaty and steamy while receiving treatment. Use light, hot packs, hot towels, steam and Nuad Prokhop. Steam, hot shower or soak before sessions. Warm your hands. Warm points before release including the Lom. Make your hands hot. At the end of the treatment session allow the client to return to normal temperature. Definitely emphasize the "Warm-up", repeat it several times as it brings energy to lower chakras #1 and 2.   (Emphasize Lines: 1, 2, 3, 9 ... Not Lines: 4, 7, 8)

1. Proper administration of strong and hot elimination therapies. Warm oil.
2. Intake of diet which is mostly ununctious (not oily) and is composed of ingredients having pungent, bitter and astringent tastes.
3. Running, jumping, swimming, whirling, keeping awake during the night, fighting, sexual intercourse, exercise, unction, bath and oil massage.
4. Intake of strong wines preserved for a long time. (Cordials, aged wines and brandies, sherries)
5. All lightening therapies along with smoking. (Please note: traditional use of various herbs including cannabis, have always been part of the general pharmacopoeia of Vedic medicine.)
6. Use of warm apparel.
7. Giving up comforts of life with a view to enjoying happiness ultimately.

For Self Balance: Treat ignorance with self education. Find the areas of life where light is not, and bring them to higher levels. Exposing oneself to teaching cultivates energy as food to support working on one's self.

Lightening Therapies: Sweats, Swedana and such lightening methods are indicated for both Vata and Kapha imbalances.

Treatment Emphasis for Dosha Balancing Sessions

Vata	Pitta	Kapha
Hot	Cool	Hot
Lom (Hold = Windy)	Medium (Light, easy on lines) Slow (Deep lines)	Fast & Light (More than Vara)
Steam Herbs	Rocking (Alternate)	Steam Herbs
Tapping/ hitting	Hold Asana	Lymphatic Emphasis
Breath/ Prana Yama	Breath/ Prana Yama	Whole Body
Colonics	Lymphatic Emphasis	Control Moisture & Odor
Hips, Pelvis, Shoulders	Abdominal	Aroma-Therapy
Oil = Sunflower/ Sandalwood	Oil = Corn/ Canola (Non-GMO)	Oil = Sesame, Colon Hydrotherapy

Chapter 13: The Srotas

Srotas are the pathways within the human body which communicate and link the different matter, structure, substance and material that make up the totality of a human being. Srotas may also be called pathways, vessels, ducts or channels. The pathways help in the manufacture and transportation of essential ingredients which support life. They support the basic amenities needed to manufacture and create all of the various tissues of the body and to flush out the unnecessary things which clog, toxify and or harm the spirit, mind and body. The pathways support the healthy existence and proper functioning of everything within us. That which defines our existence, our health and our immune status. When obstructed, blocked, choked, clogged or contaminated there may be serious damage, diseases or death. There is an infinite number of these pathways as in total there is a srota for every tissue, every cell, every structure, membrane,artery, vein and organ.

This does not count the infinite invisible channels which connect and circulate prana, vital life force and mental energy throughout the person… even extending according to classical Ayurvedic text to a distance of 50' outward in all directions from the surface of the body!

Simply stated according to the Chakrapani, commentary on Charaka Sutra "Those from which Sravana or flow of body substances take place or those through which the materials flow in the body are called Srotases"

"Those which carry or transport materials like Prana (life element or oxygen or air), anna (food), vaari (water), mamsa (muscle tissue), meda (fat) etc are called Srotases" (Ref- Sushruta Shaareera 9, Dalhana commentary)

Types of Srotas:

Basically the Srotas are of two types:
  Bahir mukha srotas (Mahanti srotas) – External openings or apertures
  Antar mukha srotas (Sukshma srotas or Yogavahi srotas) – Internal channels of the body

According to Charaka Samhita there are 13 main Antarmukha Srotases. They are:
1. Pranavaha Srotas – Channels carrying the vital life element or air
2. Annavaha Srotas – Channels transporting food
3. Udakavaha Srotas – Channels carrying water and controlling water metabolism
4. Rasavaha srotas – Channels carrying the nutritional essence
5. Raktavaha Srotas – Channels carrying the blood
6. Mamsavaha srotas – Channels carrying muscle tissue
7. Medovaha Srotas – Channels carrying fat tissue
8. Asthivaha Srotas – Channels transporting the bone tissue
9. Majjavaha Srotas – Channels carrying the bone marrow tissue
10. Shukravaha Srotas – Channels carrying the semen or reproductive tissue
11. Mutravaha srotas – Channels carrying urine out of the body
12. Purishavaha Srotas – Channels carrying stools out of the body
13. Swedavaha Srotas – Channels carrying the sweat

The Sen Lines or Prana Nadis

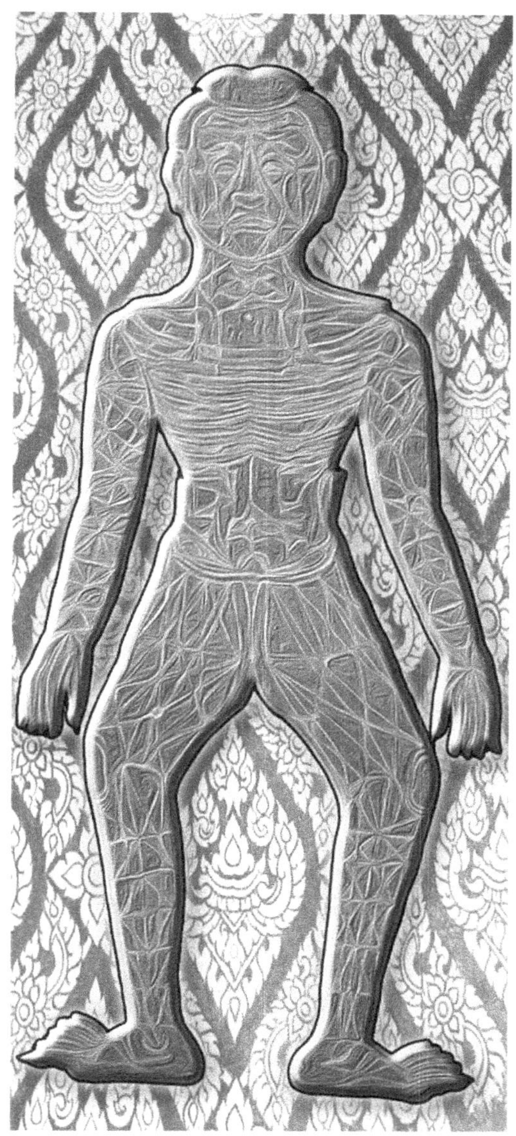

There are two kinds of Sen or subtle lines or conduits.

Subtle Nadi (Pranavaha srotas): Lines of the pranic force. The Currents and fields of vital life force, energy, light and magnetism. (Compare with Traditional Chinese Medicine concept of Meridians)

B) Gross Nadi (Manovaha srotas): Lines of the mental force. How the currents and fields of energy manifest through and animate matter, carrying the shape of the wave form. (food, water, nutritional essence, nerves, blood, lymph, semen, hair, bones, bone marrow, muscle tissue, fat tissue, fascia and connective tissue, urine, stools, sweat)

There are several kinds of gross lines, or Sen. Nerves are Sen. All of our blood supply system, the arteries and the veins and all of their capillaries are Sen. The ducts and vessels of the Lymphatic distribution system are Sen. The Osseous or bony skeletal system to the smallest bone are Sen. The length and continuous structure of connective tissue and fascia are Sen. Muscles are Sen. The integumentary system or skin organ is Sen. Some materials in the body are both Pranavaha and Manovaha Nadis (srotas). In some traditional texts, reference is made, that every single hair on the body is Sen. Perhaps this is where we obtain the historical metaphors relating to the importance of the hair in spiritual matters. Like the story of Samson and Delilah for example.

There is a gross and a Subtle line or Sen for every individual cell of our body. Each of these small and large
connecting vessels communicate instantaneously with every other Sen.

Sen is the Thai word for line. It is the same concept as Prana Nadi (Sans. Pranavaha Srotas – Channels carrying the vital life element or air) used in Yogic terminology and the terms are interchangeable. The Sanskrit word Nadi means stream or movement. Sen are thought to be energetic pathways of the life giving breath in the body. These lines actually form the Matrix, Energetic or PranaMaya Kosha body. The oldest traditional yogic texts are reputed to make reference to the existence of 350,000 lines. As recently as two thousand years ago certain references alluded to as many as 72,000 of these lines. This really makes common sense. If the Lines are how life energy is distributed through our being and body, then every part of us would need a way to receive this energy. So more likely there are billions of lines.

The earliest known references to them in the traditional medicine of Thailand is found on the premises of Phra Chetuphon more commonly known as Wat PO, in Bangkok. This record appears in the form of a series of stone carvings called the "Medical Texts which His Majesty King Rama III had engraved at Phra Chetuphon in B.E. 2375 (AD 1832)".

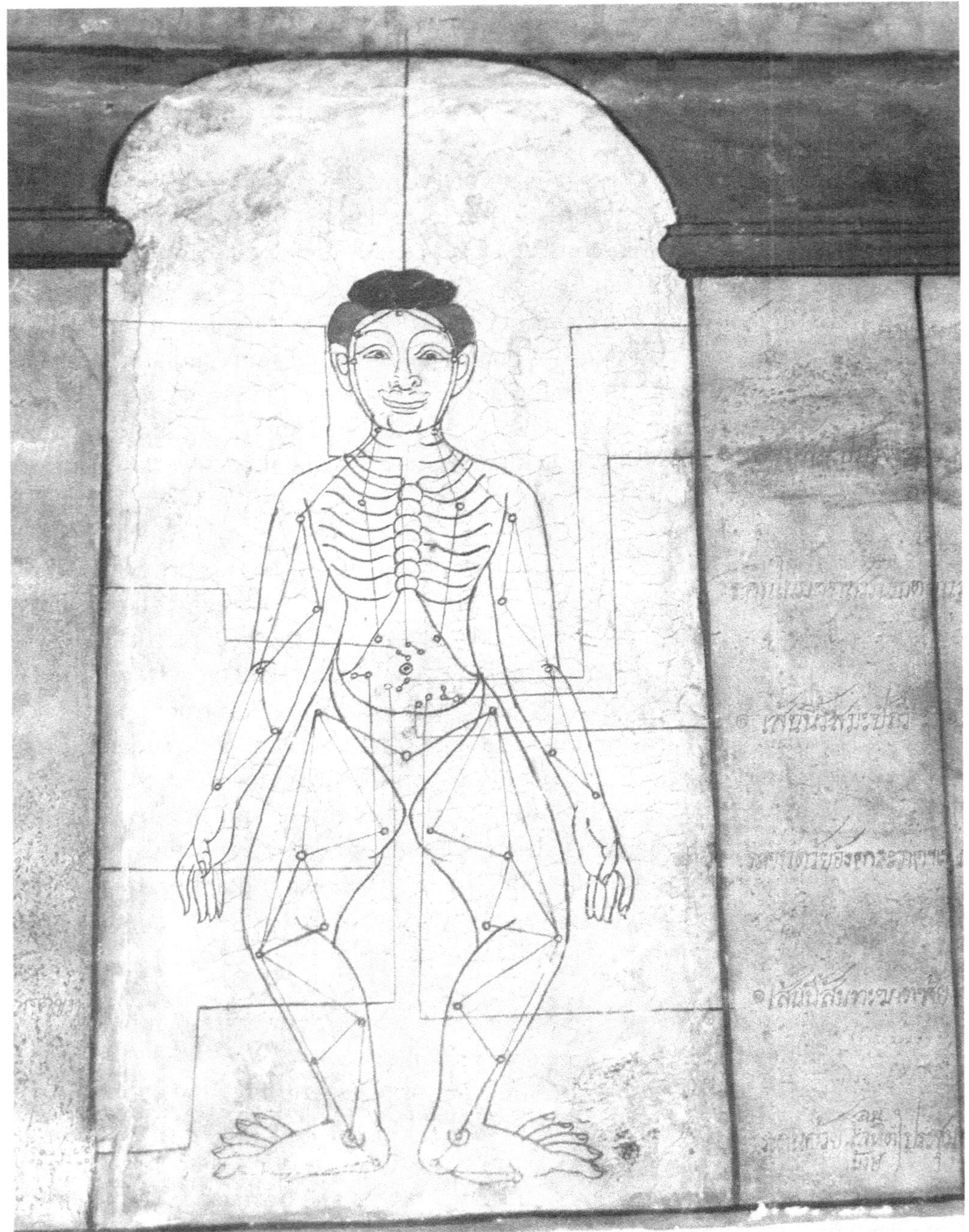

Panel depicting Sen Lines:
Wat Po Pavilion

Sen are Prana Nadis or energetic pathways of the life giving breath in the body. These lines form the matrix, or energetic body. In yoga this body is called the Pranamaya Kosha. The Sen are also charged with the transportation of the influences of the Tri-Dosha throughout as well.

These pathways correlate and communicate with each other. Their nexus of communication are the chakras, major concentrations or vortices of energy. They also flow through minor chakras which are called by many different names; muladra, granthis, knot, lom or wind gates and acupuncture points. The Sen lines move this energy to the various individual parts of us.

Upon inspection, we find many of these knots to be, in fact, the same points used in traditional acupuncture. Many also correspond with the common location of trigger points.

Page 140

In the traditional literature of Thailand, an Indian born Tibetan Yogic Doctor or Physician named Father Shivago Komolaboat, is credited with distilling the theory of 72,000 lines into ten primary lines. The Thais call these ten lines Sip Sen.

The three primary Sen (Tri-Se: Sumana, Ittha, Pingkala) develop in the embryo, and within eight weeks all the main chakras and subtle nerves are formed.

In theory, the ten lines generate, maintain and correct a harmonious balance or state in the body / mind / psyche, or spirit. Chakras function on one level as cosmic windows facilitating an exchange of energy between the human body and the universe. The various lines then move this energy to the individual parts of us. The lines, although responsive to the initial energy or stimulation from the chakras may also function to tune or assist the chakra function in turn. This picture is one of a reciprocal system. Moving, adjusting, stretching or otherwise affecting the lines into particular relationships may, in turn, focus more or less energy or Prana to (or through) one or more particular chakras. Think of a two-way transceiver. By moving the body into the various postures or Asanas, we change the relationships of the lines to each other. This may enhance or focus more or less energy to particular chakras. This concept sees the lines as a sort of antenna. Change the alignment of the antenna and get a better or a different picture.

If Chakras are the the transformers and generating stations, then the Sen/ Nadi are the network and subnets of and for the distribution of energy.

It is said that the most important of these Subtle Sen Lines are the first five of the 10 Sen originating from the Heart chakra. (5.) These energy lines (Prana Nadi) are the Sen representing the various kinds of consciousness.

Five Types of Consciousness:

> **5. Sense consciousness:** Purely Physical, Purely mechanical, tasting, touching, hearing, smelling, and seeing; together called the five doors each of which has its own Sen in turn.

> **4. One's ego sense:** The sleeping self vs. the essence or waking self

> **3. Mental consciousness:** Registering and recording incoming impressions, creates the inclination to move.: Self consciousness in the mechanical sense.

> **2. Storing consciousness:** Mechanism for storing electrical energy

> **1. Transcendental consciousness:** The sen of realization also Sen Sumana: The essence consciousness is weak or dormant in the untrained, undisciplined person. The relationship of these so called invisible lines to the tangible physical body is not so hard to envision. The lines or Sen and the nerves of the autonomic nervous system work together in much the same way as the invisible psyche works with the physiology.

For example, look at the 4th. Chakra Yantra or symbol [Page ????]. Take the 7th. Chakra [Page ????] as another example, it is referenced in some classical texts as having 1000 or more nadi emanating from it! The author believes this to be a metaphor for "the 10,000 things" or "All that there is". If in fact every cell has a Srota-Nadi-Sen or several then the actual number is infinite!

ITTM Sen Lines: Ten Pathways of Vital Life Energy

(Th. Sip Sen , Sans. Pranavaha Nadi- Pranic force lines)

CHAKRA	Number	Thai Name	Sanskrit Nadi	Dosha
#1/6	#1	SEN SUMANA (Core)	SUSHUMNA (Rajas)	V/P/K
#3/6/1	#2	SEN ITTHA (L. side)	IDA (Tamas)	V/P/K
#3/6/1	#3	SEN PINGHALA (R. side)	PINGALA (Satvic)	V/P/K
#3/4	#4	SEN KALATHARI (Core)	VISHVODARA	V/P
#3	#5	SEN SAHATSARANGSI (L)	GHANDARI	P/P-K
#3	#6	SEN THAWARI (R. side)	HASTAJIVA	P/P-K
#4/5	#7	SEN LAWUSANG (L. side)	YASHASVINI (Female)	V-P
#4/5	#8	SEN ULANGKA (Rucham) (R)	PUSHA (Male)	V-P
#1	#9	SEN NANTHAKRAWAT A) Sikhini B) Sukumang	Kuhu	K
#2	#10	SEN KHITCHANNA A) Itaken B) Kitcha	Shakhini	K/K-P

For a more detailed and complete discussion on the Thai Sen Lines see "Ayurveda of Thailand, Indigenous Traditional Thai Medicine and Thai Yoga", Anthony B. James, Meta Journal Press, p.104- 116.

Chapter 15: Shavayatra

Wind Gates Traveling Exercise

Shavayatra, the Wind Gates Traveling Exercise, will enable you to personally experience in a tangible way how flowing energy actually feels! For several years now in various classes, I have introduced the theory of 'Wind Gates.' In both the Traditional Southern or Wat PO style and the Northern or Old Medicine School of traditional Thai medical massage, there is the concept of 'Bput Bpa Tu Lom' or 'Open The Wind.' For the first time I am going to reveal not only what is this, so called, 'Wind,' but, a series of self exercises which will lead to a personal awareness of these gates and the wind which courses through them. This information should prove useful to you the practitioner, as well as to your client. I have always maintained that the Thai arts are practical arts. Even in the most esoteric of theories, we find the practical example. The Shavayatra exercise itself is a variation of the Shamatha or 'Calm Abiding' meditation. The specific object of observation or mindful focus are the wind gates themselves.

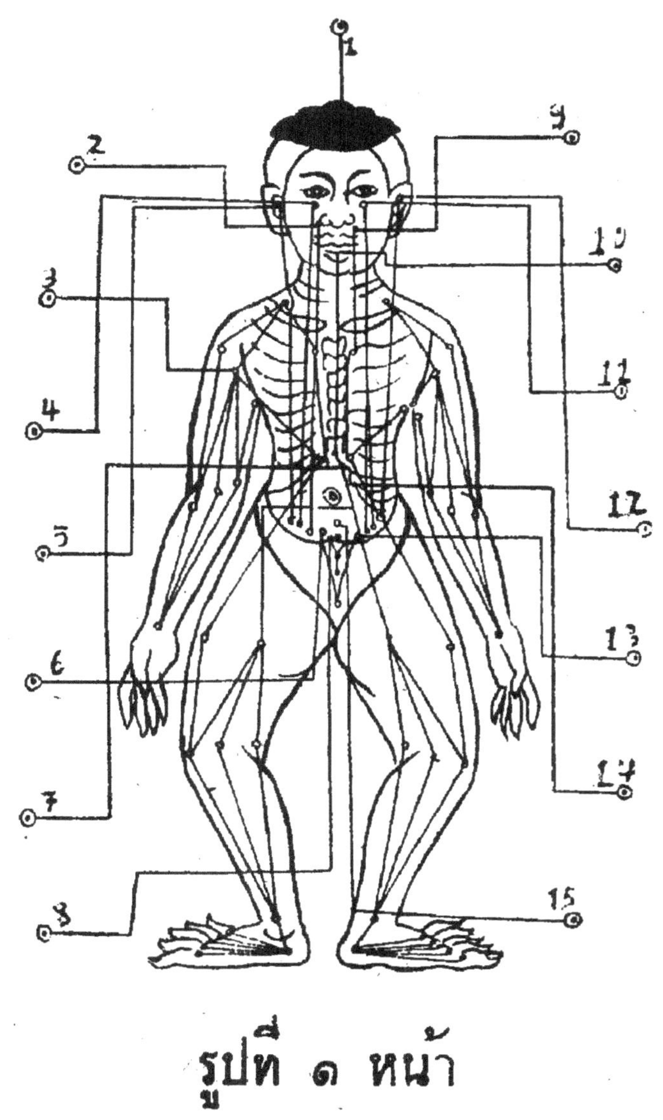

What is wind? The Tibetans call wind Humors; The Thais, prana; The Chinese, Chi; Japanese, Ki. The closest english word is air or breath, however, this can be very misleading. In all of the specific cultures I named, there has been extensive research, observation, thought and debate as to the nature of this thousands of years. Many distinctions of this breath have been clearly observed and noted.

These particular distinctions are for another time, but suffice it to say that our words for this concept are sadly lacking in nuance. So, you can say that wind is a humor or breath, of air, with life. That's still not exactly correct. It would be better to say that the wind is the essence of life. It is life and life is within it. This can be further perplexing as everything that exists is considered to have wind, or breath.

Yes, even rocks breathe! In the Thai system of energetic theory there are seen to be at least ten different kinds or types of Prana or Wind. These various Pranas have distinctive and unique properties and functions. They are considered to have specific areas of responsibility and relate to the function and distribution of Chakric energies. In order to fully appreciate the nature of winds in the body, it is good to understand a little of Chakra theory and theory of Sen (Prana Nadi.) In the traditional view, we begin with a singularity of wholeness; One point of light. This light refracted in the consciousness of the material world is diffused or seen as a spectrum of light and the centers of their influence. There are some references to as many as 88,000 Chakras. Connecting with, and communicating between, these numerous chakras have been described as many as 350,000 Sen or Prana Nadis.

This would make sense as a model if you were to consider that in the Matrix or energetic body, every living cell must have a connection or conduit for life force or Prana.

But this is really too much to consider. One of the many notable things attributed to our founder SHIVAGO KOMARPAI (Jivaka), is the distillation of this multitude of Chakras and lines into a workable format consisting of Seven primary Chakras and Ten Sen, called Sip Sen in the Thai language. All balance or imbalance is considered in one way or another to be related to the harmony or free flow of Prana, wind or life energy within this framework.

Think of this multitude of lines and chakras in communication with one another. If you can imagine points on the surface of the body where they intersect in greater numbers and these points having significant impact on the total flow of energy, you will begin to see. We have something akin to this in our material world that I can use as an illustration. The modern expressway overpass, the clover leaf.

The Cloverleaf highway bypass is a great metaphor. It is a structure designed to reconcile many different lines of energy (traffic lanes) coming from distant and different directions, (north, south, east and west), and to reconcile through traffic with local traffic. One point anyone who has ever been on a structure like this will notice: Traffic Jams. These structures provide opportunity for slow and stagnant traffic flow. It is the same in the body. There are these predictable points where the wind predictably may not be as free flowing as in other less congested areas. Another example used is that of the stream or river. In such a place, there will be deviations in the flow and direction of flow, called eddies and pools. In these places the water may even be moving in an entirely different direction.

In the traditional theory, prana not only moves on or along the surface of the body but moves within the skeletal or bony frame work within the body as well. Where you find an intersection between two bones, (a joint) and confluence of surface energy lines, you will generally find a 'Wind Gate.' Wind Gates are also referred to as Secondary Chakras, as they are the first demarcation and distribution points of the energy radiating from the seven primary chakras. I say generally, as there are many windgates located in a spiral around the Umbilicus or the navel.

All balance or imbalance is considered one way or another to be related to the harmony or free flow of Prana, wind or life energy expressed in the Dosha.

This is due, in theory, to the Umbilicus being, in essence, the origin and termination of ALL of the various pathways of the breath or Sen

Benefits of Shavayatra

There are many benefits to the exercise. As the practice is perfected, the overt effects of aging, degeneration and deterioration are reduced or avoided. The free flow of all circulation, Prana and Chi, is enhanced with corresponding benefits to all the lines, meridians and chakras, as well as the organs and soft tissue. It is said that this practice can lead one to a greater harmony of the opposing energies of the Sun and the Moon, freeing the essential nectar of the Kundalini Shakti to rise along Sen Sumana (Sushumna Nadi.) This exercise may produce much heat and vibration, signifying a release of energy. You may expect to experience a heightened awareness and connection to emotional states. You can definitely expect to have an awareness of the expansiveness of the self as the exercise is mastered. The practice is calming and enlivening at the same time. The heart rate will diminish and the respiration will become pervasive. Fluids will move and you may experience a toning effect on the digestive and sex organs. This personal exercise is a perfect partner to actually receiving hands-on SomaVeda®.

Preparation for Shavayatra

The wind gates traveling exercise may be accurately described in two ways, first as a variation of Shamatha or Calm Abiding meditation, second, as a form of Pranayama or breath development exercise. Rather than focus on the breathing pattern or effect of the breath; the idea is to focus, visualize or concentrate on the Wind Gates or important points along which the prana or breath moves. The aspirant first uses guided imagery to imagine the approximate
locations of the individual points after studying the charts. See the point clearly as vortices of energy or minor chakras where the Sen or Nadis converge and the breath congregates. In a continuous spiral, see the wind circulate in turn through each point. It may help to visualize the breath as smoke or as light.

Savasana: The Corpse Pose

Acknowledge all of the usual conventions useful for any relaxation work. Have a quite place. Have enough time allotted to allow for freedom from interruption. It is better to practice after a light meal. Wear loose comfortable clothing. Before you start have the room warm enough, so that you will be comfortable. Begin, face up, in the Supine Position for Savasana or the Corpse Posture. Allow the breath to settle as your body adjusts to the position.

Remember your greatest ally in any relaxation exercise is the proper use of the breath. Slow, not forced, natural rhythmic breathing will take you wherever your mind can see for you to go. I recommend for Shavayatra, the Mother's Breath. This is a pranayama method based on a seven/ one/ seven (7 / 1 / 7) count. If this is unfamiliar to you, do not despair. Simply breath in fully without straining for a seven count. Hold the breath stationary without straining or locking the throat for one full count. Then, breathe out slowly for a full seven count. Once you complete your exhalation, leave it out again, without straining or locking the throat for one full count. Repeat the breath pattern until it is a natural breathing rhythm without undue effort for the
duration of the exercise.

Savasana is basically moving methodically through the body first tensing then rolling and releasing each part while breathing. First, address the parts of the body most distant from the trunk or spine, and then move closer to the core of the body. For example, begin by stretching and tensing the toes of the left foot and then wiggle them a little to release them. Then tense and flex the whole foot. Follow this, by rolling it to release any tension. Move to the other foot and repeat. Now move up one leg, then the other. Stretch and hold the entire leg up and out as far as you can for a count of five then drop it hard and gently roll it back and forth a few times, not too vigorously. Repeat with the other leg. Move on to the fingers, hands, and the arms and treat them individually as you did the feet. Now lift and separate all of the arms and the legs and tense them as hard as you can for a five count before dropping as before. Roll and release. Move up the torso. First, squeeze the buttocks and then release. Follow this in the same fashion with the abdomen, only after you tense the abdomen, push it out and make it as big as you can, then release. Do the chest, shoulders, neck, and face including the mouth and eyes before moving to the next section.

The object is to see the points more than to be concerned with affecting them in any particular way; to be with the points which represent so many of the correlations between the mind, body, psyche continuum. Begin with number one at the midmost point of the perineum. Focus on this point for a few moments without straining, allowing your mind to consider the space. Move upward and continue with each point, in turn, as you make you way around the course. Each time allowing your attention to remain for approximately two breaths. The first few times it may be a little difficult to remain in a meditative state as you consider all of the points. Each time you notice that you have drifted off track, simply bring your attention back to the next gate and continue. As with all of the Thai forms, begin with your emphasis more on the flow than on the precision of the technique.

For example it is okay to visualize at first the general location of the gate. Avoid trying to be too specific, as your practice will deteriorate into just looking for points. After a few days of practice you will notice fewer distractions and discursive thinking and more of a sense of ease and flow. Remember to continue the Pranayama breathing, rhythmic and full throughout the exercise.

Wind Gates Traveling Exercise: Supine Lom/ Points

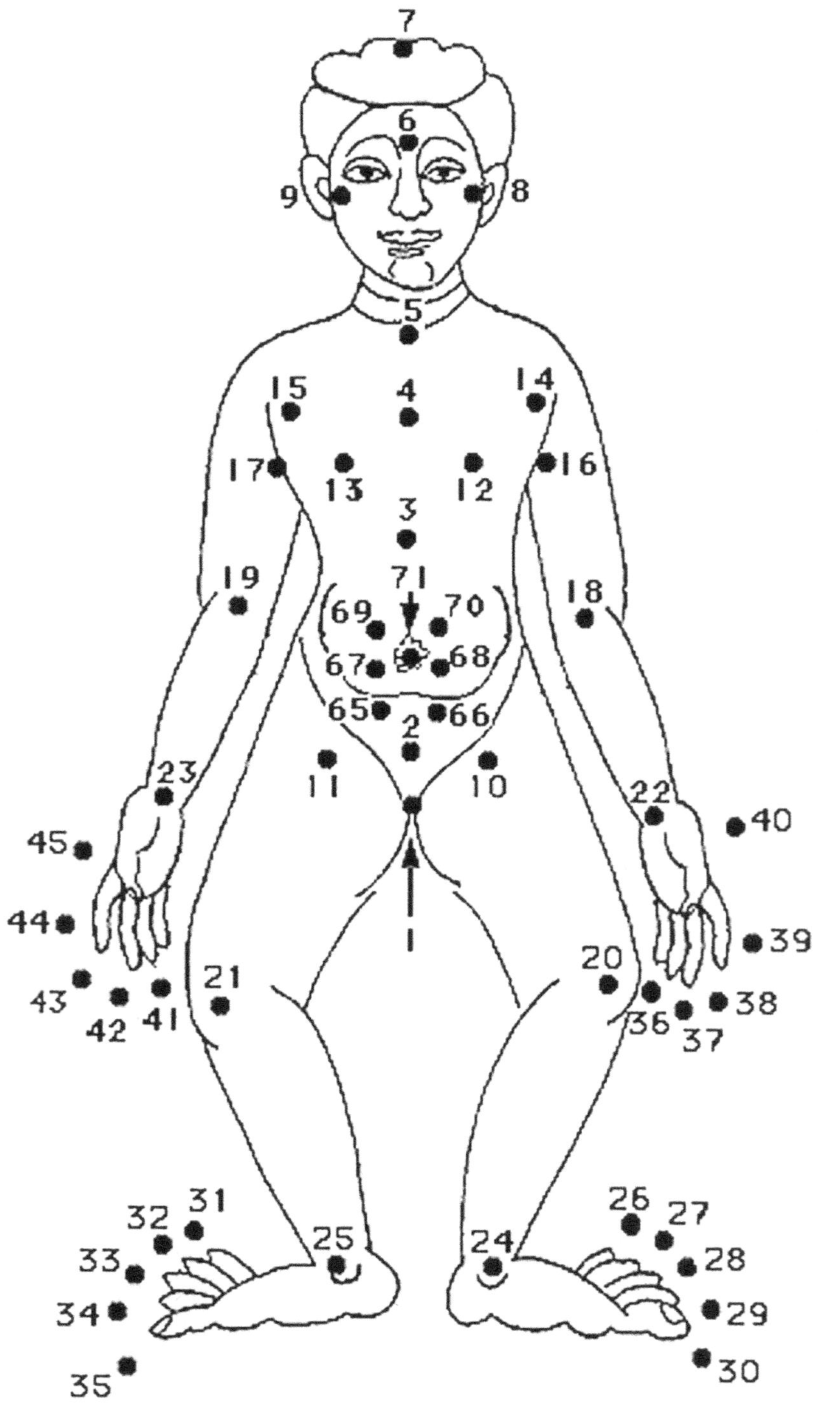

Wind Gates Traveling Exercise: Posterior Lom/ Points

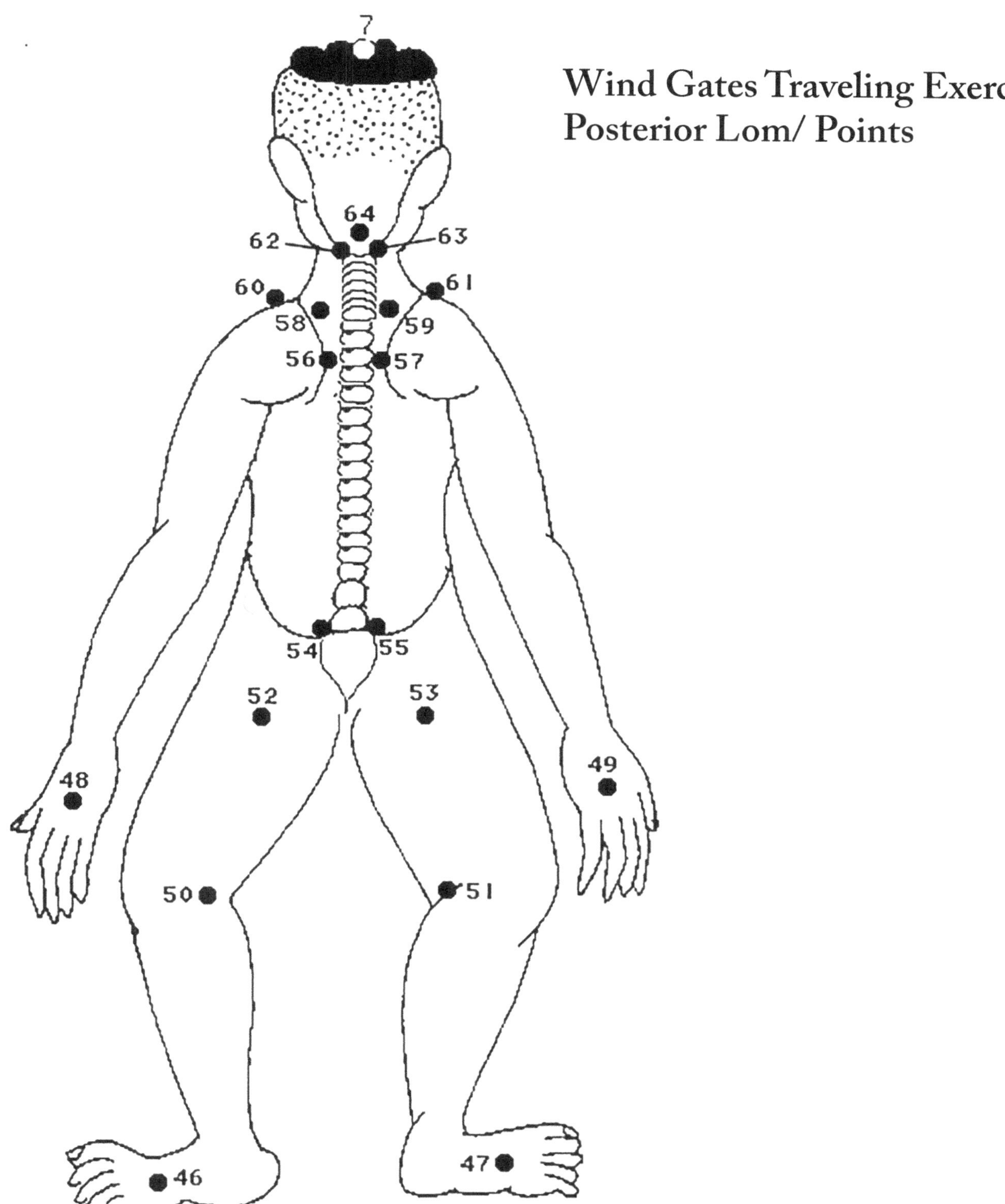

At the completion of the exercise, visualize a wave of flowing energy moving first down the front of your body, then moving upward along the spine, to the crown of the head. This circuit, called the Macrocosmic Orbit, carries all of the waste and harmful energies out of the body, while at the same time raising the kundalini shakti or vital life force awakening the higher chakras. After the wave has passed rest and allow yourself time to enjoy the well being you have brought to yourself.

Description and location of Lom used in Shavayatra

108 Lom, Wind Gates and or Marma Points are metaphors for "All that there is". There are many more constructive points. There is also the theory that there is a layering of fields of influence and paths of prana, energy and electrical fields within the same geographic locale. Simply put, one point location may in fact be many individual layers or points.

1) First Chakra (Mid most pt. of perineal area)
2) Second Chakra (Tan Din... 4 fingers below navel on CV)
3) Third Chakra (Xyphoid Process)
4) Fourth Chakra (Mid most pt. in Sternum area) (Also includes sternum and 36 rib pts.)
5) Fifth Chakra (Clavicular notch) (Also refers to 11 pts. under collar bone)
6) Sixth Chakra (Third eye area, above and between the eyebrow.)
7) Seventh Chakra (Bai Hui/ Crown Chakra point) (Can also be the 5 pts on the crown in 3 lines)

8) L. Ear Lom (hollow in front of ear, above jaw) (Also = 12 Lines and 32 facial pts.)
9) R. Ear Lom (hollow in front of ear, above jaw) (Also = 12 Lines and 32 facial pts.)

10) L. Hip Lom (Anterior, Same as in "Hold the Wind" technique)
11) R. Hip Lom (Anterior, Same as in "Hold the Wind" technique)
12) L. Nipple/ Areola area (Also includes entire breast area)
13) R. Nipple/ Areola area (Also includes entire breast area)
14) L. Shoulder Lom (Anterior, Same as in "Hold the Wind" technique) Front of Shoulder
15) R. Shoulder Lom (Anterior, Same as in "Hold the Wind" technique)
16) L. Axilla Point (Heart, Brachial Plexus) Arm Pit
17) R. Axilla Point (Heart, Brachial Plexus)
18) L. Elbow Lom (Anterior, Medial) Inside Elbow
19) R. Elbow Lom (Anterior, Medial)
20) L. Knee (Mid-most pt. Patella tendon) (Also ST36 outside below knee) Front Center of Knee
21) R. Knee (Mid-most pt. Patella tendon) (Also ST36 outside below knee)
22) L. Wrist (Carpal area) Inside of wrist
23) R. Wrist (Carpal area)
24) L. Ankle (End of outside line #1) Top of Ankle, between tendons.
25) R. Ankle (End of outside line #1)

26) L. Toe #1 (Little) Base of the toe
27) L. Toe #2
28) L. Toe # 3
29) L. Toe #4
30) L. Toe #5 (Big)

31) R. Toe #1 (Little)
32) R. Toe #2
33) R. Toe # 3
34) R. Toe #4
35) R. Toe #5 (Big)

36) L. Finger #1 (Little) 5th. Carpal- Base of the fingers.

37) L. Finger #2 (4th. Carpal juncture)
38) L.. Finger # 3 (3rd. Carpal juncture)
39) L. Finger #4 (2nd. Carpal juncture)
40) L. Finger #5 (Thumb, 1st. carpal: Point "Hoku")

41) R. Finger #1 (Little finger)(5th. Carpal- Base of the fingers.)
42) R. Finger #2 (4th. Carpal juncture)
43) R. Finger # 3 (3rd. Carpal juncture)
44) R. Finger #4 (2nd. Carpal juncture)
45) R. Finger #5 (Thumb, Point "Hoku")

46) L. Bottom of feet (Kidney reflex pt.) (Also includes pts. on 5 lines and 5 Arch Points)
47) R. Bottom of feet (Kidney reflex pt.) (Also includes pts. on 5 lines and 5 Arch Points)
48) L. Palm Lom (Palm Chakra pt.)
49) R. Palm Lom (Palm Chakra pt.)

50) L. Knee Lom (Mid Posterior Knee) (Also ST36 outside below knee) Back of knee
51) R. Knee Lom (Mid Posterior Knee) (Also ST36 outside below knee)

52) L. Prone Gluteal pt. (PIIS) Gluteal fold and upper thigh
53) R Prone Gluteal pt. (PIIS)

54) L. Low Back (SI) (Also 3 posterior hip pts.) 3 low back points.
55) R. Low Back (SI) (Also 3 posterior hip pts.)

56) L Mid back (Low scapula) (Also includes 5 pts- Lateral Scapula)
57) R Mid back (Low scapula) (Also includes 5 pts- Lateral Scapula)

58) L. Upper Back (Top inside corner, scapula) (Also includes 5 pts- Post. Scapula)
59) R. Upper Back (Top inside corner, scapula) (Also includes 5 pts- Post. Scapula)

60) L. Top of shoulder (Mid upper, Trapezius) (Also includes 5 pts- Super Scapula)
61) R. Top of shoulder (Mid upper, Trapezius) (Also includes 5 pts- Super Scapula)

62) L. Cranial Base pt. (Also includes 5 pts to over the ear) Crescent over ear
63) R. Cranial Base pt. (Also includes 5 pts to over the ear)

64) Occipital pt. (Base of cranium) (Also 5 pts. from base to Seventh Chakra pt.) GV back of head

65) R. pt. #1 Small Circle (1 cun below navel, 1/2 width of thumb lateral of centerline) (pt. #5 south)
66) L. pt. #2 Small Circle (1 cun below navel, 1/2 width of thumb lateral of centerline) (pt. #6 south)
67) R. pt. #3 Small Circle (1.5 times width of thumb, lateral of navel) (pt 3a & b, south)
68) L. pt. #4 Small Circle (1.5 times width of thumb, lateral of navel) (pt 4a & b, south)

69) R. pt. #5 Small Circle (1 cun above navel, 1/2 width of thumb lateral of centerline) (pt. #1 south)
70) L. pt. #6 Small Circle (1 cun above navel, 1/2 width of thumb lateral of centerline) (pt. #2 south)

71) Navel (Umbilicus)

72) Big Circle #1 Low right side (Clockwise)
73) Big Circle #2
74) Big Circle #3
75) Big Circle #4
76) Big Circle #5
77) Big Circle #6
78) Big Circle #7
79) Big Circle #8
80) Big Circle #9

81) R. 3 Hip pts. (pt. #1)
82) R. 3 Hip pts. (pt. #2)
83) R. 3 Hip pts. (pt. #3)

84) L. 3 Hip pts. (pt. #1)
85) L. 3 Hip pts. (pt. #2)
86) L. 3 Hip pts. (pt. #3)

87) L. Pt. #1 (5 Arch Points)
88) L. Pt. #2
89) L. Pt. #3
90) L. Pt. #4
91) L. Pt. #5
92) R. Pt. #1 (5 Arch Points)
93) R. Pt. #2
94) R. Pt. #3
95) R. Pt. #4
96) R. Pt. #5
97) L. Foot Chakra (In front of heel)
98) R. Foot Chakra (In front of heel)
99) L. Palm Chakra
100) R. Palm Chakra

101) to 108) = Extra face, shoulder, hip etc...

Please note: this list is considered complete and includes all of the primary points from the Wat Po Epigraphies and the Buddhai Sawan lineage. However, it is just a guide for practice and for meditation. There is some slight variation in exact numbers of Lom. Keep in mind also according to a Shivago legend recounted by the late grand master Aachan Sintorn of Chiang Mai... there are many more, literally infinite lom.... as many or more than there are Nadii and Sen!

The signals and information relayed and sent to and from the Chakra and Lom system completely determines our inclinations, moods, state of mind etc. This determines or at least strongly influences our predispositions to react in certain and even predictable ways to every kind of event. If you want to know what your mind was like in the past look at your body now. If you want to know what your body will be like in the future look at your mind now.

Appendix # 1: What is SomaVeda Integrated Traditional Therapies®?

Somaveda Integrated Traditional Therapies® is a system of religious therapeutics, wellness, health, sacred healing, way of life and martial arts. It is based on the integration of traditional therapeutic and healing sciences and systems of both Eastern and Western origin. The ancient and modern systems which form the basis of SomaVeda® are from several different countries and cultures such as Thailand, India, China, Tibet, Philippines, Indonesia, Malaysia, Japan and the Americas. The most important category of contribution to SomaVeda® Thai Yoga is that of the Thai Traditional Ayurvedic Medicine, Indigenous Traditional Thai Yoga and Thai Traditional Medical Massage from the Buddhai Sawan, Buntautuk, Wat Po, Anantasuk, UTTS (Union of Thai Traditional Medicine Society) and Lek Chaiya traditional schools. In particular the basis of its primary techniques are the Royal and Northern branches of Thai Traditional Medicine (TTM).

These various systems themselves forming subsets of practice in SomaVeda® are taught initially in the most strict form as originally learned from those schools by Aachan Dr. James. These systems form the working technical basis for the techniques of SomaVeda®. Additional influences of Traditional Chinese Medicine (TCM), Classical Indian Ayurveda, Western Naturopathy/ Nature Cure (ANMA), Monastic Medicine (Eastern Orthodox Catholic- Chaldean-Syrian Rite: SMOKH; Priory of Saving Grace), Traditional Japanese Shiatsu (Phipps, Miyasaki, Yamamoto) and Native American Medicine practices of the Native American Indigenous Church (NAIC) are the key therapies which are integrated into SomaVeda®.

Traditional energetic based systems such as TCM, TTM, Homeopathy, Native American Medicines and Western Medicines such as Allopathy, Osteopathy, Psychology etc. have long been portrayed as being completely at opposition with one another. This has been basically true to the present, however, it is now possible for forward thinking individuals to beat the swords we have been using to denigrate and compete with each other into the plow shares which will create the optimum environment for many types of healing experience for our clients through the vehicle of traditional religious therapy and therapeutics.

As we move away from a place where the definition of wellness and health is the "absence of disease", we will explore a model which portrays the patient as a whole. Spirit, Mind and Body cannot be taken or considered as separate unrelated parts. We separate these three components only as a mental exercise, for in reality they are one. They are variations in perspective more or less evident as one looks at a person from different angles of viewpoint and prejudice. Their functions and existence overlap and are interdependent, synergistic and sympathetic to a degree such as we only begin to suspect.

The Spirit, Mind and Body working together create the instrument by which our very soul (Sans. Atman) is manifest and able to interact and to communicate with the material world and the universe of which we are a part. In oriental medicine humans are described as being "conduits" between the twin powers of the Celestial influences and energies of Heaven and the terrestrial influences and energies of the Earth. We are how the Heavens feel wet grass between the toes and how the earth sees the stars. Native Americans simply say

"Mitakoe Oyasin" (Lakota), "we are all relatives". This infers we are living constituents of all life and related to all life in some way.

It is only when we begin to see the energetic potential and its physical manifestations expressed, that we are "seeing" the real person. There is no such thing as a body apart from the energy and vitality which animates and communicates through it. The Tibetans say our spirit, mind and body is "a perfected manifestation" of our consciousness. Take a corpse for example. No matter how intact, whole or complete, we find the semblance of a live person in merest form only. The corpse bares a superficial resemblance which diminishes immediately and continues to diminish until the corpse returns to the earth from which it was originally borrowed. We cannot isolate any of the various qualities and energies which live humans manifest apart from the physical body.

We call these qualities "Life", and traditional healing medicines have sought to define the nature of this Life force as various energies and qualities of spirit.

The Vehicle of Life

In the creation of this new and vital way of health, we will focus on the body as a dynamic vehicle with qualities of life and spirit which create a matrix of energy. This matrix of energy encourages matter to coalesce in a particular way. The end result of this is the manifestation of a human being with various attributes evidencing that which makes it up. What makes up the Stress Adaptive Human Biological Transformational Machine (living human body)?

1. Shen: The spiritual essence of being. This is the fundamental or vital elixir which calls forth for the creation of life, ultimately manifesting as men and women. The soul.

2. The Matrix Body: Existing as a pure energy field. A field with characteristics common to electromagnetic energy, but of a suspected, yet to be defined frequency. This Matrix Body is the energetic framework which our visible body emulates. I say yet to be or undefined frequency, because the matrix body, per se, is governed by properties of vibrations, and as such has universal qualities exceeding the limitations of time and space as we commonly know it. Astrology for example is an attempt to reconcile the observance of these universal properties. The construction of this Matrix Body has been better known and described in man's history than in recent times. For example, in the ancient Indian Sanskrit language, the word for "Prayer" can literally be defined as many as 64 different ways. The vocabulary to even describe sublime principles is lacking in the west. Perhaps to paraphrase Lao Tsu, from the "Dao De Jing" commonly called the "Tao", "language cannot encompass, all that there is". However we do have some information and there have been left for us clues. With these clues and traditional teachings we use our own intuitions as the ancients did, as well as our modern intelligence to reinvent, co-create the present understanding. We bring the "Science of Life" to the knowledge and awareness of mankind at a time when it is most needed.

Chi or Prana are the qualities we most associate with the Matrix Body. The medium, qualities and elements associated with the manifestation of Chi and Prana are the energetic anatomy and physiology of Meridians, Sen, Thai Lom/ Prana Nadi, Chakra, Acupoints/ Marma, Channels, vessels, Five Elements, Yin/ Yang and the like.

3. The M.E.I.S. Body: The Mental, Emotional, Instinctive and Sexual body. The MEIS body is created out of the interaction between the Matrix body, the Shen or spiritual essence and the Tangible Physical Body (TPB) (the sum of our material parts) and the reality of the environment in which the triad comes into existence. What we know of as personality and psychology of a person is generated here and reflected in the mirror of the Tangible Physical Body (TPB) also known as the Somatic Body.

More than this, physical reality may also impart to, or communicate through the MEIS body in various ways. The communication is eventually found reflected in each higher body in turn. We say that the Somatic body is the subconscious mind, the home of the personality and the psychology. The Somatic body is the end result of the process beginning with the Shen, Matrix and MEIS bodies interacting with the closest stellar bodies we know of as Sun, Moon and Earth.

On a relative scale of vibrational frequency, the Somatic body (TPB) is the lowest and slowest of the different aspects of the MEIS body. The mental, energetic, instinctive and sexual aspects all act and react much faster.

Each of these different components although part of the whole act within their own domains of influence as unique body entities with their own domains and specializations of activity. This idea also brings us to the concept of "We are Many". We call the composite the "Great" body or "Somata Magnifica". We in fact are composed of many overlapping representations of energy, material and frequency the composite that forms "I" or "Us". This is appropriate, from the beginning of creation our Great Body has been transforming higher vibrations of one order to lower and transmuting lower vibrations of one order to higher.

The TPB is the repository and storage bank for the MEIS body. It is also a material mirror or tangible image reflecting the MEIS's organization.

The construction of the TPB is well understood and documented in the biological sciences and well known through the study of anatomy and physiology of western medical science. However, no current A & P text describes the functions and components of the human body in relation to its more esoteric, energetic aspects. These are the aspects and qualities which more or less relate to the MEIS body, the Matrix body and the Shen, Astral, spirit or essence being of a person. No clear descriptions of functions will be considered complete until all of these relationships are addressed individually and in a holistic fashion. The need is to examine the role of each component, looking for additional clues as to their place and role in the Ray of Creation. The reason for this is that each different body aspect resonates with different universal frequencies. Gurdjieff Fourth Way: Enneagram studies may also provide a resource for understanding many of these processes and functions of the human organism.

SomaVeda® is a way of life originating out of a great compassion for the suffering of human beings. Our belief is that through a deeper spiritual practice and a greater understanding of ourselves that we might in the end be of some value. SomaVeda® is religious therapy in the broadest sense of the word and not meant to be taken strictly in the sense of rehabilitation. It borrows and integrates concepts and applications from the world's great traditions of sacred health and healing such as Indian Ayurveda, TCM, TTM, Native American, and Nature Cure. There is no restriction or limitation to the concept of recovering ground or function that has been lost. We explore breaking the common limitations and boundaries of our existence through the medium of healing work. We come before the seemingly insurmountable walls of our paradigms regarding life, health, consciousness, energy and capacity with a conscious perspective. The reason why rehabilitation of disability, injury or trauma is so difficult is that we do not understand what our normal is. Our views of ourselves are fragmented at best.

How can a science or an art of health truly hope to re-establish harmony, balance and function when these concepts are not understood correctly if at all? Our western science is only just now beginning to admit to the possibility that there might be other less tangible factors in the physical health of a person other than their specific pathologies! This has been understood and there is evidence of this understanding since time immemorial. It is only in the current age of man that this understanding is not generally available.

The very idea of the energetic makeup of a person should not be an esoteric concept. There exists many different likely avenues which are capable of producing, transferring and carrying or transporting the various forms of energy ascribed to the body. Simply look at the equation of the many simultaneous, overlapping and integrated bodies. The ancient Vedic scriptures for example, made reference to "350,000" Prana Nadi four thousand years ago. The people of Thailand and surrounding areas, in their traditional scriptures relate how 72,000 lines of energy within the body, referred to as Sen, were distilled into a network of 10 primary lines. The Ancient Chinese culture produced documents and teachings used for thousands of years, with similar function. They came up with 12 primary channels and 2 extraordinary vessels called Meridians. They also went further with theories incorporating Transverse Subcutaneous Muscle channels (Fascia?), muscle channels, and connecting vessels. All of these things attempt to reconcile direct observation of "Nonphysical" phenomenon of the body.

In one sense, as westerners, we have not seen the forest for the trees. Western researchers have been trying for many years to locate some set of nerves or other mechanism relative to, or similar to what is being described as Meridians, Nadi, Sen etc. One such researcher was Dr. Robert O. Becker MD. former head of research for the Veterans administration, USA. He postulated and actually demonstrated the existence of what he called a DC Potential Field or Morphogenic Field, which would allow for the possibility of acupuncture as a valid concept, even from the point of view of western science.

He postulated that this field operates as a control system through semi-conduction. A phenomena only just now being researched and understood relative to its application to living organisms. Other researchers have put forth the magnetic field theories, demonstrating the body's ability to internally produce electric currents, magnetic fields and EMF (electromotive force). Not only does the body itself produce electric and magnetic fields but there are even variations of fields of varying intensity and polarity relative to specific organs. Western science, which has been so quick to criticize traditional theories and methodologies based upon them is itself only in the last few years developing technologies and understandings to substantiate what the indigenous cultures claimed to know and experience several thousands of years ago. These ancient cultures developed these understandings not using sophisticated technologies but their abilities of intuition and observation.

 We are in a unique position in that at the present time, probably for the first time in the history of mankind, we have access to both traditional concepts, understandings and methodologies and the modern, western science's understanding and views. Not to mention that we simultaneously live in the most precarious time relating to variety and severity of health issues altogether. The watch words and concepts for SomaVeda® are respect for traditional concepts and lineage, complementation, integration, application, mastery, community, Puja (*Th. Bucha*) and compassion.

SomaVeda® Thai Yoga represents an indigenous and traditional based religious therapy. It offers a spiritually based holistic therapeutic approach, a comprehensive strategy of addressing the complex issue of spirit, mind and body, and the Biopathy or disturbance to the proper function of the stress adaptive human biologic transformational machine or person.

Appendix # 2: Master Concepts, Theories, Terms and Guidelines

SomaVeda®: Concepts & Terms

Abhyanga: Partner Thai Yoga with oil. See Samavahana. Also see "Thai Yoga and Traditional Thai Massage for Multiple Therapists".

Acupuncture: Acupuncture is one of the primary modalities found in Traditional Chinese Medicine (TCM), a 3500 year history of medicinal art and science originating in China. First brought out to the western world in middle 1970s as a result of President Nixon's "Open Door" policy. Includes the use of various sized needles placed in the body in such a way as to balance the Qi in the organs and meridians. Other tools include but are not limited to Moxa, Cupping, Scraping, electrically charged needles, spiked hammers and rollers, lancets, Magnets, various kinds of heat and cold applications, herbal science both internal and external applications and formulae. The use of needles is considered advanced and extreme. Dietary modifications and herbs along with pressure and physical therapy (Tui Na) are generally used in most cases with actual needles being for more serious or chronic conditions. It is very good with chronic syndromes and constitutional types of disorders. Basic training is about four years for medical competency. The primary textual references for this traditional form of medicine are the "Nan Jing" and the Nei Jing (Yellow Emperors Classic)".

Acute: Generally sharp and debilitating. Severe or having a rapid onset, severe symptoms with a relatively short term or course. Not chronic. Generally considered more serious and immediate.

Alchemy: Lead, Copper, Silver, Gold… Theory of transformation of influences and consciousness. May also be applied to or with Theory of Chakras. Lower chakras equate with lower alchemy and upper or higher chakras equate with higher Alchemy. Lower chakras relate to terrestrial and low vibrations, upper with celestial or higher vibrations... closer to conscious influences. Alchemy notes the results of the process but is not the process itself.

Anantasuk Thai Nuat: Hua Hin and Lak See, Thailand. Specializes in Royal Thai Ayurveda and Thai Medical Astrology. Directed by Phaa Khruu Anantasuk and Aachan, Moh Nanthipa Anantasuk.

Armoring: As a result of an imbalance or pathology of the mind body continuum, some energy will be stored in a particular region or area, other energy will be diverted from its optimal path of circulation. Over time this situation will become ingrained and habitual. For example when there is a trauma which is localized and greater than the capacity of the body /mind to resolve or cope with, this area and the communication it represents will be gradually shut off from the greater consciousness of the person. The more time elapses the greater the separation or "armoring" which will occur.

Eventually it may be seen a situation where the trauma is virtually lost. However, it is still there waiting to have resolution and it is still very much a factor in the current condition. This is actually a healthy and productive process, I suspect it to be part of a fundamental survival encoding. For example, if the trauma or injury which can not be resolved cannot be returned to function adequately or quickly enough then the body/mind must go on with living and activity promoting the wellbeing of the person, with as little interference as possible. When this process goes as nature originally intended, when things slow down a bit and perhaps there are necessary resources available, then the unresolved injury or issue is brought forward and recovered into the integrity of the whole system. However, if this resting and recovery space is not found then this recovery is postponed indefinitely.

There are evidences to be seen of this process. Energy and circulation should be going through the knee. However, because of unresolved old injury patterns this energy is diverted or thwarted in its optimal pattern of circulation. The knee will continue to work, but not well and eventually will develop a tendency toward weakness and or injury. This is the body's way of trying to bring attention to the affected body part. And that makes what we call armoring. You can have entire regions of the body armored. e.g. the whole body from the waist down. Another characteristic of armoring is that it is in layers, as it is discovered and attention brought to bear release will not be all at once but in distinctive periods. These periods of release may be accompanied with memory or sensation relating to the original trauma.

The client may regress to a moment in time, see visual images, smells or have tactile impressions that relate back to the trauma which originated the process. At some point as more attention and consciousness is brought to bear there may be a breakthrough release or catharsis that signifies the barriers being removed allowing the area of trauma to be reintegrated into the whole once again. It is not unusual to see patterns of behavior and repeated trauma locally specific disappear after this catharsis. Externally there may be many evidences of the shift, c hanges in posture, gait, stride, sensitivity and activity. Especially look for clues for this shift above and below the physical locus.

Asana: (Sanskrit) Therapeutic postures or positioning of the body. These postures may be done either in a facilitated fashion or self administered. The oldest and original Vedic texts only speak directly of four or at most five such ancient healing postures. All of the variety found in modern times, literally thousands of individual variations and progressions of variations are originally derived from these fundamental four or five. They are "Savasana " Corpse Pose, "Paschimotanasana" Full forward Bend and "Bhujangasana" The Cobra or backward bending pose. These fundamental postures can be seen literally as the resting or neutral position (reconciling) , Active posture (Backward bending) and passive posture (Forward bend). The next two are variations of twisting and inverted postures. Of course there is notice of the importance of the spine in health! These five postures in aggregate are referred to as Chakrasana or the Chakra balancing postures. Simply a r ecommendation to do these alone was considered effective in balancing or harmonizing all of the primary Chakras. Variants and derivations of these five are meant to remediate, prepare, support or to reinforce the effects and   benefits of them. The list of Asana represent the working vocabulary of the SomaVeda® therapists. There are literally thousands of individual positions and variations possible for all body types.

Asanas achieve this balancing effect in the Chakras indirectly by causing or facilitating an emphasis in the system of Sen lines or Nadi. For example: the corpse pose allows equal emphasis on all of the Sen, whereas any posture that distorts or twists the body will allow greater or lesser emphasis on one or more particular Sen over the others. In this way specific combinations of Asana can be used in cultivation of therapy for imbalance or distortion in the energy (Prana) of the Sen. Certain types of imbalance have been determined over time to relate to particular sen lines. The theory is based on this fundamental concept: the whole person is considered to be a conduit between heaven and earth, a pathway or transitional space between the twin energies of Celestial and terrestrial influences. By changing the way that our bodies relate or face these twin energies we change the proportion of them reaching the various sen and corresponding Chakra. I like to use the metaphor of the TV antenna... changing the shape or directional orientation of the antenna changes the quality of the reception!

Assembly: An Assembly is a construct of the body of the therapist in cooperation with the client in such a fashion as to allow a repetitive and precise application of pressure with as little effort as possible. Picture a seamstress sewing fabric on a machine. She does not move the machine around the fabric... no, she moves the fabric around or over the base of the machine. The fabric moves under a "foot" which centers it for the needle. Create an assembly and move one thing to move the whole. No complex movements as "push with this, pull with that."

Ayurvedic Medicine: The indigenous, traditional medicine from India, Tibet, Mongolia, Nepal, Bhutan, Burma, Sri Lanka, Thailand, Laos and Cambodia. Literally meaning "The science of long life". Based on ancient writings; Charaka Samhita Sushruta, Athara Veda and Reg Veda as well as various Tantric literature and books.

Bail-out: Every asana or application of therapeutic pressure has its "bail out " or point in which there is either a conscious or unconscious movement to release or to "Escape" from the effects of the attention, pressure or position or to escape from the internal effects i.e. emotional, mental. There are two types of bailouts that are commonly seen, those done by the client and those done by the therapist. Bailouts are seen as on a continuum from very subtle to gross. From adaptations so fine only an expert and alert practitioner would even notice to literally jumping up and running out the door! For every Asana or therapeutic posture there is for someone a point of distress, internally or externally, when this point is reached, often slightly before it is reached there will be movement to avoid it. It is traditional to not accommodate this. What I mean is it is better to have less pressure or to not go as far as possible, while keeping the mechanics of the application as strict as possible, than it is to follow or allow this deviation to steer you somewhere else.

A) Bail-out by Client: Where we see the client bail is where the action is. Right on the crisp line of transition from comfortable into uncomfortable. Even if by making this transition everyone agrees that the result will be beneficial, there will still be resistance. I am not speaking of the natural resistance to a motion or pressure that would be the normal result from a trauma as in "its broken and does not go that way". I am speaking of a more subtle characteristic as in "this is new territory", I have not been here before and don't know what to expect", There be dragons past this point!

Sometimes the bailout is a reflection that the client has not really given their permission for the interaction to occur. For example they may have submitted to the therapy externally, but have made reservations and conditions internally that you, the therapists would be completely unaware of. They may have made an internal commitment to only allow you to do certain things or to go to a certain predetermined threshold. When you violate these conditional restrictions there is a tangible resistance followed by diversion and finally escape mechanisms. The client adjusts, shifts, rolls.

Sometimes this manifests as the client "Helps". They will even say as they have completely changed the impetus of pressure that was being applied, either to reduce, transfer or to negate it, that they were "helping you". We have a saying… "Helping is Hiding!" Whenever the client helps you to apply pressure or Asana to them they always take you to somewhere slightly different than that which was originally intended. Sometimes their helpfulness ends up in a completely different place, one in which the therapeutic value of the pressure is entirely negated. By noting when and where your client decides to "Bail-out" it is possible to draw a map of restriction, lesion, trauma and the accommodations caused by short and long term disorders and imbalances of the client.

There is always a reason why they do not want to go there! Usually it is related to the problem, all though it may not necessarily be related in any way to what the client may have told you about themselves. It's a fact, clients lie! Both to you and to themselves. They may in fact be dealing with issues and traumas they have not given you a clue of. There may be underlying issues and trauma histories affecting their current state that are hidden or repressed. However your directed and focused attention and pressure will eventually reveal these things. The first sign of this revelation to come may be the Bail-out. For every postural application of pressure there is a predictable bail-out. You should know where the bail-outs are for each of the primary postures and be sensitive to when they manifest. In other words, look out for them. You try to short circuit the bail out. This is a kind of steering… like when your car on the highway wants to oversteer or veer to the side slightly and you correct with a little guiding pressure to keep it in the lane. Take this quite literally, as you feel the pressure from within the client to deviate or steer away from optimum expression of the posture, gently "steer" them back in line, on track for that specific application.

At the point of where this can no longer be maintained, this is the end of that particular   facilitation. It means you've reached the crest of their natural range of motion. You do want to reach the crest. You have done them no good at all if you stop short, getting them only to some point where they can get by themselves. "If you only take someone where they can go by themselves you haven't done them any favor. Take them a bit farther than they would go on their own...unassisted." One goal as a practitioner is to make sure that you learn all of the major bail-outs for all major applications!

B) Bail-out by Practitioner: The second type of bail-out is what the practitioner does. These are divided into two different categories. One category is when the therapist realizing a physical or other limitation on their part, simply orchestrates the client in such a way so that they do not actually have to use any effort to move the client. PTO ("Please turn over") is a sort of bail-out for the practitioner. This can be done as a matter of course, or for clients that are really too heavy for you to feel comfortable to move. In fact, you need to bail-out when they are too heavy and you can't get them out--e.g. of whale. You can say, "I'm going to touch your shoulder and push you onto your side. Once you're on your side, use your arm to sit up".

The other category is when you the therapists have either gone too fast, too far or when you have not correctly anticipated the necessary level of facilitation and control to actually move the client well and in a controlled fashion all of the way through a given posture or application. In this case the bail-out is the safest and most expeditious way that can be created or used to get you both back to a safe and neutral place to continue from. As opposed to dropping or dumping the client with unpredictable consequences. There are many known and predictable places where with any given client you might experience a loss of control depending on your own level of experience and control vs. the client's factors of size and availability to the stress being applied. Again this is the province of experience and wisdom.

B.E.T.: SomaVeda® Bio Neural Emotional Liberation Technique... A Somato-Emotional technique affecting neural and emotional states using tapping and asana on Lom and acupuncture points. Based on the integration of theory and works of Gary Craig's EFT (Emotional Freedom Technique) and SomaVeda Integrated Traditional Therapies by Anthony James.

Bodhichitta: (Pali, based on Sanskrit.) Literally a perfect thought or an example of perfected thinking or wisdom. The two examples we use are first Om Namo prayer and second the Metta Sutra. Used by Buddhists for the all encompassing prayer. "May all sentient beings be happy." "May all beings and all sentient creatures who have lived, live now, or ever will live become enlightened and conscious of their true essential nature and free of the cycle of death and rebirth." See: PUJA (Th. Bucha) pages.

Body: The physical body, yes. However, in the traditional way the body is the actual domain of the subconscious mind. Not metaphorically, literally. For example, this explains why emotional trauma can and often is associated with specific areas of pain or dysfunction.

Body Electricity: We are trying to get our clients to be in zero electrical potential, with zero electrical resistance in their muscles. When electricity (Antagonistic Muscle Stress, AMS) is at zero, healing can take place. We have a few minutes of zero activity in sleep. This occurs simultaneously with Delta brainwave activity. A corpse is in zero. There are electrical impedance devices that will scan and can specifically measure the electrical voltage of any point on the body. We are electrical chemical beings... this is actually a way to define us that makes as much sense as any other. There is a great deal to be learned of a helpful nature by investigating this perspective. Dr. Robert O. Becker pioneered this vision in his books:The Body Electric and Cross Currents.

Bottom: Refers to the limit of pressure or range of motion available in a particular point, trigger point, position, or range of motion. There are two kinds of "Bottoms"... There is a structural bottom and a functional bottom. The structural is the hypothetical limitation determined by the tissue density, elasticity of connective tissue and structural integrity of the joints or body segments involved. We could say for example that a given segment is structurally designed for 30 degrees of articulation or range of motion or that a given point should allow 1 inch of depth of penetration...however, the functional bottom is what psychology, pain tolerance and breath will allow and that is quite different. [This is the limit of what a client is capable of. They will bail out when you try to go past this point. We also say that going past the functional or "Allowable" depth or range is called "Forcing" and is considered risky or dangerous. See: [Bail-Out]

Buddha: The Awakened One. The Great Buddha is Gautama Buddha or Siddhartha, who lived in the 6th century B.C. There are thousands of other Buddhas as well. Although they are all considered to be various manifestations of one archetype of perfected consciousness.

Chakras: Literally "Wheel of Light". [Centers where many rivulets of energy come together.] See: Korosot Chakra Astrology, and or "The Chakra Poster" by Anthony B. James .

Chi: Chinese. Vital Air bringing and sustaining life. Everything has Chi and therefore everything has life to some degree or another. Bring energy to the community. Bring consciousness to it. Enhance availability of chi to the community. If you're going to raise chi, it's like raising children. You better guide and give it a place to go or there's going to be trouble.

Chinese Medicine: [From China.] Also known as Traditional Chinese Medicine or TCM. Based on several classics of Chinese literature the Nan Jing and Nei Ching (Yellow Emperors Classic) as well as the Tao Te Jing (Lao Tsu) and the I Ching. Encompasses both Taoist and Confuciust philosophies for health and longevity. The fundamental theories are The Tao, Yin/ Yang, Triple Warmer, Trigrams (Heaven, Man and Earth), Four Directions, Five Elements (Fire, Earth, Metal, Water and Wood). Five Transformations, Six Breaths (Six Yin and Six Yang Paired Meridians, in Chinese medicine all lines are bilateral. Bladder line on left = same as bladder line on right. In Thai yoga theory, lines called Sip Sen are unilateral and unique.), Eight Messengers-or Extraordinary vessels, Nine Dai Mo- Belt channels or Key, Ten Celestial Stems or Yin / Yang correspondences, Twelve Towers or Meridians, 12 months, 12 Animal attributes, 12 two hour periods of the day, 12 Tendino or trans-subcutaneous muscle channels (TSMs), 15 Da Lo or connecting vessels, 27 jing lo or connecting vessels, 81 gentlemen, 365 acupuncture points, 10,000 things... (Ah Shi, Auricular, Reflexive, Elemental, Qiao & Wei Points and all the ones we don't know yet!)

Chronic: Disorders of a lasting and long term duration. Also refers to disorders that change slowly over time or slowly progress in their development. Opposite of Acute. Long term and generally less immediate in nature.

Chronic Fatigue: Chronic fatigue syndrome can be completely related to non-elimination of waste. (See: Muscles and Soft Tissue Pain Syndromes)

Community: Energy imbalance can only exist in a person if it is in agreement with the rest of the person. We are a community, like a chorus, a chorus with different voices. For me to have a headache all the parts of me must agree that headache should abide. So don't focus so much on the problem but on the community. Bring energy, consciousness, to the community. This is based on the theory that "Every part is connected to every other part on some level".

Compassion: Compassion: practical way to manifest that love. A Thai definition of compassion: "the practical expression of love." If you say to an elder Thai monk, "Define metta (loving kindness) for me," he will get up and put his hands on your shoulders. Compassion = ACTS that you do. (Feelings are not of such importance.) You pray for the well-being of all living creatures. But then you go out and find them and do something for them.

Consciousness: People don't fully inhabit their body and consciousness doesn't fully inhabit their body. You can find someone with lots of consciousness in their stomach and chest, but none in their thighs or feet. Or vice versa. The body will shut off an area that is "consciousness challenged" to conserve energy. Energy will stop trying to go through the knee, and will go around. That makes what we call armoring. It is like a phone system. If every time you pick up the phone from a certain room there is a complaint, you will eventually disconnect the phone to that room. [In Thai Yoga Therapy the entire system needs to be connected for healing.]

Corpse Pose: Shavasana is "Corpse" or "corpse like" position in yoga. There are two traditional variations, either supine position or in prone position.

Dharma: Sanskrit: (*Th. Dhamma*) Teachings of the Buddha and the disciples of the Buddha. What is established or right. Used in Pali for the canonical works.

Din: (Thai Ayurveda) Thaat Din: The Element Earth, solid parts and physical substances in the body.

Electricity Theory: Relating to the body as a bio-electric transformational machine.

Fai: (Thai Ayurveda) Thaat Fai: The Element Fire.
Fascia: Soft Connective tissue which runs the entire length of the body. Fascia connects and distinguishes one type of soft tissue from another while at the same time lending elasticity and structure while under tension. Fascia surrounds everything in the body in its own protective sheath separating bone from muscles, muscles from viscera, viscera from organs... one organ from another etc.

Fibromyalgia: A soft tissue related pain syndrome without a specific known cause. Usually defined as so when an index of "key" hot spots or localized pains are evident. These points are usually either active or latent t rigger points as well. However, usually the pain itself is generalized over large regions of the body. Everything hurts. A. had a client who couldn't wear ordinary clothes because the seam would pain him intolerably. A. used "Somaveda® Thai Yoga as an acute fibromyalgia treatment"--which looks suspiciously like Level 1. It worked. This disease is new--only in industrialized places. Causes seem to be: environmental pollution, electromagnetic pollution, and stress.

Flow: The definition of flow: Flow is when you emphasize the transitional space or time that occurs between individual techniques to be as important or more so than the techniques themselves! The hierarchy of importance is: PUJA (Th. Bucha), Flow, Technique. The flow is where it's at - not in the positions so much as in the flow. Think of it as a dance. Seek an inner rhythm in the client, in you, between each other. As you learn to be in flow the thought of what comes next diminishes and is replaced with a simple sense of "as we are now." The Thai Yoga session as a whole is seen as a SINGLE EXECUTION, a solitary therapeutic application or event, not a series of asanas, or string of individual techniques. Without discipline and training the natural inclination is to deteriorate into technique practice. This is also the same deterioration called "trying to do it right" or correct. Flow is not about efforting it is about being. Flow is the higher art. Really focus on flowing practice. Go slow enough that you don't have to stop to figure out what comes next.

Flow Practice: Don't stop for precision. It doesn't matter if you do it wrong in flow or miss a step entirely. You'll pick it up next time through. It should just take a little bit longer to do flow practice than it takes to read it. You'll miss a step in flow but you'll remember it next time because that upsets your flow. Draw the lines. Don"t go "bit bit bit" like a machine gun. Either work the line (doing technique) or draw it (doing flow). When you get to the point of doing what comes next without thinking then you can work on technique. Don't do a stretch while flowing Just acknowledge the position. You haven't done the prerequisite warming (warning) to the body, so don't do the stretch.

Fomentation: To soak or steep with warm herbs in various forms of application. Prakhop Samun Prai or Steamed herbs applied with Compress is an example.

Four Divine States of Mind: The predictable outcome of doing Somaveda® is an increase in love, compassion, joy, and equanimity. The four boundless emotions; (*Th. Promiiwiihan Sii*): (1) love (2 compassion (3) joy (4) equanimity. The successful completion of a compassionate act brings joy. Where there is no love, compassion or joy, there is no balance in the mind. These are support for the pyramid of health. No true healing is considered possible without these and by definition a lack of or shortage in any of them is considered a sign of disease or imbalance.

Ghee: Clarified butter. Used as a lubricant for body treatment and or a carrier for herbs to be used either topically or taken internally. Does not need refrigeration and keeps in good, useful condition for a very long time. Some Ghee remedies are reputed to be hundreds of years old and still viable!

Healing: The highest art of healing is to wish a person be well and they become well. The next art is to touch them and wish them well (Positive, affirmative visualization), and they become well. Next best after that is to work on them and eventually they get well. In our tradition there's no such thing as a cure because no one gets out alive. You die of long life. That's also a terminal illness. We deal with quality of life, while you're here.

Hollow Tube: Visualization where you imagine that you are empty and spacious inside. A "Hollow Tube" for the breath and the energies to move through without interference. Your body is hollow from the top of your head to the bottom of your feet. Your arms are hollow as well as your legs and feet. Nothing is in this space except the wind of the breath and light.

Initiation: Dr. James' initiation as teacher (kruu) in the Buddhai Sawan tradition: He had three days of segregation from social places, fasting, and meditation. He had to obtain lots of incense and flowers. On the day of the graduation ceremony, he made offerings at all principal altars and little ones. (a) He made the required offerings. (b) He asked for a blessing. (c) He invited the deity of that altar to support him. A monk repeated the lineage, including Dr. J. in it, then said the name of Buddha forward and backward 108 times. At the end the top of Dr. J's head (Sahasrara, the Bi hui point) was cut with a ceremonial knife and sacred water was poured on the cut. The cut signifies that you kill or lay aside the old person. The person before and after the ceremony are not the same person. It was not a public ceremony. Only about 5 people were there. (Lopsang Tensin told him it is the same for Tibetans, but they use a hammer. They put a small shiver of wood on the crown and hammer it in. It breaks the skin and cuts the head.)

Intention: If your mind is clear and your intent is straight you can do it completely wrong and still have a good effect. An EKG will register that your thinking about their heart Chakra can get a 30% increase or decrease in your respiration. Lots can do this. (It's the principle behind Dolores Krieger's work.) Power of belief: Try chair lifting! Wright Brothers: What changed so that the Wright brothers could fly? Group thinking, 100 groups were trying by the time the Wright brothers did. France and Germany had people doing controlled flights before the Wright brothers, but the media was better here. See Puja (*Th. Bucha*) pages.

Jap Sen Nuad: Nerve Touch Traditional Massage as taught in the Mama Lek Chaiya Nerve Touch school of Chiang Mai Thailand.

Jivaka: (Sanskrit)(Th.Shivago). Jivaka was an Indian by birth who studied in Tibet. The third generation of doctors under Padmasambhava taught him. Jivaka spent the early part of his life in in Tibet, until he was 55 or 60. Jivaka was the Buddha's personal physician and highly influential of the integration and teaching of Ayurveda to the Buddhist Sangha (Order of Monks and Nuns). Also referenced in Tibetan Medicine.

Karma: (Sanskrit) ["That which is done." Used for that which happens in a life as a response to actions in past lives.] Long term problems are karmically related. Short term problems have their   origin in this life, due to external pernicious influence e.g. toxins. We say radiation; they say evil wind Holding anger, grief, and depression create their own imbalance. Karmic problems are not affected by physical manipulation. Treatments for discerned karmic imbalance are all spiritual: rituals, ceremonies, prayers. It takes a lot more finesse to be able to discern what part of difficulties are from here and what parts are not. That's another reason to focus on Puja (Th. Bucha). What they call karma is what we might call a genetic defect, etc. "Evil" as in "demonic" with intelligence to harm you" might now be called " pernicious." This might be radon gas, radiation, etc. Anthony: "I can affect DNA because DNA lives in the realm of energy and if anything can effect it, focused energy can." [And that's what Thai Yoga is about.] Always do a little Puja (Th. Bucha) when you work with a new person

Kundalini: Sanskrit. Coiled. Kundalini shakti is the energy that must go from the base of the spine to crown in order for a person to be illuminated. Also known as Vital Life Energy or Force.

Large or Heavy Clients: Working on large or oversized individuals relative to the therapist. We cannot generalize too much. As your ability to work with "Big" people, will vary according to your competency and hours of practice and the actual size and body shape variations of the clients you are working on or with. But, here are the general rules for working on clients much larger than yourself: 1) Emphasize proper technique and breathing. 2) Exhale at point of greatest exertion. 3) Do not ever strain! Select and adjust your application of pressure to favor finesse and leverage to your advantage. 4) Use your feet as much as possible, standing, walking, sitting etc. to your advantage. 5) Never try to lift with your arms and back. Always use proper lifting mechanics. Lean, perch, prop, sit, and lever... use gravity to do the work for you. 6) Use the "walking" method you were taught. Both with and without the "walker'. You can do a whole session and never have to use your hands at all. 7) Practice more flow sessions. the more practice time under your belt, the easier it is to work on clients of any size and or shape. Once you get to that 300 session mark, what a difference!

Lom: (Thai Ayurveda) Lom/ Prana: The Element Air. The secondary Chakra or "Gates of Wind" or Windgates. Generally located in or around all of the joints of the body. See "Shavayatra".

Longevity: Taoist secret of wisdom: live long. Sufis say: there are a certain number of heartbeats in your life. (Heartbeat and breath are no different.) Many traditional teachers say that the life span should be 150. It takes 50 years for an active person to become enlightened. So then 50 years of activity in the world after enlighten- ment. Then 50 years as a spiritual being. There was one Thai teacher who taught until he was 112. Then he took four years off to meditate, then he died.

Love: All healing is based on an exchange of love. In the Thai way the energy / chi / prana that   facilitates healing is love. This is kundalini shakti. In the Thai way, shakti is the essence of love. This is the only thing in the universe that can create something from nothing because it is the essence is life. One of the Four Boundless States of Mind (Promiiwihan Sii). See: Compassion.

Lymphatic Fluid: There's lots of lymphatic structures/channels under the arms. This compresses and that's the only way the lymphatic system moves. It all works by gravity and external pressure. There's no other mechanism for movement of lymph, no pump etc. 240 / 300 of the lymph nodes are not palpable - they are deep in the stomach etc. So be firm in handling the body. You want to get to deep layers of the body. (And some parts are armed by layers of muscle.) This replaces rolling on the floor, wrestling, jumping on furniture, climbing trees. Kids rolling on the ground: that's good for the body. It gives good pressure on the lymph nodes. Or getting hugs and being squeezed. Healthy adults in relationships and community will get this. You can compensate if it's absent by getting deep body work. There is little touch in our culture. Does this make us more susceptible to disease? Now there is a whole generation learning that touch is abusive. It is the official policy of national teachers union not to touch children under a certain age. No insurance, etc. It's all about liability. Kids spend more time now with caretakers than with parents and their caretakers can't touch them. You get high after bouncing a few minutes. The feeling associated with movement of lymph is euphoria. (The feeling associated with blood supply is tingling, heat.)

Martial Arts / Healing: Dr. J lived and trained in Thailand at the Buddhai Sawan Sword Fighting Institute eventually being promoted to the rank of Khruu or Teacher. His teachers were also trained in peace, and he eventually took the lessons for their healing power. One day, Grand Master Phaa Kruu Samaii Mesamarn asked, "Do you want to be a master? Yes, he answered. "How many ways do you know to break an arm?" His answer: "I know as many ways to break an arm as there are stars in the sky." Again Phaa Khruu asked "How many ways do you know to fix an arm?" His answer: "I know none." Phaa Khruu then said "When you know as many ways to fix a broken arm as you know how to break one then you're a master." This was disturbing, not a happy conversation for Dr. J. He started to get a funny feeling in his back. "No more fighting. Lastly Phaa Khruu stated "You need to learn how to dance and how to heal. Leave tomorrow morning, it's all arranged. There's a going away dinner tonight." Dr. J had been an adrenalin junkie. He lived on combat. But he found out that healing was a higher form of what he'd learned before. The most serious altercation you can engage in is the altercation inside. The fear you can never confront is your own fear. Dr. J's opponents became ignorance, spiritual deficiency, illness, disease, pain, and suffering.

Mastery: Sifu Bruce Lee's concept, further refined and taught to Dr. J. by Sifu Danny Inosanto of "How to Master Anything". 1) Research your own experience. 2) Absorb what is useful. 3) Reject what is useless and 4) Add something specifically your own.

Maw / Moh Nuad: (Thai Language) Traditional Thai Medicine Doctor. Master of indigenous, traditional Yoga Therapy (Traditional Thai Massage)

Meridians: Energy pathways according to Chinese Medicine. They are defined as the imaginary pathways connecting acupuncture points. There are 72 of them organized into various hierarchies such as the 12 major pathways, the two extraordinary vessels of Conception and Governing vessel, the 12 TSM's or Trans-subcutaneous Muscular Channels, 8 Belt channels, 12 Meridian extensions of the legs, Jing & Luo (Connecting Vessels), Chong Mo (prenatal), etc.

Morphogenic Field: First postulated by Dr. Robert O. Becker MD, former head of research for the Veterans administration, USA. He postulated and demonstrated the existence of what he called a DC Potential Field or Morphogenic Field, which would allow for the possibility of acupuncture as a valid concept, even from the point of view of western science. He postulated, this field operates as a control system through semi-conduction. A phenomena only just now being researched and understood relative to its application to living organisms. Other researchers have established the magnetic field theories, demonstrating the bodies ability to internally produce electrical, magnetic fields and EMF (Electro-Motive Force).... even variations of fields of varying intensity and polarity relative to specific organs. Details of his extensive research and documentation are found in his books "The Body Electric" & "Cross Currents".

Muscles: One of the soft tissue groups of the body. Tension in the muscular system is what gives the body structure. Without this tension we are just a "bag o' bones". If the legs move together (when you are manipulating a client) it is the nervous system or something else, not muscular. Muscle antagonism is why we can't stretch ourselves. A. reached for the hand of a friend. (Friend had his hand placed on his knee.) He couldn't budge it. The guy was just sitting there, as if holding about 40 pounds of weight. No wonder he was so tired--constant work and production of waste. There are metabolic byproducts of exercise. You need to move to get waste metabolism out of the body. So if you're sitting still and generating waste, that's a problem. These metabolites are irritants.

Storing them will manifest as less desire to move. (Student: So the less you move, the less you can move.) This would look like fatigue. (Chronic fatigue syndrome can be related to non-elimination of waste.)

Naam: (Thai Language Ayurveda) Thaad Naam: The Element Water.

Navel: Umbilicus: All meridians, Sen lines, and Chakras begin and end at the navel. Four fingers under the navel is the dan tien. The center to the body's universe. Focus there in meditation that's where you can release chi for your own healing, etc. A tight belt buckle presses the dan tien and sedates it. It is the acupuncture equivalent of immuno-depression and can give prostate & colon-rectal problems. A vessel around the navel connects the line of energy in back of a person with the line of energy in front. The umbilicus is a very important windgate. Some Thai schools do all diagnosis by looking at navel.

NMT: Neuro-Muscular Therapy: First based upon the ground breaking research and experience of Dr. Janet Travel. It was developed into a specific "soft tissue" treatment modality by Judith Walker Delaney, and then popularized by other individuals. Now an accepted sub-specialty in its own right. The NMT is really good, but as you progress more in your SomaVeda® practice you will begin to see some huge shortcomings. The biggest and most obvious is that it will cause you to become a statistic from the very same types of problems that your clients are getting.... i.e. from overuse of the wrist and hands... Also, the proper technique to do NMT work correctly must be carefully tutored and cannot be learned "On Your Own".

There are dramatic limitations on the actual theory behind NMT,

   1) first of all it is impossible to actually "work" all of the trigger points. There are millions of trigger points in an active referral, not a few key as is sometimes given the impression by some authors. The "Trigger points" occur at the precise location of nervous innervation in the muscle fiber. In your Biceps alone there are millions of individual fibers with such points of innervation.

   2) You cannot affect deep fibers directly and specifically from the surface of the body. Why? Because the various layers of tissue, fascia and connect structures of tendon, ligament etc. disperse efficiently the energy. They take specific pressure and "Spread" it around as far as possible. From the body's viewpoint, all specific pressure is a source of irritation and it will try to protect and move away from it.

   3) NMT, by itself, may make spasm worse. It may cause secondary trauma and spasm as a result of the treatment itself. Dedicated NMT treatments, run the risk of hiding or causing more fundamental stress patterns over time. This is because the pressure necessary to cause the "Gate" control mechanism to occur is more than enough to cause the client to go "defensive", they clench, strain, and cringe from the pain.... even as it "hurts so good". The relief they are getting from the "hurts so good" is reflex distraction in the nervous system and temporary. However, the strain occurrence which happens during the treatment can last from several hours to several days. Further complicating a strain pattern. This is why I say, we work with permission and avoid "defensive" reflexes, or positions and pressures, or emphasis which can cause defensive reflex from happening at all. Anything that causes this defensive reaction, shortening, tightening, straining and protecting in and of itself is enough to CAUSE more spasm.

   4) Usually, the results which are so dramatic at first (1 to 9 wks) actually do not hold up over time. (Based on personal clinical trial with over 300 patients carried out over a five year period.) Once you have been working at a higher level long enough you will see this result for yourself. They reappear and sometimes with equal or more insidious nature. We know the reason for this, is that the initial dramatic response is not from "reducing" trigger points as is alleged, but rather from a reflex in the nervous system referred to as "Counter Irritant Reflex Response". This is the same response as when you apply tiger balm to a bruise, or drop a hammer on your toe and your headache goes away. However, once the pain from the hammer blow dissipates, then the original "headache" returns. Actually it never went away! The nervous system in its efficiency will shunt neural

resources to other areas as a direct result of certain kinds of "Irritation". Basically NMT is a form of constructive and methodical irritation (CMI).

Is there a place for "point specific'" or NMT style work?

Yes, there is within the context of SomaVeda®, our treatment principle of "Distal/ proximal". The "Non specific" work is slower in producing external or obvious results. However, in the non-specific mode we are working the "Millions" of fibers, nexus of nervous innervations and nerve insertions indirectly through sympathy and synergy. The point work is in support of this, by introducing counter irritant reflex response to affect short term relief from pain specifically. However, the "Point " work is not the cure. If very specific point work would "cure" soft tissue imbalance, then the master of Chinese acupuncture would have demonstrated this as a phenomenon centuries ago. They have not. They determined that you need to address broad and sometimes apparently unrelated structures and even organs directly through herbs, external applications, and therapy (Tui Na, Amma, Chi-Gung) to effect "Cures". We do all at the same time or in logical sequence. Work as close to the problem as possible without making it worse (defensive reflex or actual secondary injury or spasm) and as far away as possible and still have relationship to the problem at the same time.

The protocol of "SomaVeda® Thai Yoga Therapeutic Day" introduces this concept. The idea is to integrate any specific point work into the context of a balanced treatment protocol which will not only give short term and perhaps dramatic results, but which will effect complete changes in and to all of the invisible structures of imbalance which are hidden or invisible to the practitioner and client alike.

Oleation: Literally to add oil topically, to the surface of the skin including the scalp and inside of the nostrils. (Th. Prokhop Samun Prai). The oil may be used as a vehicle to aid detoxification, or to carry herbs and herbal remedies into the skin. This includes the use of essential oils.

Outcomes: The predictable results from any particular or specific modality being performed, i.e. increase circulation, increase oxygenation, improve range of motion, reduce spasm, etc. See "Four Dive States of mind".

Phanaek Maw Nuat: Royal Thai Ministry of Health, Ayurveda Massage Department.

Pain: Fullest unbiased awareness of what is is always Step One. Where pain is, consciousness is not. And the reverse. Where consciousness is, pain cannot exist. Pain is not the enemy. It is not a dysfunction nor indicator of a dysfunction. It is just a communication. There are many kinds of pain. (Five major kinds.) One kind will communicate "impending possibility of injury." The other four have nothing to do with injury. It has also been demonstrated that the same signals interpreted by the brain as pain are also similar to pleasure... tickling for example generates the same type of signal to the brain. Interpretation is the key.

Past Life: Half the therapy is for this life, half for past life (Karmic Medicine).

Poultice: (Bolus) (**Th. Prakhop Samun Praii**) Wrapping herbs in a cloth and either soaking or steaming then placing on the body. generally used in treating swellings and aches and pains.

Prakhop Samun Prai (Thai): Application of Steamed herbal compress. Can be done as a stand alone application or poultice/ fomentation or as a complete session. There are many hundreds of different types of herbs used in combination depending on specific need. Many formulae follow traditional Thai Ayurveda principles of balancing affected Doshas or winds, heating, cooling and addressing specific imbalance in specific Sen lines as well.

Prana: Sanskrit. "The breath of life". Vital Life Energy. The life-energy that comes in along with breath. Prana runs in the nadis = rivers, also called the prana-nadis. These are like meridians. There are five different kinds of Prana Prana, Vyana Prana, Udana Prana, Samana Prana and Apana Prana.

Pregnancy Therapy: First of all, there are no generalities or specific contra-indications at all! That's very exciting as it means that you should absolutely be working and assisting pregnant moms with your SomaVeda® Style Thai Yoga techniques. How you will tailor your sessions will vary from person to person and the stage they are in during their pregnancy. For example, most women in their first two trimesters may be able to comfortably sustain everything you care to do, appropriate for their particular health and health history. This includes Prone Position and inversions. Inversions are especially valuable as they relieve pressure on the connective tissue supporting the uterus, improve circulation, reduce edema, pressure and swelling etc.

Of course as with all sessions you should use the "Common Sense '" rule of Contra-indications… if anything is risky for that particular client, don't do it. If it is too uncomfortable, don't do it. If you cannot do it with complete confidence, control and support… don't do it! This rule applies with all of your sessions and clients, not just the pregnant ones! In the later trimester clients, you may not want to do the "Prone" position. You may want to instead emphasize all of the remaining attitudes of the body: supine, Side Lying, Abdominal, and sitting. Thai Yoga, when practiced by a properly trained and certified practitioner is suitable for all stages. Pregnancy is not a pathologic or disease condition! Do it early on, during, and even during the delivery itself! Do it immediately following birth and during the postpartum recovery period. Do the Thai Yoga then on the newborn infant. We have even done Thai Yoga on catheterized "Preemies" in isolets with great results!

Progressive Cumulative Release Principle. (PCR): The totality of what happens when many, many points are affected in a sequential fashion. In a typical session anywhere from 200 to 700 individual points are affected "a little bit". This creates an inclination and movement toward systemic release which is profound. This is one of the secret teaching of the Thai Reishi! Instead of looking for just the "right" point, or the "Correct" point… the Reishi taught that the Kwan or essential nature and spiritual controlling mind of the person would make the correction with a little help. This is completely different from the western NMT or NeuroMuscular style of emphasizing the importance of a single point until it "releases". From the Thai point of view, the so called referral pain would still be a symptom of an overall imbalance of the spirit, Chakras and energy lines. The length and many intricate point work of the Thai is to create an overwhelming inclination for the entire support system of the imbalance to go to a corrective state.

Prone Position: Both the anatomical reference to lying on the stomach, face down and to the 2nd. major Kata taught in SomaVeda®. It is also day or session number three in the "Therapeutic Day" protocol.

Puja (*Th. Bucha*): A religious Therapeutic practice of healing using intention, visualization, affirmation and prayer. Puja is the beginning and ending of every SomaVeda® session or service. The hierarchy of importance is: Puja (*Th. Bucha*), Flow, Technique. It is considered vitally important to begin or start each session in the right frame of mind. So much so that the practitioner is directed to NOT touch the clients unless they can do so with a good frame of mind.

" He who would have the better of the end should strive to have the better of the beginning" Michael Montaigne

Five Phases or Steps of SomaVeda® Thai Yoga Puja:
Sit comfortably next to your client. Sit on Left Side for a woman and on the Right Side for a man. This practice acknowledges the natural polarity of the client and follows a traditional form of practice.

   1. Acknowledge The Space: Visualize the Energetic or Matrix body at 50', then becoming denser at 6'. Understand if any space you share is holy or sacred, it must be so for this space.

2. **Seek Refuge (Wai Khruu):** Acknowledge your lineage. You have a lineage, What is it? In their Wai Khruu, the Thais say OM NAMO SHIVAGO, paying respect to three Buddhas - Great Buddha, Boddhisatva, Inner Buddha or Conscience Teacher. Before you touch, know who you are in this encounter, why are you here and where does your energy or connection come from. Love manifests through you now.

3. **Clean House:** Ask yourself this question: Is there anything that keeps me from being with this person beside me, in the best possible healing way, now? There are only two possible answers: If the answer is no, then continue. If the answer is yes, it will fall into one of two categories: 1) Issues which can be handled now and 2) Issues which cannot be handled now and which must be postponed (if not vital). If you decide to postpone an issue in order to continue you MUST handle it when able to do so.

4. **Petition and Prayer:** Sometimes, all we need is ONE PERSON to be in agreement with us for our healing to manifest. Generate the Boddhichitta, perfect mind, perfect thought. May all living beings be happy and free from suffering. May all living beings reach enlightenment and no longer be subject to the cycle of birth death and rebirth. For your client: May this person receive all of the healing and resolution of their difficulty that they are capable of receiving, now. May all of the beneficial and healing energies, which are inclined and able to move through me to help this person, do so NOW. For an example of what is traditionally considered a perfect example of "Generating the BoddhiChitta" read the Metta Sutra.

5. **Listening and Connecting:** Continue your acknowledgement by being patient, to really get where your client is, before you proceed. This will provide a baseline to show you at any time where your client is, and how the work you are doing, is progressing. There are many different rhythms of life or as we say, pulses. Everything alive moves and the record or evidence of this movement, is its particular pulse, unique like a signature. We begin with three primary pulses: Breath, Cardio-pulmonary and Peristalsis. These are gross, physical and pervasive rhythms. Learn to see the obvious before you look for the subtle.

THE BREATH:
1) Are They Breathing?
2) Where is the breath? The breath is always somewhere
3) Where is the breath going? The breath is always going somewhere.

THE HEART
1) Is the Heart beating?
2) Describe several qualities of the heart beat. Is it fast ? Slow? Regular?

THE DIGESTION
1) Moving? Which direction?

Puja (*Th. Bucha*) is actually just a part of a larger practice referred to as Wai Khruu. Wai Khruu is the medicine appropriate for Karmic and Spiritually based disease. The Term means to literally pay respect to three Buddhas or teachers. Who are the three teachers? 1) Great Buddha, God, Great Spirit, whoever or whatever you perceive as the ultimate consciousness or creator. 2) Boddhisatvas, or Flesh and blood persons who help our progress. 3) Inner Buddha, inner teacher or conscience. the innate part of us which knows what is right. Questions about Puja (Th. Bucha): How important is the practice? How long does it take? Are there any contraindications? How many different pulses are there?

Pulses: (*Sans. Nadi Pareeksha*) "The evidence of life". Everything that has life has motion or vibration. Pulses are the evidence of the presence of life in the body. There are many kinds of pulses. The primary ones we use are the Doshic Pulses for Vata, Pitta and Kapha states in the body. There are pulses for all of the meridians, cranial pulses, peristitial pulse etc. Begin and end with pulses. By the end you should be able to feel a difference and--

better--be able to say what is the difference.

Purgative: Also Purgation... Facilitating elimination and detoxification through therapeutic vomiting and enemas.

Rongrian Sala Thaang Nuat: (Thai Language) Tourist Traditional Massage pavilion at Wat Po and other temples.

Samavahana: Pressing and kneading by hand. (Abhyanga or partner therapy with oil)

Sangha: The community of Buddhists monks and nuns who follow the teachings and precepts of the Buddha. Also a community of Yoga practitioners.

Shakti: Sanskrit. Energy.

Shiatsu: Japanese manipulation and finger pressure based on TCM. First introduced by Japanese immigrants and to the west during the period of US occupation of Japan. First training programs in the US taught by Toshiko Phipps and Kiku Myazaki in the 1950's. Famous practitioners include Namakoshi Sensei, Shizuko Yamamoto (Barefoot Shiatsu). There are many styles: Barefoot, Zen, Five Elements, Okuzaki Restorative Method, MacroBiotic, NoDaigaku etc. We don't hold points until they release, as in Shiatsu. We move the whole leg, the whole foot, we twist the whole spine. Not points. The lamina line (Lamina Groove) goes continuously from the top to the bottom of the spine. You don't want to lose continuity. In shiatsu continuity is less important or at least not as heavily emphasized. Shiatsu people press only on an exhale. Somaveda® Thai touches all 600 points. It would take forever to wait for the exhale each time.

Sleeping Position: In yoga exercise it's good to get on your stomach in a relaxed position (*Sans. Savasana*) and let your body relax. Its one of the oldest Yoga positions for relaxation. It is wonderful on your neck. Prone Savasana is one of gentlest ways to relieve neck compression, atrophy and pain. However if the bed's too soft, it's no good.

Soft Tissue: Literally anything "not hard" in the body. Generally not including the viscera or organs. This includes, but is not limited to: muscle, fascia, connective tissues, tendons, ligaments, blood vessels and capillaries etc.

Sen Lines: Ten classic Thai Energy lines or conduits of Pranic force. Sip Sen: #1 Sumana, #2 Sen Ittha, #3 Sen Pingkhala, #4 Sen Kalathari, #5 Sen Sahatsarangsi, #6 Sen Thawari, #7 Sen Lawusang, #8 Sen Ulangka, #9 Sen Nanthakrawat (Sikhini & Sukumang), #10 Sen Khitchanna (Itaken, Kitcha).

Sen Ti: (*Th. Nung, Song, Sam, Sii, Haa...*) etc: Sen line number 1, 2, 3, 4, 5 ...

Stress Adaptive Organism: Human beings are stress adaptive organisms. Our life and everything in it is based on how we adapt to stimulation and conditions... good and bad. Not only is ill health, sickness and disease stressful but all therapy is stressful as well. The trick is knowing what kind of stress is healthfully and consciously adaptive in a positive way. What kinds of stress move or bring us closer to harmonious and dynamic equilibriums.

Supine Position: Both the anatomical reference to lying on the back, face up and the first basic Kata taught in SomaVeda®. In the "Therapeutic Day" protocol, it is day number two or session number two, called the Supine Position Intensive.

Teachers: Thai monks venerate teachers. Anyone who filled you with inspiration--to be like them--is a teacher. You can get to the point where you actually see in front of you the faces of people who got you to be a good person. We say that anything that you believe is true, if you actually act as if you believe it to be true... you learned from a person. Veneration of teachers is one of the processes in our Puja (Th. Bucha).

Technique: The hierarchy of importance is Puja (Th. Bucha), Flow, Technique. "Technique is busy work. It is what you do to keep mind and body occupied while the real work happens." There is nothing wrong with technique per se... just that an overemphasis on it does not address the real or central focus of the work. Technique means "tool". Technique is to assist, to help us give the energy. It is the cart, not the horse!

Tetany: Tetany is a state of full blown catharsis. It's defined as "a condition marked by intermittent muscular spasms, caused by malfunction of the parathyroid glands and a consequent deficiency of calcium." This is a spontaneous release of pressure, an unwinding. It is unpredictable and somewhat a rare occurrence. Be warrior-like, un-threatened. The biggest component is their fear. Encourage the client to relax and keep breathing. Keep a hand on their stomach. Tell them. "STAY." "Bill, listen to me. Take a big breath now. Under my hand." They may hyperventilate. When the tetany is over, the session is over. You're done. Keep them warm as it tapers off. Stay with them until they get completely normal. They'll probably go to sleep.

Thaad Tan Sii: (Thai Ayurveda) The four Vedic Elements of Din (Earth), Naam (Water, Fai (Fire) and Lom (Air)

Three: Three Refuges: Buddha, Dharma, Sangha. or Three Buddhas: Great Buddha, Living Buddhas, Inner Buddha. The Law of Three relates the precept that there are three fundamentally   different principles or forces involved in the creation process of all that there is. These forces are 1) Active principle, 2) Receptive Principle and 3) Reconciling or Neutral principle. First force initiates, Second force sustains and Third force results or is the consequence of the interaction of the first two, and becomes the first force in the next division. Three Doshas: Vata, Pitta and Kapha. Yin, Yang and the line between the two.

Tibetan Medicine: There is very little in the way of literature regarding Traditional Thai Medicine. According to Aachan Sintorn there is only one original codex of the ancient Thai medicine. Primarily it was passed down by oral tradition. But look up Tibetan Medicine, especially the Vajrayana Tantra School of Tantric Medicine. Tibetan and Ayurvedic differ. Tibetan and Ayurvedic medicine are relatives and very similar to Thai because Tibetan and Indian Ayurveda were the origin of the Thai medicine.

Touch: There is no such thing as an inconsequential touch. Wait for the heat. Always do this. (As you learn to feel the currents in white water canoeing.) You can put a monitor inside the stomach, and can be touched any- where in your body, there is instant change in stomach--e.g. acidity, in 44/100ths. of a second. We don't have any reflex that works that fast. As far as the body is concerned, it happens at the same time.

Toxins: People may be full of toxins like a sponge. You press and they release toxins--get sick, may bruise etc. under the lightest touch. The IT band is built to armor the leg. There are toxins under IT bands. You're releas- ing toxins when you press these points, there are uric acid salts in a cake. You'll feel it, or pockets of fluid or gas. Lactic acid that has accumulated over time. A person could get get headache, nausea etc. Keep going! (This is called a "healing crisis.") You might warn them, "You may experience a headache..."

Transition: Flowing transition gives you continuity. If there is no flowing practice you get poor transitions. Anthony judges by transitions, not technique. "I don't care if the thumb is in or out, rolling or not. You can totally lose the flow and function--it's all in transition." Judging jiu jitsu: Don't watch the fighters; you'll get caught up in their mannerisms etc. Look at the space between them. That's where the action is happening.

Trigger Points: By definition a "Trigger Point " is an area of ischemia with high neurologic activity. Trigger points may be either Active or Latent. They are located at the point of nervous innervation in muscular tissue. They may or may not be sensitive to touch. Trigger points are known for throwing or referring pain and sensation to distant parts of the body. This is called the "Referral Pain Syndrome" Body ventriloquism! The process is described by Dr. Jane Travel as the operation of the "Pathologic Reflex Arc". Areas with trigger points have low oxygen and stored supplies of key sugars such as Glycogen and high residuals of waste metabolites such as Lactic Acid and Uric Acid. They may also have Edema and or other signs of inflammation... but not always. Sometimes the symptoms are that the tissue is hard and resistant (Hypotrophy) more than ordinarily it should be. Trigger point laden bands of tissue can be easily palpated with a bit of training and respond generally well to pressure, heat and cold (Cryo-) contrast therapy. In emotional terms they hold stored up tension, emotion, etc.

U Ti: (Thai Language) Nung, song, sam, sii, haa... (Thai) Point number 1, 2, 3, 4, 5... etc.

Visualizing: Energy precedes physiology. All physical phenomena are an aftermath of energy   moving. Anthony always visualizes before he touches. The touch continues the visualization, both are important and sacred. Visualize: First giving them promi wi han see. Second: facilitate flow of energy. Create a balancing, so areas less full become more full, less empty become more empty. Visualize a class before you teach. Etc. See it first. A. is not psychic but he visualizes as he does Somaveda® Thai. For example, he might visualize them talking about flowers. So he asks, "Tell me about flowers." And they say, "I can't believe you're asking me that. I was just thinking about the flowers in my aunt's garden..."

Wangklaikangwan Industrial Community and Educational College: Located in Hua Hin , Southern Thailand, this college is next to the Royal Palace and was built under patronage of the Thai King HM Bhumibol. The college is charged with developing standards of practice for vocational training for the country of Thailand and issues curriculum by way of direct class and broadcasts to over 163 schools, colleges in Thailand and 11 countries around the world. Under Director Dr. Srinoi Surasak, bi-lingual educational standards for Traditional Thai Medicine are currently being documented and distributed as a formal basis for Thai Yoga and related licensing and practice standards for Thailand.

Wind Gates: Secondary Chakra: (*Th. Lom*) Correlate with the joints of the skeletal system and navel area. There are wind gates - places where pressing down and releasing its energy to spread out, places where blockages can and do occur. In opening the wind: Keep your hand there until the heat dissipates. Then you can leave. Every time we hold a point we expect to feel heat and wait for dissipation. That determines the timing. (One doesn't wait for heat on a stretch/ facilitation of range of motion.) Wind Gates are laws unto themselves.

Yin / Yang: Universal principle of duality in the universe: Light- Dar, Male- Female, Inside- Outside, Above- Below, Hot- Col, Active and Passive etc. in Taoism and Chinese philosophy. In Nuad, Yin is the interior of leg, Yang the exterior.

Yoga Theory: The big difference between Yoga Theory and Chinese is re: lines. In Chinese medicine all lines are bilateral. In yoga theory, no. Ayurvedic: right side line corresponds to sun / ascending energy. Left side line corresponds to moon / descending energy. Etc. There are no bilateral lines. Only 2 of the 10 might be like bilateral lines--samana, sushumna nadi. See: ENERGY SYSTEM pages.

Appendix # 3: Practicing SomeVeda® Thai Yoga.

How to Master Anything:

1) Research Your Own Experience,
2) Absorb What's Useful,
3) Reject What's Useless,
4) Add Something Specifically Your Own
(Taught to me by Sifu Danny Inosanto, developed and taught to Danny by Sifu Bruce Lee).

Somaveda® Thai Yoga facilitation involves a passive, assisted/facilitated, non-ballistic, non-invasive, non-specific natural range of motion.

Passive: The client is mostly passive and is generally not required to expend much effort in order to help them during a session. It does not mean that they must always be passive. With more advanced clients they may be coached into when and when not to help. But in general less is more. If you move you too fast/hard/far, they'll participate and it won't be passive. Tell them not to help, if they are helping. (You'll feel it right away.) [You can check by dropping foot etc.] "Help" is another word for hide. They'll help you past the point they're hiding that needs help. A. tells clients, "The best way to help me is not to help."

Assisted/ Facilitated: We provide the force, the energy, for all that occurs. We assist the client into various asana we do not force. It is a matter of guidance and support as opposed to correcting to some ideal of structure or symmetrical emphasis. For example when we do a spinal twist we get right close to them and model becoming their spine. By being their spine etc. we do the work of their spine without the normal antagonism the client themselves would have under self direction. Much of the client's inhibition to range or direction of motion is due to counter strain or antagonistic muscle reflex. This reflex is greatly reduced or perhaps eliminated by working in this way. "Guided" may be a better word. Guided in a general way. It always allows the client the latitude to do what is available to them to do.

Non-ballistic: i.e. slow enough so you're not throwing the body, so there is NO MOMENTUM. Slow enough so that if I stop at any point, the body stops where I stop.

Natural: We work with a natural range of motion, no more. 99% is natural motion. (We stopped rolling the the grass when we were children, so now that motion may not seem natural.) NO OBTRUSIVE ENCOURAGEMENT OF RANGE OF MOTION. Your goal is to give them their natural available range of motion. To return them to function. 90% OF WHAT WE DO IS REMEDIAL. "If it doesn't work for you, I'm not going to challenge that." Some of us will go out with a bad knee, some not. There is no need to insist that you touch your toes before you go out. That is not a measure of your consciousness.

Non-specific: Like it sounds. Not specific means that the facilitations are general and not designed for specific corrections. For example a Chiropractor will correct a specific osseous subluxation (misaligned vertebrae) in a specific manner. We may move the spine or back , however, if something wants to move fine, if not... then that's equally as fine. Any corrections that occur within vertebrae for example are considered "Spontaneous Corrections". Much in the same way that you might experience a vertebrae moving when getting in or out of your car. Non-specific pressure means not pointed, not with a sharp point or too much emphasis on a particular point. We don't hold points until they release, as in Shiatsu. We move the whole leg or foot, we twist the whole spine. Not points.

General Rules of Engagement:

The slow, slow way is the best! (Phaa Khruu Samaii Mesamarn, Buddhai Sawan). If you have to ask yourself "Am I going to fast?" then the answer is always yes. It's not about time it's about process.

This work is not what I am doing while I wait for my life to happen, it is my life happening!

Michael Montaigne a french philosopher once is credited with saying, and I paraphrase, "If you would have the best of the end of a thing, strive for the best of the beginning".

Springing Energy: or How do you go with the flow?

(1) Enter when invited. (2) Stay while welcome. (3) Do as much as you can with what is available while your there, (4) then leave when appropriate. (5) At the very least do no harm. (It is the same with an altercation. There is a way to get into it, stay in it, and get out intact.)

1) Enter when invited: Always do Puja (*Th. Bucha*) first. We do not assume that just because our client is on the mat, that this means we have permission to go to work. We pause at the threshold and knock politely and wait a moment or two if necessary to connect and acknowledge our permission. If this sense does not come or is not given then the session should not continue. Never force someone into therapy as they are always a partner in their own healing process. Do not presume to know better what is really right for your client. This kind of presumption leads to the arrogance typical of western medicine for example. The patient can be confused, treated invasively against their intuition and wishes or contrary to their intentions or permissions as "the doctor knows best!" However, when the side effects or untoward consequences (iatragenic) occur, the therapists or doctors wash their hands of responsibility and dump back on the patient responsibility that had been removed from them in order to "help" them.

2) Stay while welcome: Sticky concept i.e. "sticky hands". Pay attention and see that often you come to a point where the client stops receiving or decreases or withdraws their permission so to speak. Work past this point may well be counter productive. Acknowledge the shift in the energy and conclude that session. Whatever was not finished is suitable for the next day.

3) Do as much as you can with what is available: We are always wishing--well, if I could only move that leg one more inch. Create an acceptance of what is in front of you even while efforting. If it changes that's OK, and if it doesn't change, that's OK, too. Get good at evaluation--knowing what's available. Go in with a positive attitude, yes, but not with false expectations. Whatever you can work with, in the sense of without restraint or inhibition from the client, then do so. I once did a full body reflexology session on a burn victim's right foot. It took an hour! Consider the saying to: "Make Hay While the Sun is Shining".

4) Then leave when appropriate: It is as useful to know when to stop or come to some completion as it is to know what is the correct course of treatment! Some of the harm that comes from western medical practices is a result of continuing treatments after their beneficial period is complete. Once it is no longer beneficial it may in the normal course of things become harmful. When you're done, you're done... Let it go!

5) When physical techniques or therapy fails try energetic and emotionally based approaches.

6) At the very least Do No Harm! Practice Ahimsa. This is the original Hippocratic Oath. Endeavor and always make every reasonable effort that at the very least you leave the client in no worse shape than that in which you found them.

Page 172

Appendix # 4: Technique Pages

The hierarchy of importance is: Puja (*Th. Bucha*), Flow, Technique.

Finesse Principle: Less effort, more result; that's the principle. Use the least effort you can for the maximum result.

Avoid Strain or Overexertion: We know that strain causes pathologic distortion in the nervous system. For example, strain is a precursor to spasm, spasm causes and is symptomatic of ischemia (low oxygen), and sugar depletion (Glycogen) and causes the nervous Reflex Arc to distort (Pathologic Reflex Arc). This distorted reflex arc can result in referral symptoms. Referral symptoms are where the signal from the brain to the referring area is so distorted that you are tricked into feeling and thinking that it is coming from somewhere else. Symptoms range from numbness and tingling to outright pain. Now, if you strain the tools that you are actually using to palpate and evaluate pressure with, then in proportion to the level of strain or strain induced spasm you will lose accuracy and sensitivity. So, basically, the more you strain, the less sensitivity you have. The more condensed you are, the less sensitive you are. So, open up as you work, be more flowing, be more open. When working allow yourself to be expansive, to take up space as you move. Relax, you'll discern and flow better.

Avoid ballistic motion: Bouncing, flinging, throwing, jerking, hard dropping and the like.

Avoid compounding the motion: Imprecise angles of pressure application

Avoid compounding the momentum: Run away acceleration

All movements are smooth and seamless: No jerking or abrupt motions. Think of the grace and deliberateness of a professional dancer and emulate their style and delivery. Dancers are quite economic as they know the real cost of overexertion and poor economics of energy usage.

Points may be more available under tension: Work the same points treated when relaxed in positions where they are under tension, notice the difference.

Do one whole side first: Then do the other side, not knee-knee, foot-foot, etc. The Thai way is to do one side at a time. Thai idea: the left side does not know the other side of the body. A different part of the brain, etc.

HOW TO DO:

Face the area you work on with your hara. Whenever you can, frame your area with your knees. Work between your legs. Facing the area gives you optimal addressment of what's before you. Always position the body for optimal addressment. Anything in front of you is in your power zone. So frame the area. Everything you face, 45 degrees on either side, is in your power zone.

Pretty much always try to keep your arms straight. The more you keep your arms straight, the more energy comes from the hara. The more you let your arms bend, the more likely you are to squeeze, push etc. We are masters of strain and counterstrain... push and pull. By developing a belly consciousness when creating pressure, to "push" if you will, from the center of your being, with the pressure being an extension of your breath, then muscular exertion will diminish for you.

Most energy goes where the arm goes. So get thumb and arm pointing at the same place. The primary conduit of Chi/ Prana is through the center of the skeleton (Bone Marrow Chi). Visualize your extremities... arms and legs as if they are hoses for water. Where would that water exit from your hands or feet? That is the "Chi" point of the hands or foot. Place the working tool, say your thumb on a line, in line with that "Chi" point or Chakra and it is then energetically, and mechanically supported. The pressure you then apply will not cause you to strain. Remember "Strain Reduces Sensitivity". Not only does strain reduce sensitivity it causes distortion.

Work toward the center of the body. Apply force in that direction. Aim toward the center (of the leg, arm, etc.).

Use your weight, don't press with muscles. When you press, the pressure is felt but it has an EMPTY QUALITY. When you apply the weight from your center, it feels FULL. In other words lean, perch, climb to create pressure. Maximum pressure that you are capable of is on a line from heaven to earth. When you are between the highest point of that Golden Thread and the point on the client's body you have maximum effect without effort. Move off of the line relative to the pressure point and you reduce pressure. Its that simple. For example: stand on someone's hands with one foot, it is impossible for you to press harder or create more pressure. Now shift your weight back to the other foot until you are holding it gently up over the hand... No pressure at all! So, you went from every possible bit of pressure back to zero pressure with no more effort than shifting the weight from one foot to the other. That is the concept. Now do this in every position.

Keep your center of gravity low, when the point you are trying to affect is low. Keep your center high when the point is high, so you can shift, perch and lean in to create pressure. The rule is when the line or point is on top so are you. When the line or point is on the side angle, so are you. When the line is high get up and over, when the line is low, put your bottom on the ground.

Lean in with with your belly, not with your butt when you're working these low side lines.

Continuous breathing; Keep breathing as you work. Anthony breathes into every palming, pressing, stretching. His breath precedes every motion. There is no time when the breath is not moving outward. From an energetic viewpoint, every creation of pressure is an extension or the breath or Prana. See your movements as extensions of your breath.

KEEP WORKING AT THE SAME SPEED ALWAYS. Develop an easy rhythm and pace to your delivery. No sharp turns.

When you're going to move the body, just do it. Don't be tentative. Pick things up with both hands.

By putting lots of pressure over an extended space you diffuse their reaction. There is not so much defensive reaction, as if you put same amount of pressure on a smaller place. We have an inborn instinct to resist thorns-- small pointy objects.

The moving hand is called the "live hand." The non-moving is called "receptive." Principle: it's usually the cranial hand that's working. The hand closer to the head. We say "Both Hands Press, Top Hand Travels."

When you work a line you should space the sequence of steps apart the length of the client's thumb. This is referred to as the stride. (That way a tall client will take no more time than a short one.) Client's thumb length is a crucial measure and often makes sense. The length of the thumb, from it's base to it's tip, represents a uniform standard of measurement. Used since ancient times. Consider Leonardo's Vitruvian (Universal) Man diagram as an illustration of the principle measurement being applied to the whole body.

"Jep" and "Bhao" in Thai--more (pressure) and less. Allow clients to give you guidance on your current pressure.

In the rolling thumb, it's the WRIST that does the RELEASE. You always push away from yourself with reinforced rolling thumb. You don't actually move your thumbs. You press in and then roll by raising your wrists. So it's press in, then roll up, then come out. You come out a different place than where you went in.
Page 174

Of all the muscles you do lifting with i.e. the gluts. are most important. If you can get the gluts. involved in any lift you can lift many times more with less effort or strain. Get your butt involved in lifting. We call the "derriere"/ rear end your "pressure adjustment mechanism." or WAM... "Weight Activation Mechanism")

"Squat before you bend" is good mechanics. The squat is a common position in Asia--for eating, reading, waiting for the bus, rocking the baby, etc.

In yoga exercise it's good to get on your stomach in a relaxed position and let your body let go, one of gentlest ways to relieve neck tension. (But it's good not to sleep on your stomach. In a soft bed it's no good.)

You start to see your hands differently. When you see what your hands are capable of, it makes you be more careful of them. Anthony is careful in what he touches, sees his hand as a loaded gun, with viable energy at all times.

The thinner the mat, the better. The thicker the mat, the more sloppy.

The optimal height of the table is such that you can set your thigh on it easily, without having to "Hike" your hip and leg to do so.

You'll get sore from doing work, but it will go away. You must do it a few times a week. Reeducate your body.

It takes 2 years to get acclimated/ conditioned to giving Thai Yoga Therapy.

For Yourself:

Do postural correction (on yourself) every time you change anything. Straighten up. (Dr. J does it many times in a therapy session.)

Put more attention on transitions. It's your chance to do movements for yourself, stretch your leg and back when you can. Engage your whole body as you work. Make corrections or movements while working that are just for you or your comfort. For example: You can put your head back when pulling in the lower leg position in Sao Nong (Bent Raised Knee Position).

General Caveats:

Never leave a person in a rotated position to get out of it himself. You'll set up antagonistic muscle responses --you can injure them. If you get someone in a good rotation and leave them, they can pinch a nerve. They did not get into the position of their own volition and their body doesn't know how to get out. For the nervous system it's as if they've been teleported into the position. We keep track: what we did to get in, we do to get out--like following a string in a cave.

Never put any direct pressure on a joint.

Don't put pressure on them while they're holding their breath.

 "Blow out" is better than saying "breathe." Get them to blow out on the greatest point of exertion. Same for giver.

Walk around them, not over them. It's more respectful. Avoid, hopping, skipping, jumping, running, pinching, poking, jabbing, jerking or other mechanical, disruptive and potentially hazardous types of movement around the client.

Avoid anything that causes acute immediate pain. Unless you are removing a splinter! Avoid anything that causes a SHARP, POINTED pain. GENERAL PAIN IS FINE. If you can't release the pain quickly--if it doesn't stop in 10-12 seconds of letting go, back out.

We work with natural range of motion, no more. We don't hold stretches or add to them in this SomaVeda® way. Never force a stretch. You can't say, "Take them as far as you can." Because you don't know their sensitivity. BUT: If you do everything with caution and slowly you can do most anything.

After the Session

The effect of a Somaveda® Thai Yoga is felt over the next four days. Wait 4-5 days, call them and talk to them. They'll tell you "story of my life over last 4 days" (Don't just ask how the Somaveda® Thai Yoga session was.) Listen to the clients story of recovery "Oh things are just the same. By the way I've been diagnosed since a kid as a chronic insomniac and funniest thing, last 3 days I've been sleeping and I'm gonna go see my doctor." File what you hear. They may say they feel terrible after the session. That will be the only thing you'll have in your notebook.

General Notes on Mongolian, Indian, Tibetan, Thai and Chinese Medicine

Thai Medicine is based upon Tibetan Medicine, which has some Mongolian roots. (Jivaka was an Indian from Tibet.) Tibetan Medicine is Indian Medicine plus. It differs from Chinese medicine primarily in the lines, Doshas and Chakra theory. Chinese lines are called meridians and are bilateral. Indian lines are nadis and are not.

Our gross body can be sensed 6 feet away. Our [energy] body goes out 50 feet in all directions. This is Indian, Tibetan. Mongolian. 4,000 years ago the Mongolians knew this. It was written in stone. They brought ideas of medicine to Tibet. Tibet added spirit.

We send out putrefactive body waste--hair, skin (which makes up 92% of dust in a room), gas coming off, (Auras: now we know there are certain elements in body that may be phosphorescent.) scents, electricity, magnetism and heat. (You can do a blindfold experiment: see if you can recognize a person from a distance. It is fun. People get it right more often than not.)

For Indian theory the Sushumna Nadi is central. It goes through the core of the body to the pineal gland and out the top of crown. It is at the absolute center of the body. A golden thread goes through sushumna, from heaven down to earth.

Thai is Sen, (Sanskrit Nadi. Sen Sumana = Sushumna Nadi.) This goes through the central core of the body. (Acupuncture people mistake it for the conception vessel, which is in front; while in back is the, governing vessel.)

In Chinese medicine there is the Chung mo = original fetal meridian, which corresponds to the sushumna nadi. (But it is taught now only as an anachronistic meridian)

The Sushumna Nadi is for the movement of the kundalini shakti. This kundalini is conceived of as a physical
Page 176

life- substance, sometimes called nectar. It is the food of the gods (Soma). It goes up the spine. When it reaches the crown, that is liberation.

In the Ayurvedic system the 7th chakra is not on the body. Sahasrara means "palace or place without support." It is the part of the lotus that is above the water--like an umbrella around you. (A metaphor for your matrix body.)

The Thais have the "Bi Hui" point (at the crown). Union of masculine and feminine. The masculine: as the sun feels the wet grass. The feminine: as the earth feels the warmth of the Sun and sees the stars.

In day to day life never put your hand up there; never interfere with the golden thread. But, all bets are off in therapy. All bets are off in therapy because we've done PUJA (Th. Bucha), set up a holy space. In Dr. J.'s initiation(Buddhai Sawan) the Bi Hui (Crown Chakrs) point was cut with a sword. It is a tough point to work on: needs cutting, grinding, burning of moxa, etc.

Chakra, Nadi, ETC:

We are one light (as in sunlight) but look through a prism (apply perception) and it separates. The Seven Primary Chakras are the first division. The secondary chakras are called Wind Gates. Wind Gates are the the first step-down transformers from Primary Chakras, which are also step-down transformers. They are the next step out-- inside hips, shoulders, knees, elbows, ankles. wrists, between toes, between fingers, and around the umbilicus. You have secondary chakras in your palm. Tertiary Chakras are the acupoints. Acupuncture knows 365 primary points. Somaveda® Thai knows 621 tertiary points. There are 88,000 chakras at the fourth level (categorized in the Vedic Upanishads, the Diamond Sutra, and the Third Vajrayana Tantra).

Prana nadis are the conduits of prana, chi, life energy. They communicate between chakras. Every cell must have breath, blood, evacuation (hence access to lymphatic system), and chakric or pranic energy. Every cell in body must have a meridian which feeds it. There are 7 chakras, 63 windgates, 621 tertiary chakras, and 88,000 chakras at the 4th level. Connect them with 10 major highways and about 144 less than major highways, and you get up to 350,000 indispensable highways. Connect every point. It winds up looking just like you!

The Warm Up is a general attention getting device for the two lowest chakras, the two earth-centered chakras. Purpose: put the person in their earth chakras. If they're already there, it just affirms them. Most people are not here yet (in session); they are still driving here, still listening to the radio, etc.

You sit close when taking the pulses. Hip to hip so that you are between the 2nd and 3rd chakra. If you sit further back you are at the survival chakra, and that can be threatening.

Figure Four Position: Figure Four facilitates energy. It is always emotional when you can't open them to the Figure Four position. Security / survival problems. There's a belt around the hip you're working with. This is second chakra stuff. (Third chakra is self image. You can argue about third chakra, talk to it. Not so with second. This is "lower emotional"--gut emotional, no mind. It is hard to talk to chakras # I and 2.) If people have undergone rape, incest, abuse, you might not be able to get them into this position. It need not be rape, incest, etc. in this life. (Half the work is for this life, half for past life.)

There are five kinds of prana. Vayana prana is the most general kind. Vayana is in leg meridian. Wei Chi: is in charge of exterior skin and interior of lungs, stomach, colon, rectum, and hair.

Meridians etc.

How many meridians are there? Chinese Medicine has: 12 primary and 2 extraordinary meridians. This is recent, since 1973-4. In a 1973 acupuncture tape there were 144 meridians.

Meridians Change. "Isn't that the gall bladder meridian?" Sometimes. Meridians cycle 60 times a day. One meridian changes into another meridian. It's gall for a minute, then heart, liver, etc. It is   predominantly gall bladder, but it cycles. All of the meridians cycle through 2 hr. periods of dominant activity. They go through 12 two hour periods per day.

Lung/large intestine. Yin (lung) / yang (large intestine) combination. Once you know lots of lines you realize you can reflex any part of the body from one part--e.g. just working on a circle at the back of the knee you can work the whole body. (So if someone is burned on most of their body, you can still work the whole body.)

Kidney 1 point on the bottom of the foot is pictured as a thousand-tiered palace. It is the most   important point on the body according to acupuncturists. Possibly second only to the navel. In Thailand the feet are considered to have lower chakra energy; the feet are completely aligned with the lowest chakra. Thai People won't let you touch part of body with the lower part of body unless your doing healing work or therapy. Don't ever point your feet at another. Never touch your feet to another. Don't put your hand on someone's shoulder. Never put your hands on their head (6-7, crown chakra). Showing foot like "flipping the bird" (giving the finger) here. The chakra way is so ingrained.

The line above the knee is different from the line below the knee. Because the first line circles around the knee and becomes the midmost line on the leg. (This is different from the Chinese meridian concept.)

More thoughts on Puja (*Th. Bucha*)

(1) Acknowledge: the Space: (the sacred space of their energy, of your intermingled energies). your Teachers, your lineage. your Inner Teacher.

How long does it take to do Puja (*Th. Bucha*)? How long does it take to appreciate beauty? The Tibetan's say it "Takes less time than snapping the fingers.

Other ways of saying it:

Acknowledge the space. I'm in his space, right now. Acknowledge just means consider the space... let that thought enter your mind. You don't have to do anything else. Like knocking at the door, ringing the doorbell. (Crow Indians don't knock.) Only go where you're invited/enter only with permission.

Establish your permission to be there. (Seek Refuge) Why are you here? Take refuge. Give credit to the three Buddhas. Acknowledging your teachers, lineage = asking for permission to be here.

Acknowledge the lineage: 'What I do, doesn't come from me. I am a hollow tube.'

Thai monks venerate teachers. Anyone who filled you with inspiration--to be like them--is a teacher. You can get to the point where you actually see in front of you the faces of people who got you to be a good person.

Anthony's sweat- lodge vision: of mirrors facing each other generating infinite images. He saw all his past teachers in one mirror up to him - a line- continuing to the future. It's all just one love seeking to manifest in humanity.
Page 178

The Great spirit, your teachers, and your Inner teacher are the three Buddhas. All three are the same. Some people refer to inner teacher as their conscience. Acknowledge the three. Wai Kruu says: paying attention to the three buddhas is an actual dance. "Give credit where credit is due."

Pay respect--honor and remember your lineage. It's like a spiritual copyright acknowledgment. You don't have to be a Buddhist to respect the Buddha. Just acknowledge there is a teacher who influenced positively hundreds of millions...

Think of flesh and blood people in your life who have brought you good teaching.

We become practitioners because of some strong contact. Now we are that contact. (A. would have been an arch criminal by now if not for early contact. He hates rigid systems and always figures out a way around them. This is good in body work. Illness is the rigid system. When he was young he felt that nothing was whole enough that he couldn't break it. Now he feels that nothing is broken enough that he can't fix it.)

Seek refuge. Buddha, Dharma, Sangha and Kruu (Khruu equals the teacher--Sensei in Japanese, Sifu in Chinese).

    (2) Generate the Boddhicitta: (Prayer and petition.) Boddhicitta = perfect mind, perfect thought. Pray for them. That is a way of generating the Boddhicitta. The Metta Sutra provides one example: May all things be happy. May all things have life, enlightenment, be free from suffering. May all living things be free from the cycle of birth and death and rebirth. May they be free from the cycle of   creation of suffering. Frame your acknowledgement or prayer like this... "May my client be happy. May my client have life, enlightenment and be free from suffering. May my client be free the the creation cycle of birth, death and rebirth. May my client be free from the cycle of the creation of suffering."

You are not saying, 'May their headache, back pain, go away." Pain will come and go. Pray that the client has what he or she needs to be whole and happy. Prayer for happiness comes first. The rest will follow.

When you address the big 4--love, compassion, joy, and equanimity pain will diminish, circulation, digestion etc. will get better. Things will tend to get better.

Pray for happiness and healing for the person. In that order; happiness is more important than   physical healing.)

A question to Buddha: how do we know we're alive? " Do you have suffering?" Yes. "Then you're alive." To be alive is to be in pain. So you can pray, 'May my client be receptive and eligible for that same healing.' Pray for everyone. Pray for client. Be sure to add the idea NOW (Present, Positive, Imperative) to prayer--not hanging in indefinite future.

Generate the Boddhicitta, generate a perfect thought. And the perfect thought is always this: "May all beings and sentient creatures who have lived, live now, or ever will live become enlightened and conscious of their true essential nature and free of the cycle of death and rebirth." This is not positive or negative. Being enlightened may be very painful. A. wishes enlightenment in little pieces, in such a way that it does not make you want to sever the bond of life. But if it must cause pain, that's his wish anyway.

(3) Clean House: Is there anything that can keep me from being wholly here? Take care of it. (You might take care of it at once: Say you don't want to work on them … Or you can promise yourself to get rest etc. afterwards, whatever is needed. Make sure to keep any promises you make to yourself. This lets you not be perfect and yet do a perfect thing.)

Is there anything inside me that keeps me from being able to be wholly and totally with him? I'll get an answer. Yes or no. Handle it right then. If it's something I can handle with him, I'm honor bound to bring it up. If I can't resolve it in mind and heart I should not touch him.

What you can handle-you do. Shower - he smells bad. "I know that you just came from your job. But we have enough time. Take a shower." Or if we need to talk about diet "You have a body odor which is related to your diet and I want to talk to you before you leave." Make a plan to take care of it at first opportunity. (Or, say, I had a fight with my wife. I need to talk to my wife. "I'll call her next break.") If I don't do it (don't phone or phone and call her names) that stays with me and I'll begin to transfer that to him. I have to do what I promised to do. Call the wife and if she doesn't want to talk to me, OK--as long as I fulfill my part. Warrior part - put aside thoughts to make the space. It gets easier with practice and discipline.

Get rid of your own "stuff" that will keep them from getting energy from you.

(4) Respect the Client: Always respect the integrity, vitality and [intelligence, competence, confidence?] of your client as of all living beings. Allow for possibility that what you are doing with this one person might reverberate to all living beings, to the whole world. See the big picture and the little simultaneously: this is the essence of Somaveda® Thai. The person you work on is the world: the only difference is the scale.

People lay hands on a whole community or country, for example, Bishop Desmond Tutu in S. Africa. (If you listen to him now he doesn't talk about S. Africa any more, he talks about the world.) It is a process--you get there from here. From one person to the world. Not all of us will get there but some or one of us may and we don't know who.

Story of rare coconut tree seed found. There were years of research. A million dollar environment was created. There was a 2 year germination. (It takes 24 years until it sets fruit.) It's like that for us. Each client represents a process over time. Look at your client as the seed. [Or yourself.]

Bow to the mat. "I respect the work that goes on here." Bow instead of saying those words.

Appendix #5 : Difference between SomaVeda® Thai Yoga Therapy and Western Therapies

Thai Yoga	Western Medicine
1) Energy and Soft Tissue Based	Blood Based
2) Corrects Cause	Treats Symptoms
3) Offers Health Care	Renders Sick Care
4) Balances and Promotes Equilibrium	Attacks and Kills Disease
5) Sees The Whole Person	Sees the Body as Parts
6) Produces Positive Effects	Causes Side Effects
7) Helps Resist Germs	Threatened by Germs
8) Revives Organs and Tissues	Removes Organs
9) Natural	Artificial
10) Wholistic Model	Reductionist Model
11) Non-invasive	Invasive
12) Drug Free	Prescribes Drugs
13) Patient is in Charge	Doctor is in Charge
14) Patient is treated with honor and respect	Patient is a test subject
15) Longevity and quality of life is important	Dead and Maimed Patients labeled "Attrition"
16) Traditionally based with thousands of year history of use and benefits	Less than 100 years, Experimental, Unproven
17) No risk of Death	Virtually every procedure has Risk of Death.
18) Food Based	Chemical and Poison Based
19) Safe	Risky
20) Acknowledges Spiritual healing as a Traditional Religious Therapeutic	Discounts the Existence of Spirit at all!
21) Based on Yoga/ Ayurveda/ Indigenous, Native Traditions	Not!

Appendix # 6: Thai and Ayurveda Specific Bibliography

[1] James, Anthony B.1983, Nuat Thai, Traditional Thai Medical Massage, Meta Journal Press, Atlanta Georgia, USA 140 pgs.

[2] Brun and Schumacher: "Traditional Herbal Medicine in Northern Thailand": 1994 edition, White Lotus, Bangkok, Thailand.

[3] Barbara Andaya, "Political Development between the Sixteenth and Eighteenth Centuries" in The Cambridge History of Southeast Asia, Volume One, Part Two, from c.1500 to c.1800 (Singapore: Cambridge University Press, 1992), 66-67.

[4] Anthony Reid, Southeast Asia in the Age of Commerce 1450-1680—Volume Two, Expansion and Crisis (New Haven and London: Yale University Press, 1993), 69.

[5] David Wyatt, Thailand: A Short History (New haven and London: Yale University Press, 1982), 104.

[6] William A. R. Wood, A History of Siam (Bangkok: Chalermnit Bookshop, 1959), 146.

[7] http://www.samurai-archives.com/jia.html

[8] Seiichi Iwao, editor and translator. Jeremias van Vliet Historiael verhael der Sieckte Ende (Tokyo: The Toyo Bunko, 1958) vii-viii.

[9] Kennon Breazeale, "Thai Maritime Trade and the Ministry Responsible" in From Japan to Arabia: Ayutthaya's Maritime Relations with Asia (Bangkok: Printing House of Thammasat University, 1999), 7.

[10] Barbara Andaya, "Political Development between the Sixteenth and Eighteenth Centuries" in The Cambridge History of Southeast Asia, Volume One, Part Two, from c.1500 to c.1800 (Singapore: Cambridge University Press, 1992), 66-67.

[11] Khien Theeravit, "Japanese-Siamese Relations 1606-1629: in Chavit Khamchoo and Reynolds Thai-Japanese Relations in Historical Perspective (Bangkok, Innomedia Co. Ltd., 1988), 19.

[12] Jivaka-Komarabhacca in Pali Cannon: http://www.palikanon.com/english/pali_names/j/jiivaka

[13] Jivaka called "Komarabhaca: "The treatment of infants", VT.ii.174; in Dvy. (506-18)

[14} Jivaka: http://nalanda-insatiableinoffering.blogspot.com/2010/06/jivaka-amravana.html

[15] Jivaka name documented in Pali Cannon: Studies in Traditional Indian Medicine in the Pāli Canon: Jīvaka and yurveda", (Kenneth G. Zysk, Journal of the International Association of Buddhist Studies 5, pp. 309–13, 1982)

[16] Jivaka: "Giving of Robes" (Vin.i.268-81; AA.i.216)

[17] Jivaka treats Buddha's ailments: Buddha reads Jivaka's thoughts and bathed as required: Vin.i.279f; DhA. (ii.164f)

[18] Jivaka declared by the Buddha chief among his lay followers loved by the people (aggam puggalappasannā-nam) (A.i.26)

[19] Jivaka included in a list of good men who have been assured of the realization of deathlessness (A.iii.451; DhA.i.244, 247; J.i.116f)

[20] Jivaka and Vejjavatapada: In the seven articles, excerpts from four passages in the Pali canon, the Buddha lays down the attitudes and skills which would make "one who would wait on the sick qualified to nurse the sick." "Doctors Code of Conduct": Anguttara Nikaya III, p.144 (The Vejjavatapada likely predates the Greek Hippocratic Oath.)

[21] Provide for the sick: Brahma Net Sutra, STCUSC, New York, 1998, VI,9.

[22] Traditional Medicine in Kingdom of Thailand: http://www.searo.who.int/entity/medicines/topics/tradi-tional_medicines_in_the_kingdom_of_thailand.pdf?ua=1

[23] Traditional knowledge and traditional medicine: https://www.wto.org/english/tratop_e/trips_e/trilatweb_e/ch2d_trilat_web_13_e.htm

[24] Ministry of Public Health also controls the curricula of the institutions which provides teaching and practicing of Thai traditional medicine.: http://www.thailawforum.com/articles/Thai-traditional-medicine-protection-part1-3.html#64

[25] The efficacies of trance possession ritual performances in contemporary Thai Theravada Buddhism, p. 120: https://ore.exeter.ac.uk/repository/bitstream/handle/10871/15758/ChamchoyP_TPC.pdf?sequence=3&isAllowed=y

[26] The Use of Traditional Medicine in the Thai Health Care System: P. 146: http://thaiyogacenter.com/wp-content/uploads/2017/05/Thai-Healthcare.pdf

[27] Ayurveda of Thailand: Anthony B. James, Meta Journal Press, Brooksville, FL 34602, 2016

[27] The Role of Thai Traditional Medicine in Health Promotion: Vichai Chokevivat, M.D., M.P.H. and Anchalee Chuthaputti, Ph.D. Department for the Development of Thai Traditional and Alternative Medicine, Ministry of Public Health, Thailand

[28] Ban Chiang Archaeological Site: http://whc.unesco.org/en/list/575

[29] Kennon Breazeale, "Thai Maritime Trade and the Ministry Responsible" in From Japan to Arabia: Ayutthaya's Maritime Relations with Asia (Bangkok: Printing House of Thammasat University, 1999), 7.[30] Legal Status of Traditional Medicine and Complimentary/ Alternative Medicine: A Worldwide Review: Thailand: Kennon Breazeale, "Thai Maritime Trade and the Ministry Responsible" in From Japan to Arabia: Ayutthaya's Maritime Relations with Asia (Bangkok: Printing House of Thammasat University, 1999), 7.

[31] Vichi Chockevivat and Anchalee Chuthaputti, 'The Role of Thai Traditional Medicine in Health Promotion' (Paper presented at the 6th Global Conference on Health Promotion, Bangkok, Thailand, 7-11 August 2005) 2.

[32] Angkor influenced Architecture in Thailand: http://www.hellosiam.com/html/Thailand/thailand-history.htm

[33] Traditional Thai Medicine: https://en.wikipedia.org/wiki/Traditional_Thai_medicine

[34] Ratarasarn, Somchintana. The Principles and Concepts of Thai classical medicine. Bangkok: Thai Khadi Research Institute, Thammasat University, 1986

[35] Beyer, C. 1907, Journal of the Siam Society, vol. 4, part 1:1-9 Bangkok, Thailand. The Siam Society. 9p.

[36] Hofbauer, Rudolf 1943 (Lecture delivered before the Thailand Research Society on 13 December 1942) Journal of the Siam Society, vol. 34, part 1:183-201 Bangkok, Thailand. The Siam Society. 19p.

[37] Bruce, Helen 1960 Nine_Temples of Bangkok, Bangkok, Thailand. Progress Book Store Publishers. 93p

[38] Cunningham, Clark E, 1 970 Antibiotic Mediators In: Social Science & Medicine, vol.4, pp.1-24 England. Pergarnon Press. I 4p.

[39] Hinderling, Paul, 1972 Mit traditionellen Arzten Uber ErkIarungssysteme und Therapien. Aspekte der lnteraktion zwischen Arzten und Patlenten.[Folk medicine in Thailand - Interviews   with traditional doctors about explanatory systems and therapies. Aspects of interaction between doctors and patients] Saarbrucken, Germany. Sozialpsychoi. Forschungsst. d. Univer. S. 140p

[40] Larr, Stephen, 1984 Bangkok's Other Massage Is an Euphoric Experience, If a Little Painful Bangkok Post, Bangkok, Thailand. Pp.

[41] Krungkrai Jenphanid, 1986 Traditional Thai Massage Therapy [in Thai]: • Lak phueen thaan kha'awng kaan nuad thai [Basics of Thai massage, Sp.] • Khunatham 16e jaryatham khaawng maaw nCiad thai [Qualities and ethics of the Thai massage doctor. 1p.] - In: A compilation of pirated text material Chiang Mai, Thailand. Old Medicine Hospital. Gp

[42] Krungkrai Jeenphaanid, 1986 Noad thai phua chiiwid mai [Thai Massage for a New Life, Status of Thai Massage Today] In: Raangkaai khawng rao: ph0uen thaan kaan nuad thai. [Our body: Basics of Thai massage; pp. 19-22], Bangkok, Thailand. Thai Massage Revival Programme. 4p.

[43] Krungkrai Jeenphaanid, 1986, Lak phuuen thaan lae jariyatham kha'awng kaan nuad thai. [Basic Rules and Ethics of Thai Massage] In: Raangkaai khaawng rao: phuen thaan kaan nuad thai. [Our body: Basics of Thai massage; pp. 42-50], Bangkok, Thailand. Thai Massage Revival Programme. 9p.

[44] Krungkrai Jenphanid Somboon Kidniyom 1988 Traditional Thai Massage Therapy [in Thai]: • Kham nam rueng kaan na'e naaew kaan jab sen phaaen boran [Introduction to traditional massage] • Bot wa' khruu kaawn long mooe tham kaan jab sen [Paying respect to the teacher before starting massage] • Lak ph0een tha'an kha'awng kaan nuad thai [Basics of Thai massage] • Khunatham lae jariyatham khawng ma'aw nuad thai [Qualities and ethics of the Thai massage doctor]   [A compilation of pirated text material] Chiang Mai, Thailand. Old Medicine Hospital. 126p.

[45] Thai Massage Revival Programme, 1986 Raangkaai khawng rao: phuen thaan kaan nuad thai. Eekasaan prakawb kaan obrom khaawng khroongkaan kaan nuad thai [Our body: Basics of Thai massage. Document complementing training by the Thai Massage Revival Programme], Bangkok, Thailand. Thai Massage Revival Programme. 165p. Thai Massage Revival Programme

[46] 1986 Khroongkaan fuek obrom kaan ndad thai sa'mrab chaaw ba'an [The training program in Thai massage for villagers] In: Ra'angkaai khaawng rao: phduen thaan kaan nuad thai. [Our body: Basics of Thai massage; pp. S-Il] Bangkok, Thailand. Thai Massage Reviva(Programme. 7p.

[47] Lorentzen, Fridtjof H- 1988 Traditional Thai Massage - A Handbook, [An independent study project, College Semester Abroad Program] Chiang Mai, Thailand. School for International Training. 51 p

[48] Meyer, Walter 1988 Beyond the Mask Toward a Transdisciplinary Approach of Selected Social Problems Related to the Evolution and Context of International Tourism in Thailand [Traditional Thai Massage: 327-329] Saarbrucken, Germany. Verlag Breitenbach Publishers. 533p.

[49] Prayood Bunsinsuk, Lukas Earnst , Peng Sarnkam, 1988 Khruu muue kaan nuad thai (nai kaan saatharana suk muun Tha'an) [Thai Massage Handbook (for Public Health], 2nd ed.(1985) Bangkok, Thailand. Thai Massage Revival Programme. 139p

[50] Somboon Kidniyom, 1988, Traditional Thai Massage Therapy [in Thai]: • Kham nam rueng kaan nae nasew kaan jab sen phaen boran [Introducing traditional massage. 2 p.] • Bot wai khruu kaawn long mooe tham kaan jab sen [Paying respect to the teacher before starting massage, 1 p.] -In: A compilation of pirated text material Chiang Mai, Thailand. Old Medicine Hospital. 3p.

[51] Sharpe, Elizabeth A., 1989 Traditional Thai Massage (Man An Independent Study Project Paper. School for International Training. College Semester Abroad Program. Chiang Mai, Thailand. Personal copy. 31p.

[52] Krungkrai Jeenphaanid, 1989 Kaan nuad thai. NOad ton eeng dai - ma tawng phueng yaa. Thai Massage. You Can Massage Yourself - No Need to Depend on Medicine. By: KIum su.eksa'a panha'a yaa & Khrongkaan fuenfuu ka-an -nUad thai: Muulanjthi saathaaranasuk kab kaan phaflhanaa. [By: Drug Study Group & Thai Massage Revival Project.], Bangkok, Thailand. Foundation for Public Health & Development. 16p.

[53] Krungkrai Jeenphaanid, 1989 Kaan nuad. Thanaawm raksaa sa'aftaa ddai ton eeng & Kod jtid yud aakaan Massage. Conserve Eyesight by Yourself & Point Pressure to Stop Symptoms By: Klm sueksaa panha'a yaa & Khropgkaan fciuenfuu kaan nuad thai. Muulanithi saathaaranasuk kab kaan phaflhanaa. [By: Drug Study Group & Thai Massage Revival   Project.] Bangkok, Thailand. Foundation for Public Health & Development. 12p.

[54] James, Anthony B., 1 991 Nuat Thai, Traditional Thai Medical Massage, Revised. 1995; Chicago, IL, USA. Meta Journal Press. 140p.

[55] Phatraa Saengdaanuch & Mongkhon Plianbaangcha'ang, 1991Hiip nuad baaeb booraan thai [Traditional Thai Massage As a Profession] Bangkok, Thailand. Tdn Aaw Co. Ltd. 64 p.

[56] Phatraa Saengdaanuch & Mongkhon Plianbaangcha'ang, 1991 Aachiip nad baaeb booraan thai [Traditional Thai Massage As a Profession] Bangkok, Thailand. Tdn Aaw Co. Ltd. 64 p.

[57] Roullet, Claude & Foury, Patrick, 1 991 Le Massage Traditione. Les formationsem (1) [Presentation of the Wat Pho Thai traditional massage school: The setting, techniques, and teaching] In: KA Sant 6 Magazine, no. 390,   France. 1p.

[58] Roullet, Claude & Foury, Patrick, 1991 [Presentation of the Old Medicine Hospital in Chiang Mai, Thailand], In: KA Sante Magazine, no. 391; 27 Sept.; rePlace: n. a., France. 1p.

[59] Kannika Piyapong & Uthai (Illustrations), 1992 Traditional_Thai...Massage. - A Handbook Bangkok, Thailand. Wat Pho Traditional Thai Massage School. 27p.

[59] Gaurier, Thierry, 1992 Pratique médicale du massage traditionnel thaïlandais; (I3.nd.ai.s. Paris, France.

Encre/Ste Ary. 83p.

[60] James, Anthony B, 1993   Nuat Thai Traditional Thai Medical Massage- The Northern Style, Chicago, IL, USA. Metta Journal Press. 144 p.

[61] Sawaeng Thaenthaisong, 1993 Book 1 [A bilingual handbook] Khu'u muue kaan nuad phaaen booraan. Lm 1, Bangkok, Thailand. Chulalongkorn Rajavithayalai, Wat Mahathat. 79p.

[62] Yantra Tatooing: WIkipedia: https://en.wikipedia.org/wiki/Yantra_tattooing

[64] Jon Wetlesen, Did Santideva Destroy the Bodhisattva Path? Jnl Buddhist Ethics, Vol. 9, 2002 (accessed March 2010)

[65] AN 4.125, Metta Sutta. See note 2 on the different kinds of Brahmas mentioned.

[66] Metta Sutta: https://en.wikipedia.org/wiki/Metta_Sutta

[66] James, Anthony B., Ayurveda of Thailand, Indigenous Traditional Thai Medicine and Yoga Therapy, Meta Journal Press, Brooksville, FL, 2016 (https://www.amazon.com/Ayurveda-Thailand-Indigenous-Traditional-Medicine/dp/1886338051/ref=sr_1_1?s=books&ie=UTF8&qid=1495727024&sr=1-1&keywords=ayurveda+of+thailand)

[67] Prakruti and Vikruti, http://ayurveda.iloveindia.com/ , Blog Post, http://ayurveda.iloveindia.com/prakruti-vikruti/#d9P0hIzxYiEk2zCs.99

[68] Amazing Thai Yoga for the Hands: Reusi Dottan Based Restorative and Regenerative Yoga for Hands, Shoulders and Heart. Meta Journal Press, Brooksville, Florida https://www.amazon.com/Amazing-Thai-Yoga-Therapy-Hands/dp/1886338159/ref=sr_1_1?s=books&ie=UTF8&qid=1496266190&sr=1-1&keywords=amazing+thai+yoga+for+the+hands

Appendix # 7: Thoughts on the course...

This textbook was created for the "Lines, Wheels, Points and Specific Remedies" course known as the "SomaVeda® Thai Traditional Medicine Theory: Level Four" It's SomaVeda theory, philosophy and therapeutic ideas. Right on the first page the Lessons begin, notice that we are talking about SomaVeda Integrated Traditional Therapies. We are in the Thai Yoga component of the SomaVeda Integrated Traditional Therapies. In the logo, there are other components like Naturopathy, TCM (Traditional Chinese Medicine), Ayurveda and Native American Medicine.

Native medicine is the concept of indigenous medicine. In other words, medical and healing principles which are promoted by native and indigenous people who are either in the past or currently associated with the land and have a naturalistic way of looking at the world and healing. Along with that, we have this idea of Thai Medicine and Western Naturopathy. There is a strong western component in SomaVeda theory. In the United States, the natural or holistic or organic non-invasive, non-drug based, noncommercial based medicine has been practiced under the heading of Naturopathic medicine. In the United States we have a group of doctors and therapists who have always practiced natural, medical principles from the beginning to the present day. We have several different associations of naturopaths, which have been around for a very long time. In various states, there are varying degrees of legalities for that practice.

The principles at the core of Naturopathy are: natural, noninvasive, nondrug, nonsurgical, organic, healing methods using tools that cause no or the very least amount of side effects possible. Naturopaths and or Nature Cure practitioners are different from allopaths in that they take oaths to practice non-injury to their patients. I know you might have heard of the Hippocratic Oath [Appendix #13, Page ???] that Allopaths used to take. It talks about 'physician heal thyself' and 'do no harm'. You can look up the formal oath. Medical doctors are no longer required to take such an oath or to make such an ethic statement in order to pass their boards and become medical doctors. It's more of a feely-good thing that a doctor might have on their office wall. They might, on a personal level, subscribe to a philosophy like that. As an industry, it's not required. It hasn't been for quite a long time. In the Western medical model, there is such a thing as medical attrition. Medical attrition is all the harmful effects that people are being exposed to in proximity with western or in a western medical environment up to and including horrific side effects, injuries and high rates of death. It is not death from disease but death from medical practice, which we call malpractice. When you die as a direct result of a doctor's attempt to help you, malpractice. We tend to emphasize that when the doctor does something wrong like if they amputate the wrong body part or they do a surgical procedure which was not called for and you had a side effect, which causes you to die prematurely.

Western medicine in our culture today is flawed. It's flawed in about every way conceivable. It's flawed majorly in some areas and minorly in other areas and there are reasons for that. We represent an alternative paradigm in healing and medicine. It is a completely different viewpoint. I know a lot of my cohorts and myself say we practice complementary and alternative medicine.

Everything you can think of as a healing technique can be put under the umbrella of complementary and alternative medicine. I have to say that we are not quite so complimentary. We don't like seeing people die as a result of ineptitude, malpractice, unethical behavior and twisted philosophies that place profits above individual health. That is the biggest single criticism of Western medicine. It is a profit-based system entirely about making money. Health services are the products sold to make money. The primary motivation is to make money. The reason for the deterioration of the practice of medicine is this. If the fundamental philosophy of why medicine is performed is to produce income and profit, then that overtime changes the definition of what is medicine. That's how we got here.

We represent systems, like SomaVeda®, which never were and still are not profit-based systems. As soon as I say that, I often have this question that pops up. Don't we still have to make a living right? Isn't that profit? Don't we have to make a profit to make a living? Don't we still have to pay mortgages and pay our bills? The answer is, yes. However, there is a concept called "Way of Right Livelihood." Just because my life in the world requires that I have to generate income to pay my rent to have a life and vehicle to get groceries doesn't mean I have to make 10,000 times the amount of income that I need to have this good life.

It doesn't mean that I need to make a million times the amount of income that any reasonable person would need to have a fabulous life for themselves, their family and their community. That's the problem, when we have this idea of, 'yes I'm a healer and have a right to make an income.' It sometimes translates to 'I have a right to make all of the income, not just from you but from everyone that I touch.

Medical practices bankrupt tens of thousands of people a year. They may devastate whole families, income wise. They contribute to keeping children from being able to get food. They keep young people from being able to go to school. Medical bills will keep whole generations of people from being able to go to college because their college and retirement funds were all spent to support the personal lifestyle of so called healers..

I think that's crazy. The people who do this are not crazy. They are very smart and in some sense, our society says that they are the model citizens. They are the people we want to be. We want our children to grow up and be doctors and health professionals. We want them to marry doctors. It's an ideal that is perpetuated that we want to be like these people. And yet, as an industry, the medical industry and the people in it perpetuate so much harm on the public that it is unconscionable and should be illegal. It's not. That's the dominant culture and that's just the way it is. We have to make our way in it.

We represent an alternative paradigm of these traditional systems and ideas; even the modern western one.

The SomaVeda® Thai Yoga or Indigenous, Traditional Thai Ayurveda and Medicine which we've primarily studied up to this point, is a derivative of Classical Hindu Indian Ayurveda and Yoga, Tibetan medicine, Traditional Chinese Medicine and Muslim Unani medicine from the Muslim countries of Indonesia and Malaysia immigrating to the North.

All these cultures come together and integrate with the original Hindu and Buddhist medicine practiced by the core of the Thai people and especially the Thai kings. Their medicine has always been natural and the least invasive possible. In other words, if there is a choice between two or three therapies that give similar effects, we always start with the least invasive therapy with the least side effects.

We should also not forget that there has for hundreds of years been influence of western medical ideas and practices in Thailand as well. As I discussed in the history of Thai medicine previously there were western doctors in Ayudthaya consulting with the royal family from the 1500's forward.

Traditional Chinese medicine is strongly influential. A third of the population of Thailand is ethnically Chinese. Northern Thailand is only 65-70 km from Southern China. It's walking distance from Southern China. There has always been, through the various trade routes and so on, a lot of Chinese influence that has come together. TCM is about acupuncture, acupressure, Chinese herbology, Chinese theory of meridians (all 72 of them, not just the 12 commonly demonstrated on an acupuncture chart), and influenced by the Tao all the way to the theory of 10,000 things.

Astrology has also always been part of traditional indigenous medicine principles. Thai medical astrology is called Korosot. In India the Ayurvedic version is called Jyotish. Naturopaths can use western astrology. The idea of observing natural phenomenon with their impact and influences is also very important in Native American medicine. In this there are very strong ideas about how the sky and the earth influence us in every way including mentally, physically, emotionally, spiritually, and sexually. We are connected to the universe so it affects us.

Lines, Wheels, Points and Specific Remedies. Lines refers to the energetic anatomy and physiology of us. You see the little man on the cover? That's a reverse or negative of a photograph of a stone carving that is one of the Wat Pho Epigraphies in one of the Sala's or therapeutic pavilions in Bangkok, Thailand. It illustrates both energy lines and points. Like in Western anatomy and physiology we have the parts, the systems, the chemistry and how all of these things interact to give the sum of the expression of life in organic bodies. In natural ways of looking at a person, we see them differently.

We have an energy anatomy. We have energetic organs, biology and chemistry; how these various frequencies interplay and impact each other. We have a completely alternative anatomy and physiology that overlies the anatomical anatomy and physiology of the organic tissue. We are not really going to go into the organic anatomy and physiology in this class, although, on the record, it's very important to have a good working knowledge of the physical structure and function of the body. I also have to acknowledge that knowing A&P (Anatomy and Physiology) does not have any impact on your ability to practice. In fact, in the 980 years of our school Buddhai Sawan, there never was an A&P component to training. Previous to my lifetime, no master or grand master was ever required to name the bones in the body or the organs. No one was required to differentiate soft tissue, from fascia and viscera. The anatomy required was external landmarks like bony protuberances.

It was simpler, like knowing the belly from the kneecap. The names themselves and organs, tissues, blood, lymphatic fluid and so on was never part of the system. This system has been valid enough to have generated 100s of 1000s of teachers and millions of practitioners who have been the primary health givers for 100s of millions of people over the last 900 years. Consider that for a moment. When we talk about how what we are doing is an alternative. That puts it into context. What has been the impact of this work in the life of the world? As the primary form of health giving for 100s of millions of people for a thousand years is a fairly substantial contribution to the progress of the world.

Sometimes there is criticism about what we do because people say it's unproven, it's not scientific, etc. Western medicine is not proven. Western medicine has only been around for a few years. So far, it's coming up short. The further it goes, the more it is critically looked at and seen that it may not be functional. There might be a point in time where it will have to be abandoned completely because of the damage it engenders physically, emotionally and it's false advertising. It doesn't do what it claims to. Eventually the body politic of people of the world is going to have a very clear idea that they've been sold a pig in a poke. They've been sold a bill of goods. They've been lied to, misinformed, and propagandized to their detriment. Every year that goes by, more people in the world are interested in reassuming the preeminence of natural based medicines as the way of the future.

We are not only practicing ancient based healing technologies. We are on the cutting edge of what medicine will look like 100 years from now. We are it. We are high tech. We are as far on the forward edge of the future of medicine as any people on this planet could claim to be right here, right now. It's a different paradigm. It doesn't have to happen in multibillion-dollar edifices of learning. It's not required. The conversation that we are having today; the subject matter that we are talking about is being simultaneously considered in small and large groups all over the country and world right now. There are tens of thousands of teachers like me having the same conversation from their own particular background, perspective and style. You are part of that. We want to operate in the most knowledgeable way, since we will be the representatives of natural medicine and healing in the future. We want to be articulate, defensible, and clear. We are counterculture. We are flowing against the current. Jim Hightower says, "Even a dead fish can swim with the current". We want to move against the current of the dominant culture's idea of what is health and healing and medicine.

We practice yoga therapy. SomaVeda style, yoga therapy incorporates all of these ideas. That's why I say SomaVeda is integrated traditional therapies. I have permission and a moral obligation to research, to absorb, to expose myself to and to integrate with any healthful, beneficial idea or therapy that I can bring to bear to help my fellow human in any way that I see fit to the best of my ability. I will not hesitate to integrate any healthful, non-invasive, non-drug and non-surgery based therapy into the practice. I keep emphasizing the non-drug and non-surgery basis from which I work. That is the core of SomaVeda. Part of the reason for that is that 99 out of 100 health practitioners are drug and surgery based therapists. We don't need any more of them. We need more of the non-drug, non-surgery based practitioners. That's where our opportunities for growth lie.

You need to be clear with people. When you say you are non-drug and non-surgery based, you draw a line in the sand. Many people don't even know that there are non-drug based therapies. Just like in the Eating video and in the Healing Cancer documentary, by law in the United States, you cannot say the world heal or claim to have healed anything that does not involve the application of a prescription drug.

When we talk about healing, we say it's non-drug and non-surgical. Everything we do here is non-medical based training because we don't use drugs or surgery.

Student: According to the law, could you have a sign in front of your business that says Holistic Healing? If you use no drugs or surgery?

D. J: That's controversial because technically the answer is no. Technically, if you advertise that you can heal anything, that's medical malpractice. That's practicing medicine without a license. If you can't prescribe drugs, you cannot legally claim to heal. We live in this wacky, litigious society of laws. We have what's called the separation of church and state. We also have what's called the first amendment rights. It is common, for example, for a turn of phrase as a concept in religious philosophy to use the word Heal and Healer as in 'Jesus was a healer'. Jesus didn't use drugs or surgery. If Jesus had a practice healing the blind, the lame and bringing the newly deceased back to life right now and used the word healing, he would go directly to jail. In every instance he would have committed a felony crime.

However, n the context of religion and spiritual practice and philosophy, you are allowed to use this term. It also goes under the expression of free speech. However, there are problems with free speech right now. For example, in federal airports, you can't say the word bomb. You can't say, 'she's the bomb'. You can't say, 'that's a bomb of an idea'. If you said, 'a bomb went off in my head,' that would be a felony. In every airport and Federal building in the United States, if you say that out loud, you will be taken with uniformed people with guns who will drag you to some basement and then interview you over the next several hours over your possible terrorist affiliations. 'What did you mean exactly when you used that word? Where are you from? What's your social security number? What's your phone number? Who do you know? Who are you traveling with? What's the purpose of your travel?" This happens everyday. Even though we think we are in the land of free speech, it's not true. We are in a litigious land and the use of words is being legislated. You can't say you practice "massage", for example.

No where are we doing or promoting the practice of massage or massage therapy. I'm not prejudiced in that I believe it's wonderful that massage and massage therapists want to learn alternative and energy based healing technologies. I think that's beautiful, just like I think it's beautiful that carpenters and painters and dancers and yoga people want to learn these things too. Just because we have "massage therapists" in the class doesn't mean it's a massage therapy class...no more so than if you went to a painting class and you were a massage therapist the painting class would suddenly become a "massage" class.

For example, a bunch of massage therapists are in a fish horticulture class and decide that fish are therapeutic and having fish tanks would reduce stress. They want to incorporate fish tanks as a common practice in a massage therapy office so they all went to Petco and signed up for aquarium technology classes and fish identification and purification processes. Would that make fish horticulture now massage therapy? No, because they are completely unrelated. The problem is, because we often use the word massage, which has been around for centuries in the English language, in the last 10 or 15 years, there is movement around the country to license the use of the word and words for politics and profit. The reason to license the word or any word is to create a monopoly for a specific franchise of people with very specific educational criteria, very specific political affiliations. For example, organizations such as the NCBTMB (National Certification Board for Therapeutic Massage and Bodywork) and mBlex are political organizations. When people belong to these kinds of organizations, they are supporting a political agenda. That's what their dues are used for. They are used to promote laws. An organization whose primary function is to promote laws is a political organization. That's how it works. It has nothing to do with the practice of healing or medicine or for that matter with massage.

We don't teach massage and we don't teach "massage therapy" although sometimes we may use the words. As I use the words, I will be very clear about what our definitions for the use of those words are and how we mean something different from the common use of the word. I'm suggesting, as we go further, that we use the word less and less because it is becoming more and more controversial because of the push to control the use of it. Just like, I don't use the word 'bomb' in airports anymore. I never have any ideas go off in my head anymore when I'm in an airport. I do not have explosive concepts or ideas. I no longer have explosive realizations in airports anymore. The bomb never goes off in my head because it's illegal.

When I first started talking about Traditional Thai Ayurveda and Thai Yoga Therapy (Traditional Thai Massage) and when I published the first book on "Traditional Thai Medical Massage", ("Nuat Thai: Traditional Thai Medical Massage", Meta Journal Press, Atlanta, GA) in 1983, there was no such thing as a massage school.

There were no massage laws and there was no litigation over the use of healing words. It didn't exist so I used what seemed like the most natural, reasonable terms to describe to common people who had no idea about Ayurveda or yoga or Thai anything…didn't even know where Thailand was…most people had never heard of it. I used common, simple and easy words to describe what we did. Now, over the last 15 years, since there is push to legislate these words, I encourage equally for us to change the way that we describe what we do so we can remain less controversial and stay out of the way of the juggernaut (mercilessly destructive and unstoppable) of the dominant culture's push to control every thought, idea and activity that human beings have a right to engage in as a matter of human liberty and dignity.

This is part of what the course is about. As you understand the actual theories, concepts and traditional language, you can begin to use those as they enter your vocabulary. We can educate our clients with new words. If you look into, for example, research by Joseph Bandler, and J. Sargent and the trans-humanist psychology movement, the rebirthing movement, the alternative psychological movement, the NLP (neuro-linguistic programming) movement…the one thing I agree with that all of these groups share is the idea of the importance of language and the words we use to describe what we do, who we are and who we are in relation to what we do. These are very important because they create what is called in linguistic terms, frames and frame sets. The frame sets that the words create and the mental images and pictures the words create influence our behavior.

One of the premises of NLP, for example, is that if you want to change any behavior, one of the simplest tools is to change the words you use to describe it both out loud and inside your head. There is the idea of creating scripts. In other words, I want to change the way I feel about myself so I create a new script and a new set of words describing myself and I memorize them. I practice that until I have done it enough times that I create
Page 190

a new frame. That new frame, based on those words, causes a concurrent change in my behavior and thinking, feeling and actual being. I have trained in NLP to become a certified NLP trainer from Joseph Bandler. He was the guy who supposedly invented it. I did that after I had this training. I did that because I saw the truth in it.

In Ayurveda we understand the concept of mantra and how powerful the spoken word is in a meditation or a prayer. Even the Lord's Prayer is a mantra. When you recite the Lord's Prayer in various languages, you get different frames and these frames actually engender an emotional set that goes with the mental image. We would like to think that mental image in relation to your mental illness is positive.

There have been many people that have said you can cure certain kinds of mental illness simply by meditating on and reciting healing prayers and mantras. In Ayurveda we call it mantra medicine. In Christian theology, it's called the power of prayer. In other words, a passage from the Bible is used as a form of prayer itself. There is a healing effect. The way the words are phrased and translated has an intention of a positive nature. When we use those words correctly, we create the frames and we get the behavioral modification, that's on purpose. We can use this idea to create any mental frame of reference we would like to consider and to then create spontaneous behaviors that are based on it.

Learning traditional theory is about a new language, first of all. We have to learn new words to describe concepts for which there are no words in the English language. We are learning concepts that were never considered in the English language previously. There are now words for these concepts. That's one reason why we go to other cultures like India, Thailand, China, and to Native American traditions of healing. They have the words to describe the concepts. They have the behaviors based on the frames that using the words created. Now that we want to create the behaviors that are positive and reflective of these frame sets, we have to learn the words and engage ourselves in speaking them and thinking about them, reading them. That's another function for why I have to have a theory and definitions course before I can say I have a complete program. I have to have definitions. If we can't agree on our use of common words and terms, then we cannot actually say we agree on anything. Your frame set for using one word will be different from mine so your behavior will always be different. Even though at different points there may appear to be intersection and common support and beliefs, as long as we are still thinking two completely different thoughts, even though externally we might appear congenial, internally we're still going in opposite directions.

That's why, for example, you can have systems of healing that still operate in support of the western paradigm of the commercial model and still funnel people into it. Even though they're promoting they are an alternative concept and a different way, their language is still the same as the western model. As long as the language is the same as the western model, and the language outcomes are the same, then the frame sets in these people's heads will always be the same. The psychology will still model that mindset and they will have no choice but to direct their support and energy into that model. The words control that function.

When we consider these ideas of origins and Samkhya principles in Ayurveda, the principles of truth knowing. Knowing the truth, in and of itself and learning how to describe and consider the truth will actually create different ways of thinking. As these different ways of thinking manifest in your life, they will manifest as new behaviors. Most of the time it will be subtle and you won't really realize how differently you are behaving until you see it juxtaposed against something that used to have been common for you but now is not. Literally it is completely separate from a way of being that just a year ago or two years ago you wouldn't even have considered for one second as being different. All of sudden you look at something and you see it completely differently.

Sometimes it happens dramatically and we call that a realization, revelation or relevation (A realization or revelation that elevates) — or the idea that we have these spontaneous shifts that seem very dramatic in our consciousness. Most of the time, it will take hard work and effort over time to get to that point.

I wanted to give you a little explanation about SomaVeda® in that context and even about the name.

Soma is a Vedic term.

"Soma (Sanskrit: सोम) connotes the Moon as well as a deity in post-Vedic Hindu mythology.[3] In Puranic mythology, Soma is moon deity, but sometimes also used to refer to Vishnu, Shiva (as Somanatha), Yama and Kubera.[4] In some Indian texts, Soma is a name of an Apsara, alternatively it is the name of any medicinal concoction, or rice-water gruel, or heaven and sky, as well as the name of certain places of pilgrimage. [4]" (https://en.wikipedia.org/wiki/Soma_(deity))

Soma was referred to in those ancient texts as an actual substance or item or food, which a person who was less than enlightened could actually ingest. As a result of consuming that food, they could attain an enlightened state of consciousness of being. They could obtain a supernormal consciousness as a result of eating that food. That's soma.

I believe that food is a metaphor, that the concept of food as it's translated from this word soma is a metaphor for what we call 'the foods'. We are organic, human, biologic, transformational, electro, stress-adaptive entities. This human transformational organism needs certain input to grow and survive. We call that input food. We don't just need one kind of food. We need many kinds of food. For example, according to traditional principles, we need the food of impressions, the food of light. We need to be stimulated visually. Certain kinds of visual stimulation create certain kinds of concomitant mental, emotional, psychological and physical states. I'll give you an example. If you see something greatly beautiful, in that moment it changes your entire being. It changes the way you think and feel. It actually changes your chemistry in your body. Conversely, if you are exposed to great trauma or something that is horrible and devastating it does the same thing but in a different way.

We have food like grains, proteins, and organic vegetables. These are what we put in our mouth and have to chew up and swallow to preserve, maintain and grow life.

According to the Vedas, air itself – prana is one completely separate food group. The idea of breathing, inhalation and exhalation is a sharing of the nutrition of this space or air.

We have many kinds of food. When I think of the word soma and I think about the substance…we don't know the recipe of soma. I use the word as a metaphor for all the kinds of things that come to us from outside of us which nurture and support our organic, mental, psychological, emotional and physical life in this world. All of those things are Soma.

T: Could I consider the word nutrient as a full sense of what you're telling us?

Dr J: If light, air and water are nutrients as well as all organic substances and the inorganic minerals and elements, then yes.

Veda…as mentioned in the documentary on the "Art of Being". Veda has several meanings. Veda is the original, contemporaneous books, poems, songs, mantras, that the ancients codified in various ways from clay tablets to papyrus, detailing what it actually takes to be a whole human being in life. Veda refers to the Vedas, the ancient, particularly Indian and Tibetan books, tantras, codices, and scriptures written down and passed on from generation to generation as collections of anecdotal evidence on what it takes to be a whole human being in life. When I think of the word Veda, I think of it in terms of what we saw in the documentary – the art of being. Veda means the art of being, the art and science of how to be.

SomaVeda® is this word I've created which relates to the acquisition of food, which supports the art of being.

That's the origin of the name. That's what was in my mind when I made up that word. Sometime in your life, as a little sidebar, as a practice, if it ever occurs to you to make up a word write it down and have your word. I've made up other words like 'Relevation' – a revelation and realization that elevates. If words have impact and meaning and if words are what generate frames, which then generate behaviors, emotionally, psychologically and physically, then how much more powerful are words that you make up for your life? As an exercise in being, I occasionally recommend that you should make up a new word and then use it. Use that word to create your frame for your life and to empower people around you. This is the essence of the 5th chakra (**Sans. Vishudda**) - communication and expression of being. I invent a word that codifies how I believe myself to be in some way, shape or fashion. I then use that word, as I speak to other people to create a possible way of you seeing me, as I really believe myself to be. I just want to put that out as a little sidebar of an empowering concept. It is also the origin of this class and this work.

We have just gotten to the bottom of the cover. The eclectic and comprehensive introduction to the Ayurvedic based, energetic anatomy and physiology concepts of SomaVeda® Theory of Ryksaa Thaang Nuat Phaen Boran Thai: Indigenous, Traditional Thai Ayurveda and Yoga Therapy (Religious Therapeutics).

Appendix # 8:
Links And References To Energy Medicine- Radionic Sites

Modern western articles, research, books, studies and other resources which support the idea of vital life energy beyond the purely mechanical. Research suggest that healing based on mind and spirit, on prayer and visualization is genuine and there is science to support this. Spiritually based, systems of religious therapeutics and the healing they manifest are not just placebo effect!

1. Innovative devices at www.biophysica.com
2. Browse the Keyword Map of Raydionics.com at http://www.kwmap.com
3. Water purification and Ionization at http://www.antivirol.com
4. Zero Point Energy and useful links at The Calphysics Institute at http://www.calphysics.org/zpe.html
5. Zero Point Energy and Revolutionary Energy Technologies at http://www.zpenergy.com
6. Casimir Force and Zero Point Energy at Rutherford Appleton Laboratory of Space Science and Technology http://www.casimir.rl.ac.uk/zero_point_energy.htm
7. PEAR "Scientific study of consciousness-related physical phenomena" at Princeton Engineering Anomalies Research
8. The Metaphysics Research Lab, Stanford University at http://mally.stanford.edu/
9. Institute of Metaphysical Science at http://www.scientificmetaphysics.org/
10.   White Mountain Innovations for Radionic Potentiser devices at: http://www.remedydevices.com
11. "Alternative-medicine Resources" related news, books and web resources at http://www.utyx.com/alternative-medicine/
12. Umugisha.com for air and water filters, Chinese herbs, organic products
13. Article on History of Radionics: http://www.radionic.co.uk/Franks%20A4.1.htm
14. Radionic Journal: http://www.radionic.co.uk/Rad%20Journ.htm
15. Books on Radionics: http://www.radionic.co.uk/Books.htm
16. Useful Radionic links: http://www.radionic.co.uk/Links.htm
17. Dowsers Canada: http://www.dowsers.ca/
18. Meridian Associates: http://www.felfield.u-net.com/links.htm
19. Zero Point Energy: http://www.flantech.com/crystalenergy/microcluster/zeropoint/zeropoint.html
20. Dr J. Benveniste at http://www.digibio.com/
21. Memory of Water and Digital Biology at http://www.digibio.com/cgi-bin/node.pl?nd=n3
22. Subtle Energies and Energy Medicine Journal at http://www.issseem.org/journal.html
23. "Scalar Waves" at US Psychotronics Association: http://www.psychotronics.org/scalars.htm
24.   "Scalar Waves (Precursor Engineering): Directly Altering Physical Reality" 2004 T. E. Bearden at http://www.psychotronics.org/Precursor_Engineering.htm
25. Other Interesting Spiritual and Healing Links at http://www.healer.ch/LinksAwards.html
26. Dr Thomas Bearden on Scalar Waves at http://www.cheniere.org/books/ferdelance/
27. Radionics and "witness" theory at http://www.cheniere.org/correspondence/121602a.htm
28. Memory in Water; Basis of Homeopathy at http://www.newscientist.com/news/news.jsp?id=ns99993817
29. A Spirituality Web Directory at http://www.the-insight.com
30. Edgar Cayce is considered to be the father of holistic medicine by JAMA, the prestigious medical journal. Cayce was a wonder to the medical community because of his ability to diagnose and specify a treatment for gravely ill people often hundreds of miles away through his out-of-body journeys. Look at http://www.near-death.com/cayce.html
31. Brief history of Radionics at http://www.strayreality.com/plants2
32. Keyword map of Radionics at http://www.kwmap.com
33. Dr William Tiller (Physics & Consciousness) at http://www.tiller.org/
34. Article on Dowsing techniques at http://go.to/LetterToRobin

35. Journal of Consciousness Studies at http://www.imprint.co.uk/jcs.html

36. The Emerging Mind at http://www.bbc.co.uk/radio4/reith2003/links.shtml

37. An interdisciplinary journal of research on consciousness at http://psyche.cs.monash.edu.au/

38. Consciousness Research Laboratory at http://www.psiresearch.org/   and at http://consc.net/online.html Online papers on consciousness. Part I: Philosophy of Consciousness [718 papers]; Part II: Other Philosophy of Mind [884 papers]; Part III: Science of Consciousness [558 papers]

39. ASSC: Association for the Scientific Study of Consciousness at http://assc.caltech.edu/index.htm and at http://www.lifetechnology.org/teslashield.htm   Life Technology Research International® The Tesla Purple Energy Shield®

40. Consciousness & the Brain at http://home.earthlink.net/~dravita/

41. Connection between phenomenal consciousness and intentionality; by Charles Siewert at http://plato.stanford.edu/entries/consciousness-intentionality/

42. Imagination, Mental Imagery, Consciousness, and Cognition: Scientific, Philosophical and Historical Approaches at http://www.calstatela.edu/faculty/nthomas/

43. Great links at The Field: http://www.wddty.co.uk/thefield/noflash/links.asp

44. "Teleporting larger objects becomes real possibility" at http://www.newscientist.com/news/news.jsp?id=ns99991888

45. "Vacuum is beginning to look like a substance in its own right" at http://www.newscientist.com/hottopics/quantum/quantum.jsp?id=23154400

46. "Signal from molecules of heparin (a component of the blood-clotting system) slows down coagulation of blood when transmitted over the Internet from a laboratory in Europe to another in the US" at : http://www.tcm.phy.cam.ac.uk/~bdj10/water.memory/milgrom.html

47. "Patients have a right to choose unscientific treatments" at http://www.independent.co.uk/story.jsp?story=41160

48. Institute of Heart Math publications at: http://www.heartmath.org/ResearchPapers/soh/soh_70.html

49. "Experiment could reveal 'extra dimensions,' exotic forces" at: http://news.uns.purdue.edu/UNS/html3month/021029.Fischbach.Casimir.html

50. "String theory calls for 6 extra dimensions": at http://www.nature.com/nature/links/030227/030227-6.html

51. String theory is an all-embracing theory unifying the feeble force of gravity with the other forces of nature described by the Standard Model of particle physics. It states that point-like elementary particles are in fact tiny, string-like entities, and calls for six extra dimensions beyond the three we inhabit. We can't see them, theorists argue, because they are curled up into small spaces. But gravity derives from the properties of space-time itself, in however many dimensions it exists. So the largest of these invisible compact dimensions may have a detectable effect on gravity at small but measurable distances. Several experiments are under way to test this prediction, and the group from Boulder, Colorado, now reports final results. No new force was observed at distances of ~100 Ìm, putting a upper limit on the exotic and still hypothetical 'dilaton' and 'radion' forces.

52. Letters to nature "Upper limits to submillimetre-range forces from extra space-time dimensions" Joshua C. Long, Hilton w. Chan, Allison B. Churnside, Eric A. Gulbis, Michael C. M. Varney & John C. Price: Nature 421, 922–925 (2003); doi:10.1038/nature01432

53. Parallel Universes: Not just a staple of science fiction, other universes are a direct implication of cosmological observations at http://www.sciam.com/article.cfm?chanID=sa006&articleID=000F1EDD-B48A-1E90-8EA5809EC5880000

54. Good links about Universal Field at: http://www.wddty.co.uk/thefield/noflash/links.asp

55. Mystical Healing Art-Enhancing people's lives with Inspirations and unique spiritual Art in many interesting categories. Browse our 125 galleries with over 1,500 pages and our many free services. at http://www.mystichealingart.com/

56. Innovative devices at our other site   www.biophysica.com

57. "Alternative-medicine Resources" related news, books and web resources at

http://www.utyx.com/alternative-medicine/

58. Memory of Water and Digital Biology at http://www.digibio.com/cgi-bin/node.pl?nd=n3
59. Subtle Energies and Energy Medicine Journal at http://www.issseem.org/journal.html
60. Other Interesting Spiritual and Healing Links at http://www.healer.ch/LinksAwards.html
61. Dr Thomas Bearden on Scalar Waves at http://www.cheniere.org/books/ferdelance/
62. Radionics and "witness" theory at http://www.cheniere.org/correspondence/121602a.htm
63. Article on Schumann resonance at http://www.2012.com.au/SchumannResonance.html
64. Schumann Resonance at http://www.crystalinks.com/schumannresonance.html

General Vibrational Medicine References

1. Recommended text for this Course "A Practical Guide to Vibrational Medicine: Energy healing and Spiritual Transformation" by Dr. Richard Gerber MD, Quill, 2000, $23 (replaces "Vibrational   Medicine for the 21st Century" Hardcover).
2. "Vibrational Medicine: The #1 Handbook of Subtle-Energy Therapies", Third Edition by Dr. Richard Gerber MD, Bear & Co., 2001
3. "Virtual Medicine" by Dr Keith Scott-Mumby M.D., Thorsons, 1999.
4. "Harry Oldfield's Invisible Universe", by J & G Solomon, Thorsons, 1998.
5. "The Dark Side of the Brain", by H. Oldfield & R. Coghill, Element, 1988.
6.   "Radionics Interface with the Ether Fields" by Dr. David Tansley, 1975.
7. "Chakras, Rays and Radionics" by Dr. David Tansley, 1984.
8. "Esoteric Healing" by Alice Bailey, Lucis, 1971.
9. "My Search for Radionic Truths" by R Murray Denning, 1988.
10. "Cure of all Cancers" by Dr. Hulda Clark, 1993.
11. "Cure of all Diseases" by Dr. Hulda Clark.
12. "Rays of Truth – Crystals of Light" by Dr Fred Bell, Bear Publ., 1999
13. "The Complete Guide to Dowsing" by George Applegate, Element Books, 1997
14. "Towards a new Alchemy" by Dr Nick Begich, Patrick Flanagan Earthpulse Press, 1996
15. "Beyond the Quantum" by Michael Talbot, Bantam, 1988
16. "The Holographic Universe" by Michael Talbot 1992
17. "Cross Currents : The Promise of Electromedicine, the Perils of Electropollution"by Dr Robert O. Becker MD
18. "Tachyon Energy : A New Paradigm in Holistic Healing" by Gabriel Cousens, David Wagner
19. "Esoteric Anatomy : The Body As Consciousness" by Bruce Burger
20. "The Body Electric : Electromagnetism and the Foundation of Life" by Gary Selden, Robert O. Becker M.D.
21. "Brain Longevity: The Breakthrough Medical Program that Improves Your Mind and Memory" -- by Dr Dharma Singh Khalsa M.D. & Cameron Stauth
22. "Margins of Reality : The Role of Consciousness in the Physical World" report by Princeton Engineering Anomalous Research (PEAR) by Robert G. Jahn, Brenda J. Dunne
23. "The Time Travel Handbook: A Manual of Practice Teleportation & Time Travel" by David Hatcher Childress
24. "The Presence of the Past : Morphic Resonance & the Habits of Nature" by Rupert Sheldrake
25. "Hyperspace : A Scientific Odyssey Through Parallel Universes, Time Warps and the Tenth Dimension" by Michio Kaku
26. "Mind into Matter: A New Alchemy of Science and Spirit" by Fred Alan Wolf
27. "Bridging Science and Spirit : Common Elements in David Bohm's Physics, the Perennial Philosophy and Seth" by Norman Friedman, Fred Alan Wolf
28. "Dogs That Know When Their Owners Are Coming Home : And Other Unexplained Powers of Animals"

by Rupert Sheldrake

29. "Messages from Water: How Water Responds to Subtle Energies and Consciousness" by Masaru Emoto
30. "Living Energies : The Schauberger's Work With Trees, Light, Air, and Water" by Callum Coats
31. "The Deepening Complexity of Crop Circles: Scientific Research and Urban Legends" by Eltjo H. Haselhoff
32. "Mysterious Lights and Crop Circles" by Linda Moulton Howe
33. "DMT: The Spirit Molecule from the Pineal: A Doctor's Revolutionary Research into the Biology of Near-Death and Mystical Experiences" by Rick Strassman MD
34. "The HeartMath Solution: The Intelligence of the Heart" by Doc Childre and Howard Martin
35. "The Conscious Universe : The Scientific Truth of Psychic Phenomena" by Dean I. Radin 1997)
36. "Miracles of Mind: Exploring Nonlocal Consciousness and Spiritual Healing" by Russell Targ, Jane Katra 1999
37. "Body Mind Spirit: Exploring the Parapsychology of Spirituality" by Charles T. Tart (Editor)
38. "Parallel Universes: The Search for Other Worlds" by Fred Alan Wolf
39. "Wholeness and the Implicate Order" by David Bohm
40. "Spiritual Healing: Scientific Validation of a Revolution (191 Published Controlled Studies)" collected by Dr Daniel J. Benor, M.D. forward by Dr Larry Dossey, M.D., Vision Publications, 2002
41. "Rational Mysticism: Borders of Science and Spirituality" by John Horgan (Author of "End of Science"), Houghton Mifflin,2003
42. "The Evolutionary Mind: Conversations on Science, Imagination and Spirit" by Rupert Sheldrake, Terence McKenna, Ralph Abraham, Monkfish Books, 2005
43. "Chaos, Creativity and Cosmic Consciousness" by Rupert Sheldrake, Terence McKenna, Ralph Abraham, Park Street Press, 1992
44. "Truth versus Falsehood: Applied Kinesiology Techniques to Calibrate Consciousness" by David Hawkins M.D." Axial Publishing, 2005
45. "Can We Be Good Without God" by Robert Buckman M.D., Prometheus Books, 2002
46. "Sense and Goodness Without God: A Defense of Metaphysical Naturalism" by Richard Carrier, Author House, 2005
47. "The Disappearance of the Universe: Elaborations on A Course on Miracles" by Gary Renard, Hay House, 2002,
48. "Rational Mysticism: Dispatches from the Border Between Science and Spirituality"
49. "The practice of Medical Radiesthesia" by Vernon D. Wethered, B. Sc., C.W. Daniel Co. LTD, London, England, revised edition 1977
50. "Animal Healing and Vibrational Medicine" by Sage Holloway, Sharon Callahan
51. "An Introduction to Medical Radiesthesia and Radionics" by Vernon D. Wethered (Hardcover - June 1957)
52. "Automated Radionic Detecting Devices" by Jorge Resines, Borderline Sciences, 1989
53. "Dimensions of Radionics : a manual of radionic theory and practice for the health-care professional" by David V. Tansley 1997
54. "Dimensions of Radionics: Techniques of Instrumented Distant Healing" by David Foster (Designer), et al (Paperback - May 1992)
55. "Electronic Medicine" by Bruce Copen
56. "Energy Diagnostic and Treatment Methods" by Fred P. Gallo - February 2000)
57. "Energy Medicine: The Scientific Basis of Bioenergy Therapies" by James L., Ph.D. Oschman, Candace Pert Ph.D
58. "Energy Medicine" by Donna Eden, et al; Paperback
59. "Geopathic Stress : How Earth Energies Affect Our Lives" by Jane Thurnell-Read 1996
60. "Harry Oldfield's Invisible Universe", J & G Solomon, Thorsons, 1998.
61. "Healing With Radionics : The Science of Healing Energy" by A.L.G. Dower
62. "Healing with the Rainbow rays : the art of color energy therapy" by Alijandra
63. Introduction to Medical Radiesthesia & Radionics" by Vernon D. Wethered 1992

64. "Intuition Medicine: The Science of Energy" by Francesca McCartney

65. "Practical Introduction to Radionics and Dowsing"

66. "Quantum Biology: Healing with Subtle Energy" by Dr Glen Rein, 1992

67. "Radionics & Radiesthesia: A Guide to Working with Energy Patterns" by Jane E. Hartman, Ellen Kleiner 1999

68. "Radionics : A Compilation of Experimental Rates"

69. "Radionics : Science or Magic? : An Holistic Paradigm of Radionic Theory and Practice" by David V. Tansley (Paperback - December 1982)

70. "Radionics and Progressive Energies" by Keith Mason 1984

71. "Radionics and Radiesthesia" by Dr Jane Hartman, Aquarian Publ., 1999

72. "Radionics and the Subtle Anatomy of Man" by David V. Tansley (Paperback - December 1983)

73. "Radionics Interface With the Ether Fields" -- by David V. Tansley; 1992

74. "Radionics Manual" by John Williams (Paperback - July 2000)

75. "The Radionic computer handbook" by Bruce Copen

76. "The Radionics Handbook" by Keith Mason, Piatkus & Co.,2001

77. "Ray Paths and Chakra Gateways and the Subtle Anatomy of Man" by David V.Tansley, D.C.

78. "Report on Radionics" by Edward W. Russell 1994)

79. "Report on Radionics" by Edward W. Russell, Neville Spearman Ltd., 1975

80. "Shaman, Healer, Sage : How to Heal Yourself and Others With the Energy Medicine of the Americas" by Alberto, Phd Villoldo (Hardcover - December 2000)

81. "Shamanism for the New Age : A Guide to Radionics and Radiesthesia" by Jane E. Hartman

82. "Talismanes radiâonicos" by Eduardo A. Herrero

83. "The Dark Side of the Brain", H. Oldfield & R. Coghill, Element, 1988.

84. "The Divining Heart" by Patricia C. Wright, Richard D. Wright (Contributor)

85. "The Subtle Energetic Aspects of DNA" by Dr Glen Rein, 1997

86. "Vibrational Medicine for the 21st Century", chapter 9, by Dr. Richard Gerber, Bear & Co., 2000.

87. "Vibrational Medicine" by Dr. Richard Gerber, Bear & Co.,1996.

88. "Vibrations : Healing Through Color, Homeopathy and Radionics" by Virginia Mac Ivor, Sandra LaForest

89. "Virtual Medicine: A New Dimension in Energy Healing" by Dr Keith Scott-Mumby, Thorsons, 1999

90. "Spiritual Healing: Scientific Validation of a Revolution (191 Published Controlled Studies)"collected by Dr Daniel J. Benor, M.D. forward by Dr Larry Dossey, M.D., Vision Publications, 2002

91. James Trefil, "Dark Matter", Smithsonian, June 1993, p.27.

92. "Studies Shed Light on Universe in the Moments of Creation". Los Angeles Times, April 30, 2001.

93. James Glanz, "First Direct Evidence of Negative Gravity". National Post Online, April 4, 2001.

94. Gary Taubes, "Everything's Now Tied to Strings", Discover Magazine, Nov. 1986.

95. Henry B. Pullen-Burry, M.D., "Qabalism" The Yogi Publication Society, Chicago, 1925.

96. Zev ben Shimon Halevi, "Adam and the Kabbalistic Tree", Samuel Weiser, Inc. 1990.

97. Aryeh Kaplan, "Sefer Yetzirah. The Book of Creation", Samuel Weiser, Inc., 1990.

98. Will Parfitt, "The New Living Qabalah", Element, 1998.

99. Annie Besant and C.W. Leadbeater, "Occult Chemistry, Investigations by Clairvoyant Magnification into the Structure of the Atoms of the Periodic Table and Some Compounds", The Theosophical Publishing House, 1951.

100.   Edwin D. Babbit, "The Principles of Light and Color", Malaga, N.J., 1925.

101.   Stephen M. Phillips, "Extrasensory Perception of Subatomic Particles: 1.Historical Evidence", Journal of Scientific Exploration, volume 9: Number 4 Article 2.

102.   Dr. Jacques Benveniste, from a talk given in the Cavendish Lab on March 10th, 1999, http://twm. co.nz/benveniste99.htme.

103.   Milan Smrz, "Experiments Made Together with Robert Pavlita", Proceedings of International Conference on Psychotronic Research, West Georgia College, Carrolton, GA, 1988, p.B18

104.   D. Dean, Ph.D. "Physical Changes in Water by Laying-On of Hands", ibid, p.B2.

105.	L.A. Volf, Ph.D., "Some Chemical and Physical-Chemical Aspects of the N.S. Kulugina Phenomenon", ibid, p.B20 (in Russian).
106.	Wilhelm Pelikan, "The Secrets of Metals", Anthroposophic Press, 1973, p.35
107.	Alastair Couper, "Subtle Energy and Astrology", http://shaka.com/~kalepa/subtle.htm.
108.	The Complete Works of Lao Tzu. Translation and Elucidation by Hua Ching Ni. Seven Star Communications, 1997.
109.	C.W. Leadbeater. "The Chakras" Quest books, 1990.
110.	A.E.Powell. "The Etheric Double" and " The Astral body". The theosophical Publishing House. London UK 1925, 1927.
111.	Rosaline L. Bruyere. "Wheels of Light. A study of the Chakras". Bon Productions 1989.
112.	Richard Gerber M.D. " Vibrational Medicine". Bear & Co. 1988.
113.	Jay Barbree and Martin Caidin, "A Journey Through Time" (Exploring the Universe with the Hubble Space Telescope), Penguin Books, 1995 p.198.

Appendix # 9: A Modern Version of the Hippocratic Oath

I swear to fulfill, to the best of my ability and judgment, this covenant:

I will respect the hard-won scientific gains of those physicians in whose steps I walk, and gladly share such knowledge as is mine with those who are to follow.

I will apply, for the benefit of the sick, all measures which are required, avoiding those twin traps of overtreatment and therapeutic nihilism.

I will remember that there is art to medicine as well as science, and that warmth, sympathy, and understanding may outweigh the surgeon's knife or the chemist's drug.

I will not be ashamed to say "I know not," nor will I fail to call in my colleagues when the skills of another are needed for a patient's recovery.

I will respect the privacy of my patients, for their problems are not disclosed to me that the world may know. Most especially must I tread with care in matters of life and death. If it is given me to save a life, all thanks. But it may also be within my power to take a life; this awesome responsibility must be faced with great humbleness and awareness of my own frailty.

Above all, I must not play at God.

I will remember that I do not treat a fever chart, a cancerous growth, but a sick human being, whose illness may affect the pedix #9rson's family and economic stability. My responsibility includes these related problems, if I am to care adequately for the sick.

I will prevent disease whenever I can, for prevention is preferable to cure.
I will remember that I remain a member of society, with special obligations to all my fellow human beings, those sound of mind and body as well as the infirm.

If I do not violate this oath, may I enjoy life and art, respected while I live and remembered with affection thereafter. May I always act so as to preserve the finest traditions of my calling and may I long experience the joy of healing those who seek my help.

The modern version of the Hippocratic Oath was written in 1964 by Louis Lasagna, Dean of the School of Medicine at Tufts University.

Appendix # 10: The Metta Sutra

Generating The Boddhichitta

The Bodhichita is an example of the most perfect thinking a person can do. It is a perfect petition for the well being of all sentient beings. As a Mantra, it powerfully manifests the loving and compassionate energies of all of the Saints and Sages, and as such, is suitable for inclusion in your Puja.

METTA SUTRA (*Pali. Karanīyamettā Sutta*)

This is what should be accomplished by the one who is wise,
who seeks the good and has obtained peace:

Let one be strenuous, upright and sincere, without pride, easily contented and
joyous;
Let one not be submerged by the things of the world.
Let one not take upon oneself the burden of riches;
Let one's senses be controlled;
Let one be wise but not puffed up;
Let one not desire great possessions even for one's family;
Let one do nothing that is mean or that the wise would reprove.

May all beings be happy.
May they be joyous and live in safety.
All living beings, whether weak or strong, in high or middle or low realms of
existence, small or great, visible or invisible, near or far, born or to be born,
May all beings be happy.

Let no one deceive another, nor despise any being in any state;
Let none by anger or hatred wish harm to another.

Even as a mother at the risk of her life watches over and protects her only child, so
with a boundless mind should one cherish all living things, suffusing love over the
entire world, above, below and all around without limit; So let one cultivate an
infinite good will toward the whole world.

Standing or walking, sitting or lying down, during all one's waking hours
let one cherish the thought that this way of living is the best in the world.

Abandoning vain discussion, having a clear vision, freed from sense appetites, one
who is made perfect will never again know rebirth in the cycle of creation of
suffering for ourselves or for others. [65][66]

Appendix # 11: List of Illustrations, Graphics and Photo's

Indonesian 12, 26
Insight meditation 41
Intention 27, 93, 161
Isvara Pranidhana 33
ITTM 8, 16, 17, 18, 19, 20, 21, 26, 142, 202

J

Japanese 14, 23, 24, 143, 151, 168, 179, 182
Jap Sen Nuad 161
Jittanamai, 57
Joy 9, 11, 27, 45, 46, 47, 50
Jyotish 25, 187

K

Kabri- Kabrong 24
Kalaripayattu 26
Kampuchea 4
Kapha 7, 68, 83, 100, 106, 111, 112, 118, 119, 120, 121, 122, 123, 124, 125, 127, 128, 129, 130, 131, 133, 134, 136, 137, 167, 169, 202
Kayanamai 57
Khmer Kingdom 25
King Naresuan 14, 24
King Ramathibodi 22
Korosot 25, 57, 119, 132, 159, 187
Korosot Astrology 57, 132
Kosha 6, 70, 72, 73, 74, 75, 76, 77, 80, 131, 132, 139, 140
Kundalini 144, 162

L

Laos 4
Laotian 11, 12
Lineage 6, 9, 49, 50, 52, 202
Lom 8, 10, 11, 18, 55, 88, 89, 90, 91, 92, 94, 95, 96, 105, 111, 114, 134, 136, 137, 143, 146, 147, 148, 149, 150, 152, 158, 162, 169, 170
Love 9, 11, 27, 45, 46, 50, 122, 162, 167
Lymphatic Fluid 162

M

Majapahit Empire 26
Mala 110, 133
Malaysia 4
Malaysian 12, 26
Marma 16, 18, 55, 132, 148, 152
Martial Arts 27, 51, 57, 163
Maw Nuad 10, 18
MEIS body 152, 153
Meridians 50, 111, 114, 139, 152, 154, 159, 163, 178
Meta 3, 4, 40, 119, 142, 182, 183, 184, 185, 190
Metta Sutra 8, 10, 28, 158, 167, 179, 201
Midwifery 21, 51, 55
Mon-Khymer 12
Morphogenic Field 154, 163
Mr. Surasak Srinoi 5, 52
Muslim 12, 26, 187
Myanmar 4, 12, 14, 24

N

Naam 10, 89, 90, 91, 92, 94, 99, 105, 164, 169
Nadi Pareeksha 128, 167
Nalanda 11, 15, 16

Page 206

Shavayatra 8, 134, 143, 144, 145, 148, 162
Shiva 62, 63, 192
Somatic Body 152
Spirit 38, 66, 151, 167, 181, 196, 197
Srotas 8, 87, 138, 139
Sukhothai 14, 22, 43, 67
Surgery & Healing of Bone Injuries 55
Swasthya 31, 33

T

Tamas 6, 66, 67, 68, 69, 70, 90, 92, 105, 132, 142
Tangible Physical Body 72, 152
Tao 5, 52, 62, 152, 159, 187, 202
Tapas 33
Tawee 5, 20, 52, 97
Tecudhatu 89, 94
Tejasdhatu 10, 90, 96
Thaat Thang Sii 6, 68, 88, 89, 92, 94, 112
Thai Ayurveda 4, 9, 10, 11, 12, 56, 58, 59, 68, 88, 89, 94, 155, 160, 162, 165, 169, 187, 190, 193, 202
Thai cupping 59
THAILAND 4
The Code of Manu 21
Theravada 9, 14, 16, 26, 183
The Royal Favorable Art 19
Thrice Crowned King of Medicine 16
Tibetan Book of the Dead 39
Toxicology 56
TPB 72, 152, 153
Traditional Chinese Medicine 20, 50, 53, 61, 65, 92, 93, 139, 151, 155, 159, 186, 187
Treatment of Disorders of the Head and Neck 55

U

Union of Thai Traditional Medicine Society 5, 9, 20, 52, 151
UTTS 5, 9, 20, 151

V

Vampire metaphor 81
Vata 7, 68, 95, 106, 111, 112, 114, 117, 119, 120, 121, 122, 123, 124, 125, 127, 128, 129, 130, 131, 132, 133, 134, 135, 136, 137, 167, 169, 202
Vayudhatu 10, 89, 90, 94, 95
Vejjavatapada 6, 16, 17, 182
Venerable Prakhru Pipitpattanapirat 5, 52, 202
Vietnamese 12, 44
Vikruti 7, 10, 112, 124, 132, 133, 185
Vipassana 6, 35, 36, 41, 42, 43, 44, 45, 51, 57, 62, 71, 80, 94, 95, 135, 136
Virilification 56
Virility 56, 57
Vishnu 5, 14, 67, 192, 202

W

Wai Khruu 6, 17, 38, 39, 50, 51, 167, 202
Wangklaikangwon Industrial Community & Educational College 5, 9, 52
Wat Buddhai Swan 22
Water Element 7, 10, 90, 99, 100, 101, 202
Wat Po 5, 9, 10, 12, 17, 18, 19, 20, 22, 23, 24, 26, 52, 140, 150, 151, 168, 202
Wat Po Association for Traditional Thai Medicine 5, 52
Wat Raja Orasaram Ratchaworawiharn 18, 19, 202
Wat Sawankhalok 5, 9, 20, 52

Other Titles By Author

James, Anthony B., Ayurveda of Thailand, Indigenous Traditional Thai Medicine and Yoga Therapy, Meta Journal Press, Brooksville, FL, USA 2016 Available on Amazon.

Angels Speak: The Art and Work of Crafting Consciousness, Meta Journal Press, Brooksville, Florida. USA Available on Amazon.

Amazing Thai Yoga for the Hands: Reusi Dottan Based Restorative and Regenerative Yoga for Hands, Shoulders and Heart. Meta Journal Press, Brooksville, Florida. USA Available on Amazon.
Korosot Chakra Astrology

James, Anthony B, 1993   Nuat Thai Traditional Thai Medical Massage- The Northern Style, Chicago, IL, USA. Metta Journal Press. 144 p. Available on Amazon.

What is SomaVeda® Thai Yoga: 49 Systems of Self Expression and Healing?

The BET book

James, Anthony B.1983, Nuat Thai, Traditional Thai Medical Massage, Meta Journal Press, Atlanta Georgia, USA 140 pgs.

Additional Resources

Learn more about SomaVeda Integrated Traditional Therapies® Thai Yoga Therapy

1. www.ThaiYogaCenter.Com (Gain Professional Training and Certification)
2. www.SomaVeda.Org (Gain a College Degree based in Indigenous Traditional Natural Medicine)
3. www.SomaVeda.Com (Native American Indigenous Church, NAIC)
4. www.ThaiMassage.Com (Information and resources on Traditional Thai Medicine and Yoga Therapy)
5. www.FindYogaTherapy.Com (Find a qualified and certified practitioner near you)
6. www.BeardedMedia.Com (Books, Videos, Genuine Thai Mats and more!)
7. www.CafePress.Com/thaimassage (All thing promotional Thai Yoga. T-shirts to coffee mugs!)
8. www.ThailandStudyTours.Com   (Join us for authorized Thai Yoga Training and culture excursion in Thailand)